Y0-BPT-577

Zion's Glad Morning

Zion's Glad Morning

by Willard A. Ramsey

Millennium III Publishers
Simpsonville, South Carolina
1990

©1990 by Willard A. Ramsey. All rights reserved
ISBN 0-9625220-0-7
ISBN 0-9625220-1-5 pbk.

Printed in the United States of America

To Nita . . .

for all that she is and for creating a home

in which a man can be content

and can think and can serve his God and hers.

Hail to the Brightness

Hail to the brightness of Zion's glad morning!
Joy to the lands that in darkness have lain!
Hushed be the accents of sorrow and mourning;
Zion in triumph begins her mild reign.

Hail to the brightness of Zion's glad morning,
Long by the prophets of Israel foretold!
Hail to the millions from bondage returning!
Gentiles and Jews the blest vision behold.

Lo, in the desert rich flowers are springing,
Streams ever copious are gliding along;
Loud from the mountaintops echoes are ringing,
Wastes rise in verdure and mingle in song.

See, from all lands, from the isles of the ocean,
Praise to Jehovah ascending on high;
Fallen are the engines of war and commotion,
Shouts of salvation are rending the sky.

Thomas Hastings (1784-1872)

Contents

Foreword

"An Eschatology of Triumph." I like that!

I'm tired of losing. I'm tired of the same "business-as-usual" mentality that allows Lucifer the freedom to conquer the Saints of God at will. I'm tired of the "woe-is-me" attitude that dominates the theologies and pulpits of our churches. It is high time Royal Saints of the King of Kings claimed their birthright . . . possession and joint rulership of the creation!

Lucifer is a false god and a usurper of the rule of this earth. The great Creator-God delegated that rule to His magnificent crowning creation, Man. Man, in a foolish attempt to side in rebellion with Lucifer against God, was overthrown, banished from the presence of God, and taken over by Lucifer and his fiendish demons. Jesus, the great I Am, the Only Begotten Son and Son of Man, won back that authority lost to Lucifer, and, as the Anointed One, conquered all that was against the Holy God and established His throne in the heavens, there to reign until all enemies become His "footstool."

Jesus left behind Him His "Assembly," a small band of some 120 followers who faced a whole world of hostile unbelievers dominated by a system of civilization and a philosophy of life that was alien to the very thought of the Holy God. Yet the Bible said that His Assembly would go on the attack against "every high and lofty thing that exalts itself against the knowledge of God," and that the very "gates of hell" would not be able to withstand that attack. That sure sounds like Jesus planned for His Assembly to win! The idea that the great *Ecclesia* of Jesus Christ is to stumble and bumble its way through an unknown parenthesis in time, ultimately to be embarrassingly rescued by Jesus after having miserably failed at its assigned task, is foreign to the Word of God. It is foreign to the very nature of God! God does not fail. His plans are not thwarted. His agencies do not crumble before the enemy. Praise God! There *is* an "Eschatology of Triumph!"

Dr. Henry M. Morris, III
Canoga Park, California

Acknowledgments

Seldom has there been a written work which was the product of a single individual, and I am conscious in this case of a considerable indebtedness to many others. But there are four men to whom I owe a special debt of gratitude. The first is my older brother Carroll C. Ramsey, who, many years ago, through discussion and counsel opened my vision to a serious search of the Scriptures on the subject of eschatology. I only regret that I have not had much opportunity to study further with him.

However, my early studies on this subject were done in frequent consultation with Henry M. Morris, III, who consented to write the foreword for this work. At that time we were co-pastors in Hallmark Baptist Church, and we spent many profitable hours together in search of a biblical eschatology. And now William C. Hawkins and Glenn J. Kerr are fellow pastors with me in the same church, and I have leaned heavily upon their wisdom and advice while writing this work. Also, Glenn has been especially helpful in the area of the original biblical languages as well as in many editorial chores. To all these men I am grateful.

Then I want to express a special word of thanks to Rebecca Kerr who typed the initial manuscripts, and also to my daughter, Nikki Turner, who has been my "right hand" in preparing this publication. Thanks also to my daughter, Prudence Hawkins, for the front cover art, and to Anne Hawkins, Mary Sue Jones, Keith Campbell, Robert Augustine, Sue Salmon, and Nina Laidlaw for proofing and other helpful chores.

The title of this book was borrowed from the lyrics of a hymn written by Thomas Hastings entitled "Hail to the Brightness" (cited elsewhere). This theme, of which he so eloquently wrote, has been a special inspiration to me and to many of God's people.

To all of these, and others as well, I want to express my warmest appreciation.

Willard A. Ramsey

Charts and Illustrations

Introduction 1

The eighteenth and nineteenth centuries brought upon two continents that glorious period celebrated in history as the First and Second Great Awakenings. During this time when the fires of revival swept over the Western world for nearly two centuries, there was a wholly different understanding of the prophetic future than that which prevails today. It was an eschatology of gladness. There was hope abroad. There was the zeal of expectation. There was power. The eschatology that drove these revivals was known then as "the latter-day glory" (of which I will have more to say in the last chapter of this book). In those days God blessed this response of faith to His prophetic truth by pouring out the Spirit of revival upon His waiting people until the mid-nineteenth century. He can and will do it again in a measure surpassing anything known in prior history.

The greatest work of the Gospel through the church is yet to come. In the pages ahead, I want to show that the biblical picture of the future is a picture of the hope of salvation through the Gospel for millions of lost souls — hope for the hungry, suffering, war-weary nations of earth.

Though clouds darken the immediate horizon as we move into the third millennium in the year 2000 A.D., I believe it is premature to proclaim this planet which God has made and the church which Jesus has built as "down for the last count." Throughout the early decades of the twenty-first century, events will doubtless continue to unfold which will perplex and confuse God's people beyond measure if interpreted in the climate of popular twentieth-century eschatology. Among our most urgent needs is an accurate understanding of biblical prophecy to guide us effectively through the stormy years that lie ahead until we reach the clearing — until "Zion's Glad Morning" breaks and righteousness spreads over the earth "as the waters cover the sea." It is this truth that must once again be seen by the people of God.

I know the views I am about to set forth will be controversial. I will challenge the most popular views held today by millions of well-meaning people — a challenge which I hope will be received as it is given, in charity. We will all live through the events of the future together, and the events themselves will inevitably force doctrinal concessions. Eschatology is a doctrine that will be settled by the unfolding of time. Yet God has given the outline of the future in Scripture that His churches might know how to conduct themselves in the prosecution of His purposes on earth, and so much the more as time wears on toward the events of the consummation. Though the doctrines of eschatology will inevitably be settled by these events, how much better it would be to settle them now by charitable dialogue in Scripture truth that we might be properly guided in the days to come.

Therefore, as I present this challenge of an eschatology of Gospel victory, I trust it will be received as the biblical expression of hope for the billions now lost, even though it will challenge the widely held premillennial view of the day. Toward the many godly men who hold a premillennial position, I hold no ill will. I long for their fellowship in the work of Christ and for a charitable spirit of Christian dialogue solely in the interest of truth. I acknowledge also that a thorough understanding of the premillennial doctrines has helped me to avoid the needless "spiritualizing" errors of amillennialism and evolutionary postmillennialism.

I simply want to reason concerning the things of the Scriptures. I want to be candid, and I will be tough-minded on the doctrines I consider to be in error. But at the same time, I want to be charitable toward men, remembering both my errors of the past and those that are yet to be corrected. I simply want to analyze Scripture on this subject and allow it to speak. And I invite everyone to join me in a consideration of these things with an unbiased and a charitable spirit, so that we all might come closer to knowing exactly what God's truth is.

Due to the difficulty of the subject of eschatology, I think it is a mistake to make it a matter of Christian or church fellowship as some have done since the revival of the premillennial view — and the origin of the pre-tribulation rapture view — in the last century. Still, it is a very important doctrine primarily because it conditions our attitudes toward the power of the Gospel, the purpose of the church, the restoration of its unity, and the maintenance of its purity.

A century, then, is too long for the premillennial doctrine to have been so widely disseminated without being called to serious scriptural accountability.

The premillennial doctrine that the greatest work of salvation will be accomplished *after* the rapture of the church and the return of the Lord, in contrast to the biblical truth that His return forever fixes the destiny of every person then living on earth (2 Thess. 1:7-10), has caused immeasurable harm to the progress of truth and the power of the Gospel in the earth.

In the first half of the nineteenth century when the doctrine of "the latter-day glory" was still stirring a revival impulse in the churches, the Gospel was flourishing. Then came the nineteenth-century revival of premillennialism, and the glad impulse of "the latter-day glory" gave way to a theology of failure. The glad impulse turned to gloom. The church came to be seen as only an intercalation, "a parenthesis," in God's supposed plan for the earthly theocratic kingdom of Israel with Christ physically reigning on earth over sinful, fallen, flesh-and-blood men.

In this view the church is not seen as the earthly centerpiece and apex of God's purpose to make known the "manifold wisdom of God, according to the eternal purpose which he purposed in Christ Jesus our Lord" (Eph. 3:10, 11). Inherent in the premillennial position is the concept that the church will ultimately dwindle to almost nothing and be raptured without ever having made much of an impact on the world through the Gospel. The church will essentially fail. The preaching of the Gospel of the grace of God will inevitably become powerless. And since this is presumed to be true, it seems useless to try to purify and unify the church. The degenerate, splintered, condition of the churches today, under this doctrine, is what is expected. Few have the vision to believe that the churches by the power of the Holy Spirit through the Gospel can improve, be unified, and reap the vast harvest of souls now living on earth. Since the premillennial understanding of prophecy essentially negates the power and future success of the church, and since any minute now Christ is to return, it is hard to muster the courage, faith, and vision necessary to launch into a long term work of unifying the churches around Scripture truth, purging them of the immorality and doctrinal heresies by which Satan has divided and weakened them. It is a very debilitating thing to be facing a harvest of five billion souls in an institution that has no prophetic future on earth.

Jesus, the night before He went to the cross, prayed "that they may be one . . . that the world may believe that thou hast sent me" (John 17:21). If we take this passage of Scripture seriously, we must know that the masses of the world will *not* respond to the Gospel unless they see God's people unified, visibly, *not* "mystically." Since the first century, when the churches were unified, the power and impact they had on the world has never been equaled. During the Great Awakenings, the people of God began to look up with a new vision to see God's power through the Gospel again, and God blessed them in some measure. But they were still divided.

It is now time to return to the vision of "the latter-day glory" and seek again that unity for which Christ prayed. It is time that the words and sentences of the Scriptures be examined minutely for what they say and what they mean and a biblical eschatology derived from them. When that is done, we will again see an eschatology of hope and success for the Gospel message on earth.

My determination to make a detailed search of the words

and sentences of Scripture on the subject of eschatology came after a long struggle to sustain a system of eschatology that could not even bear the surface implications of Scripture — especially of the New Testament. This discomfort grew until I knew I would have to reevaluate my eschatology, and the following is an account of how it came about:

In 1954 and for several years after, I came under the influence of strong premillennial, pretribulation-rapturist ministries under the preaching and teaching of several godly pastors and churches who loved souls and who loved the Word of God. I was twenty-four years old and had not yet formulated, by personal study, any kind of eschatological position. At first I found difficulty in reconciling a premillennial position with the surface statements of Scripture. I began to read books on the subject. I read widely — Ironside, Pettingill, Larkin, Scofield, Thiessen, Bancroft, Pentecost, and a myriad of others — until I thoroughly understood the system of thought and had learned all the presuppositions that one must bring to every Scripture passage in order to sustain a premillennial interpretation. Thus was I conditioned to receive this view, and I defended it with great vigor for about fourteen years.

Then in 1967 I began a serious study of many other doctrines of Scripture, and my discomfort with premillennial eschatology increased. As I studied and discussed these matters with others, for the first time I began to notice the presuppositions that I had been applying to every passage of Scripture to make it compatible with a premillennial interpretation.

For example, when I came to Matthew chapter 24, I presupposed that since Matthew is a "Jewish" book, that (even though spoken to Christian disciples being trained as pillars in the church) this chapter had little of church-age significance in it. I automatically rejected the notion that the tribulation period could apply to church-age people, even though no rapture is mentioned until after the tribulation period. This was a "Jewish" book. The "elect" who were raptured after the tribulation (Matt. 24:31), I presupposed unhesitatingly, were the non-church-age Jews because the church-age saints, everyone knew, had already been raptured at a different time. But the Scripture nowhere makes such a distinction.

Then, too, the stars that were falling from heaven (v. 29) were not *real* stars, only meteorites; and the powers of heaven shaken was only a little shaking; and the black-out of the sun would not seriously affect life on earth. And although it was a bad time, flesh and blood would survive to inherit the "kingdom of heaven" which Christ was coming to establish. I also distinguished between the "kingdom of God" and the "kingdom of heaven," for "flesh and blood cannot inherit the kingdom of God" (1 Cor. 15:50). Yet by making categorical and distinctive entities out of the general phrases that the Bible uses interchangeably (e.g., kingdom of God vs. kingdom of heaven, day of the Lord vs. day of Christ, end of age vs. end of world), I was able to satisfy my mind for a decade and a half that this premillennial picture really was the view God was trying to convey in His Bible.

Thus did I precondition every great and clear passage of Scripture in preparation for a premillennial conclusion in each case. The New Testament passages on prophecy were not taken literally at face value. But when I saw and admitted what I had been doing, my conscience was smitten and I determined to restudy all the prophetic passages of Scripture, taking them at face value.

I decided I would simply let the Scriptures speak to me. I would then formulate a view of the doctrines of prophecy that would be comfortably compatible with what I read without any preconditioning or tampering with the passages of Scripture that were before me. I would simply let the Bible speak and then continue to adjust my views and to structure a framework of thought that would fit what they said, without having to make explanations that seemed needless, unnatural, and unreasonable. And when I came to that conclusion, I found a great liberty of conscience in the interpretation of Scripture. Things grew simple. They made sense. I found a real peace having reached the conclusion that I would permit Scripture to shape my view of things, rather than for me to try to modify the meaning in some way in order to be compatible with what I had been previously taught. That problem is primarily what makes eschatology a "hard" subject for most people.

Before long I saw a totally different framework of eschatology emerging — so much simpler, easier to maintain by the unvarnished words and sentences of Scripture. Soon I began to see that God had a wholly different plan for the course of the future than I had formerly thought.

Now in consideration of a subject such as this, it is almost always necessary to consider both the negative aspects as well as the positive aspects. So in the course of this study, I will be dealing with both sides of this issue. It is necessary to present positively what the Bible actually teaches concerning the framework of prophecy, but then I also want to treat negatively the prophetic errors and look at the areas of Scripture where we have misinterpreted and have gone astray. I want to discover how it is that so many good men have reached wrong conclusions.

But my primary desire is to help to establish in the minds of the people of God a true picture of God's purpose and His plans for the future. It has to be disappointing to God (I speak as a man) to have His people looking toward, expecting, and confidently surging ahead toward a future that will never occur. He wants "friends" who know what their Lord does, ". . . for all things that I have heard of my Father I have made known unto you" (John 15:15). It makes a vast difference in the end result if a friend invites you to come for a week and help him reap a massive harvest of grain if you get the message garbled. If you think he is coming to pick you up and whisk you away to enjoy a seven-day wedding feast and — instead of work clothes, sun helmet, and implements of harvest — you are ready in tux and tails in a partying frame of mind rather than girded for the long summer days of toil, he will be disappointed in you.

Just so, an accurate knowledge of the Lord's plans for future events makes a vast practical difference. It is inevitable that our behavior and mental disposition will be influenced by what we *think* the future holds. The zeal with which we attack the problems that hinder the Lord's churches in their ministry of the Gospel is going to depend in great measure on whether we *think* it will do any good — or whether we *think* there is time. It is both to the advantage of His purpose and to the personal advantage of each of us that we think accurately about the general framework, not dates and minute details, the general shape of future events.

The advantage to the harvest of knowing accurately what God has revealed is so great that it becomes an urgent matter for an accurate framework of eschatology to be established. Such knowledge would wholly change the mentality of the churches today. It would root out shallowness and flippancy. An earnest purpose would replace the attitude that the work is all about over here. The thought that any minute now we will be on our way to the great wedding feast deadens the motivation for the long-range work of correcting the wrongs, building strong disciples, purging the corruption, and banishing heresies and discord in the churches today.

In my efforts to try to promote the unity of the faith in truth, I have been told by a number of premillennialists (but, thank God, not by all) that "there can never be unity until Jesus returns to set up His kingdom." It is not necessary to hold this opinion just because one holds a premillennial view, but this widespread attitude is a serious impediment to unity.

An accurate framework of eschatology would focus attention on the harvest, on sharpening our implements, on studying the methods of the Lord of the harvest, on cleansing the institution Christ established to reap the harvest — the church. It would highlight, as never before, the need for a unified mission of the churches in the harvest, for "unfeigned love of the brethren" (1 Pet. 1:22), for the unity of the faith (see John 17:21).

But it is psychologically impossible for all these central and vital qualities to accrue to God's people as long as they sincerely expect their work to be cut short at any moment and expect that those who have not heard the Gospel when Christ comes will have a second chance. It is urgent therefore that we gain an accurate understanding of God's revealed plan for the future.

The Framework of Eschatology 2

The first issue to be confronted in determining the outline of future things is the question: What framework[1] of prophecy does the Bible actually establish — premillennial, amillennial,[2] or postmillennial? The most important single

---

[1] For those who may not be familiar with the general terms of eschatology (which refers to final things or things to come), the terms *premillennial*, *postmillennial*, and *amillennial* refer to the second coming of Christ in its relation to a period of "a thousand years" (Rev. 20; see also Isa. 2:1-5; 11:5-9) or *millennium* in which righteousness, peace, and prosperity will prevail over the earth. *Premillennial* means Christ will come *pre-* or before the millennium and physically reign as an earthly king. *Postmillennial* means Christ will come *post-* or after the millennium and take the saints to be with Him in a new heaven and new earth. *Amillennial* means *a-* or *no* millennium. Also the term *great tribulation* is a short period of unparalleled wickedness, war, and suffering on earth (see Matt. 24:15-24).

[2] Though I will not deal extensively with the amillennial position in this work, its main features are: (1) The millennium is not understood literally as a real, unique millennial period but only the Gospel era. (2) It relies heavily on a spiritualizing approach to the interpretation of Scripture, especially with regard to the basic covenants of Israel. (3) Its most serious problem is the rationalization of the binding and loosing of Satan (Rev. 20:2, 3, 7; cf. 1 Pet. 5:8) and the implication that Satan is now bound and that we have been in the millennium since the death of Christ.

factor in the consideration of future things is to get the second coming of Christ oriented at the proper end of the millennium. Only then can we accurately interpret other details of prophecy.

To do this, I want to present five rigorous (inflexible, rigid) propositional truths which I believe will rigorously establish a framework of prophecy that is true to the Bible. But first a few words should be said about the reality of a unique millennium.

The Millennium: A Unique Era on This Earth

The Scriptures teach that there will be an extended period of time during which righteousness will predominantly prevail over the whole earth just as wickedness now predominantly prevails and has prevailed since the sin of Adam. This concept is set forth in several Old Testament passages such as: Isaiah 2:1-5; 11:6-16; 60:1-18; 65:18-25. One of the clearest expressions of this unique period is found in Isaiah: "for the earth shall be full of the knowledge of the Lord, as the waters cover the sea" (11:9).

In the New Testament this period of time is implied in a few Scripture passages (e.g. Matt. 24:14), but it is plainly stated and explained only in Revelation 20:1-6. In this passage we learn that the millennium is initiated by the supernatural binding and imprisonment of Satan in such a measure that he will not be able to "deceive the nations" during this period (v. 3). We also learn that the loosing of Satan terminates the millennium and that he does deceive the nations again (v. 7, 8). The fact of the postmillennial loosing of Satan unequivocally confines the millennium to this present earth, not the new heaven and new earth.

It is here that the amillennial position breaks down. It claims that Satan is bound at the death of Christ and that the Gospel era is all that is meant by the millennium. But there are a number of serious problems with that. The New Testament Scriptures expressly teach after the death of Christ that Satan is not now confined or bound: "Be sober, be vigilant; because your adversary the devil, as a roaring lion, walketh about, seeking whom he may devour" (1 Pet. 5:8; see also Acts 5:3; 2 Cor. 4:4; 11:3, 14; Eph. 2:2; 6:11, 12; 2 Thess. 2:9; 2 Tim. 2:26; Rev. 2:9-13; 20:8, 10). He is called the "God of this world." He is the "prince of the power of the air." He does deceive the world right now. But during the millennium he does not do these things; therefore the millennium is a unique period of time yet future. Moreover, after the millennium, Satan will be allowed to return to these deceitful works for a short time (Rev. 20:7, 8).

Now it is true that the Bible teaches that Satan was destroyed, defeated, judged by the death of Christ, but it is obvious that the sentence of that judgement has not yet been, and will not be, fully executed until Satan is finally cast into the lake of fire (Rev. 20:10). Whatever the angel does in binding Satan at the beginning of the millennium will be undone at the end of it (Rev. 20:3), but what Christ did at His death will *never* be undone. Therefore, these two works are not the same thing. There is definitely a unique millennium.

Moreover, a biblical sense of the righteous standards of God tells us that the centuries of gross suffering, the debauchery of sin, the violence and wickedness of the nations, which has been to this day the unbroken record of history, cannot be God's notion of a time when men "shall beat their swords into plowshares, and their spears into pruning hooks: nation shall not lift up sword against nation, neither shall they learn war any more" (Isa. 2:4). No, the amillennial theory is flawed. Scripture will not support it. There is to be a unique millennium on this earth.

Returning now to the five rigorous propositional truths, we will not "spiritualize" except where the Scripture spiritualizes for us or except in those rare cases where a literal interpretation would trivialize God or otherwise contradict His Word. We will take the words of Scripture at their literal, face-value meaning. I do not, as do the amillennial and some postmillennial interpreters, spiritualize the covenants to Israel. I take them at the literal meaning of the words of Scripture written about them. The Scripture itself "spiritualizes" some things for us, and a literal interpretation of the words of such a passage requires us to understand it in a "spiritual" or symbolic way. But otherwise we must take it directly at face value.

The First Rigorous Propositional Truth

Now let me turn to the first of five rigorous propositional truths and see what framework of eschatology begins to develop. The first passage of Scripture I want to examine is found in the book of Hebrews (12:26f). The context of this passage is the great prophecy concerning "mount sion . . . the city of the living God, the heavenly Jerusalem" (vs. 22, 23). The writer of Hebrews compares this time over against the time when God came down on Mount Sinai and gave the law to Moses. He said that God's voice then (at Sinai) shook the earth, but now there is a promise yet pending that God will shake *both heaven and earth* once more:

> Whose voice then shook the earth: but now he hath promised, saying, Yet *once more I shake* not the earth only, but also heaven. And this word, *Yet once more*, signifieth the *removing* of those things that are shaken, as of *things that are made*, that those things which cannot be shaken may remain (Heb. 12:26, 27).[3]

Applying the direct, literal, face-value approach to interpretation, this passage refers to a time "*once* more" when God will "shake" the earth again and at the same time will also "shake" the heavens. Now this is to happen *one* more time; not *twice* more. And the writer, you will note, explains what is meant by this phrase "yet once more." He says "this word," and he quotes again, "yet once more" signifies the *removing* of the things that are *shaken*. So there is to be one more shaking; and when that shaking occurs it means the removing, the destruction, or the termination of the things that are shaken.

The things that are shaken (which are to be destroyed) are both the heavens and earth, i.e., the "things that are made." All that God made as recorded in the first chapter of

---

[3] The italics in all the Scripture quotations throughout this book are added for emphasis and to highlight specific issues for further discussion.

Genesis — the heavens and the earth and every physical thing in them — is to be destroyed when God shakes the earth and the heavens one more time. That is all this passage proves, but that is a rigorous, inflexible proposition made and interpreted by the Bible itself and will not admit of preconditioning or twisting when literally received.

Naturally the question arises: when, or upon what occasion, is God going to *shake* the heavens and the earth once again? And I turn now to the Gospel of Matthew to see when this will happen:

> *Immediately* after the tribulation of those days shall the sun be darkened, and the moon shall not give her light, and *the stars shall fall from heaven*, and the *powers of the heavens shall be shaken* (Matt. 24:29).

Upon reading this verse, the premillennial interpreter must at once begin a mental process to interpret this list of severe catastrophic phenomena in such a way that living things on earth, plants, animals, and human beings, are not seriously affected. It is necessary, in that view, to insist that the environment on earth when Christ returns remain sufficiently benign to sustain life. This means that crops must grow, that men must work, that children must be born and reared. Now, when the sun and moon give no light, the stars fall from heaven, and the power (forces, energy) of the heavens are "shaken," survival on this earth (let alone millennial conditions) will be impossible.

Then to face the task of interpreting this passage with the mental necessity to clear the way for a premillennial conclusion, requires that these serious catastrophic phenomena be extenuated in some way to allow flesh-and-blood life on earth to continue in a more or less normal biological pattern.

Now let me pause to make a few surface observations on this passage. First notice the time. The timing is *immediately* — not a long time — *immediately* after the tribulation. In the preceding verses the Lord had just finished discussing the events of the great tribulation — a period when there will be a time of trouble such as never has been. So then immediately after the tribulation there will appear visual indications that a physical calamity is near; the sun will be darkened and the moon shall not give her light. This is the first manifestation of some great, impending catastrophic event in the celestial bodies. The sun darkens; and of course if the sun is dark, the moon would not give its light because it is a reflector of the light of the sun.

One premillennial brother said the "powers of the heavens" and the "stars," etc., were not referring to the physical heavens. He spiritualized it and said it meant demonic powers — like Paul's "principalities and powers" or "spiritual wickedness in high [or heavenly] places" (Eph. 6:12).

But the occasion of which Christ is speaking (Matt. 24:29, 30) is of His second "coming," and Haggai identifies His second coming with the one and only "shaking" of heaven and earth: "Yet once, it is a little while, and I will shake the heavens, and the earth, and the sea, and the dry land; and I will shake all nations, and the *desire of all nations shall come:* and I will fill this house with glory, saith the Lord of hosts" (2:6, 7). This is without a doubt the revelation of Jesus Christ, and it is this very passage that the writer of Hebrews interprets as being the end of this physical universe "things that are made" (12:26, 27) not just demonic powers. It is a dangerous thing to rationalize so positive an identification.

Some premillennial interpreters have held tenaciously to the error that this present heavens and earth is eternal and that there will be no serious destruction. To settle this issue requires an analysis of all the applicable passages in Scripture. We have made such an analysis (see page 19) and the conclusion is positively clear that the present heavens and earth are destroyed at the second coming of Christ and a new heaven and new earth is then established.

Should it be objected that since Haggai says "I will fill *this* house with glory" that it refers to a reign on earth, I would point out that this cannot refer to the temple of Haggai's day, but some future aspect of the House of God. In view of all the light on this passage, Hebrews 12, Matthew 24, etc., "This House" has to be the final abode of God and men — the new

The Shaking of the Heavens and the Earth

This cluster of Scripture verses demonstrates that the terms *shake, shaking* are used consistently in many eschatological passages in connection with the destruction of the present heavens and earth. This peculiar usage is clear enough from the contexts of these many passages, but in addition we have a rigorous interpretation to this effect by Scripture itself.

The Holy Spirit Interprets Shake

Hebrews 12:26, 27 interprets *shake* as used in Haggai 2:6, 7 and thus as used in all other references of similar context, i. e., the destruction at the revelation of Christ:

Whose voice then shook the earth: but now he hath promised, saying, Yet once more I *shake* not the earth only, but also heaven. And this word, *Yet once more, signifieth the removing of those things that are shaken,* as of things that are made, that those things which cannot be shaken may remain (Heb. 12:26, 27).

For thus saith the Lord of hosts; Yet once, it is a little while, and I will *shake* the heavens, and the earth, and the sea, and the dry land; And I will *shake* all nations, and the desire of all nations shall come: and I will fill this house with glory, saith the Lord of hosts (Hag. 2:6, 7).

The Peculiar Eschatological Usage of Shake

For the day of the Lord of hosts shall be upon every one that is proud and lofty, and upon every one that is lifted up; and he shall be brought low.... To go into the clefts of the rocks, and into the tops of the ragged rocks, for fear of the Lord, and for the glory of his majesty, when he ariseth to *shake* terribly the earth (Isa. 2:12, 21).

Behold, the day of the Lord cometh, cruel both with wrath and fierce anger, to lay the land desolate: and he shall destroy the sinners thereof out of it. For the stars of heaven and the constellations thereof shall not give their light: the sun shall be darkened in his going forth, and the moon shall not cause her light to shine.... Therefore I will *shake* the heavens, and the earth shall remove out of her place, in the wrath of the Lord of hosts, and in the day of his fierce anger (Isa. 13:9,10, 13).

. . . and the foundations of the earth do *shake.* The earth is utterly broken down, the earth is clean dissolved . . . it shall fall, and not rise again (Isa. 24:18, 19, 20).

The sun and the moon shall be darkened, and the stars shall withdraw their shining. The Lord also shall roar out of Zion, and utter his voice from Jerusalem; and the heavens and the earth shall *shake* . . . (Joel 3:15-16).

Immediately after the tribulation of those days shall the sun be darkened, and the moon shall not give her light, and the stars shall fall from heaven, and the powers of the heavens shall be *shaken:* And then shall appear the sign of the Son of man in heaven . . . (Matt. 24:29, 30).

And there shall be signs in the sun, and in the moon, and in the stars . . . for the powers of heaven shall be *shaken.* And then shall they see the Son of man coming in a cloud with power and great glory (Luke 21:25-27).

See also Ezek. 38:18-20; Hag. 2:21; Mark 13:24, 25; Rev. 6:13, 14).

Jerusalem (Rev. 21:2). "Behold the tabernacle of God is with men . . . ," (21:3).

"Shaking" the powers and principalities will hardly involve the sun, moon, stars, the heavens, the sea, the dry land, and the nations. Then compare Matthew 24:35: "Heaven and earth shall *pass away.*" Also consider 2 Peter 3:10: "The heavens shall *pass away,*" and Hebrews 12:26, 27: "The removing of those things that are shaken." Then note Revelation 6:13, 14: "The heaven *departed.*" How — upon what exegetical principle — shall we spiritualize all these literal, physical passages that testify uniformly with one voice to the destruction of the universe?

But let us examine more closely the persistent claim in Scripture that the stars will not give their light and will fall from heaven (Isa. 13:10; Ezk. 32:7; Joel 2:10, 31; 3:15; Matt. 24:29; Mark 13:25; Rev. 6:13). "The stars," with the definite article, implies all stars. This language, in every case, is in the context of the sun and moon being darkened which is expressly tied to the great and terrible day of the Lord (Joel 2:31; 3:14, 15; cf. Matt. 24:29; Acts 2:20; 2 Pet. 3:10; Rev. 6:13). This phenomena cannot be interpreted merely as meteorites as many want to make it. In Revelation 6:13 a vision from God, as reliably recorded by an apostle, says expressly that "*the* stars" fall. A star is a gigantic, sustained hydrogen reaction. It is like millions of hydrogen bombs going off at the same time continuously. Our sun is a medium-sized star. And should one star come anywhere near this earth, the earth would vaporize like a drop of water in a hot furnace. And yet the text says that the stars will fall from heaven.[4]

---

[4] In the process of the destruction of the universe, God has chosen to hurtle the stars toward the earth. In an interesting unpublished monograph, H. Ron Elliott shows how the convergence of the stars would very likely produce these visual effects described in Scripture. Elliott postulates the convergence of the stars at a rate near the velocity of light and shows that a gravitational "shock-wave" preceding the oncoming mass by a short time (hours or days) would "red shift" the light of the sun causing it to appear red then finally dark. The moon would mirror this change. But as the sun dims, a "blue-shifted" eerie light from the converging stars would lighten the earth on every side (see Zech. 14:6, 7). The gravitational shock-

Therefore, when we read that the powers of heaven shall be *shaken*, this denotes the terminal event. Obviously, if the stars are to fall from heaven, there has to be a mighty shaking of the powers or forces that have held the heavens and earth in the order we now see. Then all the incredible mass of the universe will converge toward a point of impact of which the earth is at or near the center.

But remember what we read in the book of Hebrews, that when there is once more a shaking of the heavens and the earth, that means the *removing* of the things that are shaken. Also we are told in Revelation that the "first heaven and the first earth were passed away" (21:1), and this event of the "shaking" (Matt. 24:29, 35) tells us when this present earth will perish. The creation of the heavens and earth, as recorded in the first chapter of Genesis, comprises the entire material universe. This great shaking then, according to Hebrews 12:27, means the destruction, the removing, the perishing of the "things that are made," namely, the whole material universe.

In Matthew 24:29 then, we have words which clearly establish the end of this present universe. It will implode upon itself undoing what God had previously done in creation.

Since we have seen from Matthew (24:29) that immediately after the great tribulation the earth will be terminated by the shaking of the heavens and the earth and the falling of the stars, we now read:

---

wave would produce severe tidal effects in the earth's crust, and "every mountain and island" (Rev. 6:13, 14) would be moved as the solar system and earth is finally engulfed in coalescing "black holes."

Another startling aspect in Elliott's discussion of the high velocity convergence of the stars is that star light (most stars being many light years away) would require several years to arrive at earth. Hence if the stars themselves had been miraculously accelerated toward the earth to near light velocity, they would be only a short time (hours or days) behind their own light emissions. This means there would be no possible way to detect the approach of the stars until a short time before their actual arrival even though some of the more distant stars may, even now, be hurtling toward earth and may have been so doing for thousands of years.

> And then [that is, as these great catastrophic events are proceeding] shall appear the *sign of the Son of man in heaven*: and then shall all the tribes of the earth mourn [that is, the wicked will certainly realize that doom is upon them and they will mourn], and *they shall see the Son of man coming* in the *clouds* of heaven *with power and great glory* (Matt. 24:30).

Here is the *second coming* of the Lord Jesus Christ (cf. Acts 1:9-11), and, as I believe everyone would agree, Matthew 24:30 describes what we call the *revelation* of Christ. Then reading further:

> And he shall send his angels with a great sound of a trumpet, and they shall gather together his elect from the four winds, from one end of heaven to the other (24:31).

We see then, there is a rapture. The word "rapture" is not found in the Scripture as such; it means a taking up. And here the Lord Jesus is taking up (see Matt. 24:40, 41) the elect from the four winds. Now I used to have a problem with that Scripture passage, because I did not want to understand it to be saying that the saints would be raptured at this time. Others have had the same problem: One premillennial preacher emphasized, "It says they were gathered from *heaven*; it doesn't say *earth*." He was vainly trying to make the point, for obvious reasons, that the saints were not caught up or raptured from the earth at the revelation of Christ. But now in the book of Mark (the parallel passage to this one) we read this:

> And then shall he send his angels, and shall gather together his elect *from* the four winds, *from* the uttermost part of the *earth* to the uttermost part of heaven (Mark 13:27).

The gathering or the rapture at the *revelation* of Christ is going to be *from the earth* to heaven. It is a universal gathering; therefore, it is the same gathering as in Hebrews (12:21, 22) when God gathers together the souls of just men made perfect from the foundations of the earth with all of the angels present. There can only be one universal gathering.

Just to let those passages mean what they say, it is certain when Christ is revealed from heaven that: (1) the

Studies on the Temporality of this Present Earth

By gathering together a cluster of the main passages throughout the Bible that pertain to the destiny of earth, we find: four passages teach or imply that the earth is eternal; fourteen passages teach categorically that this present earth will perish; and sixteen more strongly imply it. Some see this as a dilemma, but as we review all the data below, the resolution will be very simple.

Passages that Teach or Imply an Eternal Earth

1. And he built his sanctuary like high palaces, like the earth which he hath established for ever (Psalm 78:69).
2. Who laid the foundations of the earth, that it should not be removed for ever (Psalm 104:5).
3. One generation passeth away, and another generation cometh: but the earth abideth for ever (Eccl. 1:4; see also Deut. 4:40).

Scriptures Showing the Destruction of the Present Heavens and Earth

1. Therefore I will shake the heavens, and the earth shall remove out of her place . . . in the day of his fierce anger (Isa. 13:13).
2. The earth shall reel to and fro like a drunkard . . . it shall fall, and not rise again (Isa. 24:20).
3. . . . the heavens shall vanish away like smoke, and the earth shall wax old like a garment . . . (Isa. 51:6).
4. For, behold, I create new heavens and a new earth: and the former shall not be remembered, nor come into mind (Isa. 65:17).
5. I beheld the earth, and, lo, it was without form, and void; and the heavens, and they had no light (Jer. 4:23).
6. Heaven and earth shall pass away, but my words shall not pass away (Matt. 24:35; Mark 13:31; Luke 21:33).
7. . . . Yet once more I shake not the earth only, but also heaven. And this word, Yet once more, signifieth the removing of those things that are shaken (Heb. 12:26, 27). See Cluster Study 1, p. 15.
8. . . . the heavens shall pass away with a great noise, and the elements shall melt with fervent heat, the earth also and the works that are therein shall be burned up (2 Pet. 3:7, 10; see also Heb. 1:10, 11; Rev. 6:13, 14; 20:11; 21:1;).

Passages Resolving the Supposed Dilemma

1. For as the new heavens and the new earth, which I will make, shall remain before me, saith the Lord, so shall your seed and your name remain (Isa. 66:22; see 65:17 above).
2. Nevertheless we, according to his promise, look for new heavens and a new earth, wherein dwelleth righteousness (2 Pet. 3:13; see Rev. 21:1 above).
3. . . . he that sat upon the throne said, Behold, I make all things new (Rev. 21:5).

Conclusion

The teaching of the Scripture is now obvious: God will destroy this present sin-cursed heavens and earth and will create a new heaven and a new earth which is sin-free and eternal. All passages actually teaching eternality of earth must be applied to the latter; all passages teaching destruction must be applied to the former. There is no dilemma.

heavens and earth are to be utterly destroyed; (2) just before this happens He will come and rapture all of the elect from the four winds of earth to heaven. Just as Jesus promised, "if I go and prepare a place for you, I will come again, and receive you unto myself . . ." (John 14:2-4). Jesus has not "prepared a place" on this earth; therefore the righteous all will be taken up out of the earth. Then (3) the wicked will be left (Matt. 24:40, 41) to perish in the holocaust that is coming as the stars fall and converge upon the earth.

Now I can make the first rigorous point. Simply stated, the first of the five rigorous propositional truths is this: *When Christ leaves the heavens and comes the second time, this terminates the entire history and existence of this present universe. It will be no more.*

This analysis is rigorous, but there is yet more proof. I want to turn to Revelation chapter six, and there we find a passage that parallels Matthew 24:29, 30. It has to be the same event, because the same things happen. You do not have the destruction of the world two or three times, just "once more." The same event is described in these two different places:

> And I beheld when he had opened the sixth seal, and, lo, there was a great earthquake; and the *sun became black* as sackcloth of hair, and the *moon became as blood* (Rev. 6:12).

We read about the sun being darkened in Matthew 24:29 and Acts 2:20 in connection with the great shaking of the heavens, the falling of the stars, the second coming of the Lord, and the "great and notable day of the Lord" (cf. 2 Pet. 3:10). Now we read also in Revelation:

> And the *stars* of heaven *fell unto the earth*, even as a fig tree casteth her untimely figs, when she is shaken of a mighty wind (6:13).

Again the same events are related — the stars fall; the sun is blackened. This is the same occasion as in Matthew 24, because it only happens once. This is the destruction and the end of all things that God made in Genesis. Now notice:

> And the *heaven departed* as a scroll when it is rolled together;

and every mountain and island were moved out of their places (Rev. 6:14).

This is a universal catastrophe involving the heavens and the earth. The heavens perish as the converging stars destroy the earth and any human or other life that is left on the earth. This is a total "wipe-out" of the heavens and of the earth as plainly as words can make it. If I were to sit down and try to describe the destruction of the heavens and the earth, I would not know words that would be less ambiguous than these. What we have in these passages, just interpreting the Scriptures literally, is the termination of the heavens and the earth, and it takes place at the *revelation* of the Lord Jesus Christ. There is no ambiguity about these passages.

Now when I faced these things with no preconditioning, I knew I had to adjust my view. I knew I dared not twist those clear passages and make the Word of God of none effect by my traditions. I had formerly been taught that chapter four through chapter nineteen of Revelation described the great tribulation period. I thought the rapture occurred about the beginning of chapter four, and that all the events from chapter four on through chapter nineteen were events that took place during the great tribulation. Yet here in chapter six, right near the beginning of that period, I found the heavens and the earth being destroyed as plainly as language could teach it.

Now I had a problem. I had to rationalize or spiritualize that passage or give up my position. And other premillennialists have had to rationalize it too. For example, Dr. Ironside, a great old premillennial scholar now dead, said that this passage did not mean the literal, physical destruction of the heavens and the earth, but rather it had reference to the turmoil in the political, social, and ecclesiastical affairs of the world, that were coming during this tribulation period.[5] That conclusion was necessitated on his part to

---

[5] Ironside is quoted to this effect by John F. Walvoord, *The Revelation of Jesus Christ* (Chicago: Moody Press, 1966), p. 136. Walvoord himself commenting on this passage, while giving tacit consent to a quasi-literal

avoid the obvious implications of a literal interpretation here. A truly literal interpretation here would have forced him to give up his position.

Dr. Henry M. Morris, to whom the Christian world owes a great debt of gratitude for his work in creation science, has published a volume on each of the biblical books that bracket the Scripture, Genesis and Revelation. His book on Genesis is for the most part a careful, objective work of immense value. His book on Revelation, however, is seriously flawed by his premillennial background.

In the verses under consideration, Revelation 6:12-14, Dr. Morris, like Dr. Ironside, stumbles seriously, as every premillennialist must. He does not acknowledge that the heavens actually depart or that the real stars, the great nuclear "suns" as we know them today, converge upon the earth. What happens, he says, is that a "swarm of asteroids . . . pummel the earth." Concerning the statement that the "heaven departed," Dr. Morris comments that it is the result of one of two possibilities: 1) "clouds of dust will gradually spread across the sky, making it appear that the sky is being 'rolled up'" or 2) that people who live on "shifting crustal plates will observe the heavens appearing to move in the opposite direction."[6] Surely there is at least one other possibility — that it actually will happen as written.

The implications in taking this approach to the interpretation of Scripture is rather serious. We do not have here the words of a casual bystander observing a limited calamity and mistaking a dust storm or shifting plates for the departing of the heavens! And we would hardly expect the Lord to use this language to reveal political, social, or ecclesiastical turmoil, especially since we have so many other direct passages with similar wording to establish a literal

---

interpretation, makes what might be considered the understatement of the century in saying: ". . . it does seem to indicate that . . . God is taking a direct intervention into human affairs." He does not admit that the heavens really *depart*.

[6] Henry M. Morris, *The Revelation Record* (San Diego: Creation-Life Publishers, 1983), pp. 122, 123.

destruction of the heavens and earth. We have here a vision created by God, observed and reported by a mature and reliable apostle, chosen and verbally inspired by God to render a precise account of the falling of the stars, the departing of the heavens, and the chaotic breakup of the whole earth. That is the actual literal message of the passage. The "scroll" is only poetic description: "*like* a scroll."

However well-meaning these interpretations by premillennial writers may have been, they seriously impugn the integrity of the Apostle John making him appear as an ignorant or confused observer who would mistake a dust cloud or other phenomenon for the departing of the heavens. Not only does it impugn John, but it impugns the very vehicle of God's revelation as having little or no ability to describe an event as colossal as the destruction of the universe in language that can be understood.

Then too, if the crustal plates of the earth were shifting fast enough to give the illusion that the heavens were departing in the opposite direction, the earthquake damage, "every mountain and island moved," the surface buckling and tilting, the magma flows, and the tidal waves and flooding, would mean destruction so universal that no human could survive on earth. And even if a few did somehow survive, the earth would be essentially uninhabitable for at least centuries — a calamity far worse than a universal flood. This is not what I would call the best environment in which to start the golden age of the millennium.

But the Lord has promised that the waters, at least, shall not destroy the earth with its creatures again (Gen. 9:15). Moreover, He has promised: ". . . neither will I again smite any more every thing living, as I have done. *While the earth remaineth*, seedtime and harvest, and cold and heat, and summer and winter, and day and night shall not cease" (Gen. 8:21, 22).

The next destructive action from the Lord that will disrupt the normal agricultural and seasonal cycles of the earth will be the destruction of the earth itself, and that by fire (2 Pet. 3:10). There will be no direct intermediate calamitous judgment of the human race of the order described by Revelation 6:12-14 while the earth remains. Only once more will it be so shaken (Heb. 12:26, 27; Hag. 2:6, 7), and that is the end.

I need not belabor the weakness of the premillennial rationalizations of this passage and their obvious incompatibility with biblical eschatology and its persistent teachings that when Jesus comes this present earth is destroyed in preparation for a new heaven and new earth. Premillennial interpreters pride themselves on being literal in their interpretations; but they cannot take the language of this passage at its literal meaning. Since it literally says the stars fall and the heavens depart, they must spiritualize or rationalize it, which thing they decry in amillennialists and postmillennialists. We should adjust our views of prophecy to be able, with great ease and confidence, to interpret this passage at face value just as in Matthew (24:29-31) and others. These passages are rigorous, but there is yet more proof.

In the book of 2 Peter, chapter three, we have another passage that gives yet more detail concerning the destruction of the heavens and the earth, at the revelation of Christ, with intensive fire. It begins by pointing out that scoffers will come in the last days saying, "Where is the promise of his *coming*?" This shows that in Peter's mind he is dealing here with the *second coming*, the revelation, of Christ. I once had to precondition this passage with the presupposition that Christ had already been on earth a thousand years before the events described in this passage. But this will not do; Peter is clearly anticipating the events relating to the second coming of Christ. If Peter anticipated Christ as present on earth for a thousand years before the events described, where is the relevancy of the question?

Peter is describing the "great and notable day of the Lord" (Acts 2:20, 2 Pet. 3:10, 12) "in which the heavens shall pass away with a great noise" — precisely what we saw happening in Matthew (24:29-31) and in Revelation (6:12f). This can happen, as we saw in Hebrews (12:26, 27), only once. Therefore, all these passages describe the same event. In Revelation (6:14) the heavens departed as a scroll when it is rolled together. In Matthew (24:29) the heavens are *shaken*

The Great and Notable Day of the Lord

This cluster of Scripture references has been brought together for convenience in the evaluation of the phenomenon of "The Day of the Lord." Every place this phrase is mentioned in the Bible is referenced below, some more than once. We have set these references in categories for simplicity in understanding their usage in Scripture.

Judgments Upon Israel
Isaiah 2:12
Ezekiel 7:19
Hosea 9:5
Joel 1:15; 2:1
Amos 5:18, 20

Judgments Upon Egypt
Jeremiah 46:10
Ezekiel 30:30

Judgment Upon the Prophets of Israel
Ezekiel 13:5

Judgment Upon Edom
Obadiah 1:15

The Great and Notable Day
Isaiah 13:6, 9, 13;
Joel 2:4, 31; 3:14
Zephaniah 1:7, 14; 2:2, 3; 3:8
Malachi 4:5
Acts 2:2
1 Corinthians 1:8; 5:5
2 Corinthians 1:14
1 Thessalonians 5:2
2 Thessalonians 2:2
2 Peter 3:10, 12
Revelation 6:17; 16:14, 15

Telescopc Prohetic Vision
We use this term to describe the very instructive prophetic device wherein a prophet sees a local event of limited judgment on a people and uses it as an occasion to project beyond the local to the principle of the final judgment in the "great and notable day of the Lord." By this means God has both taught and confirmed the fact of the great final judgment of earth.

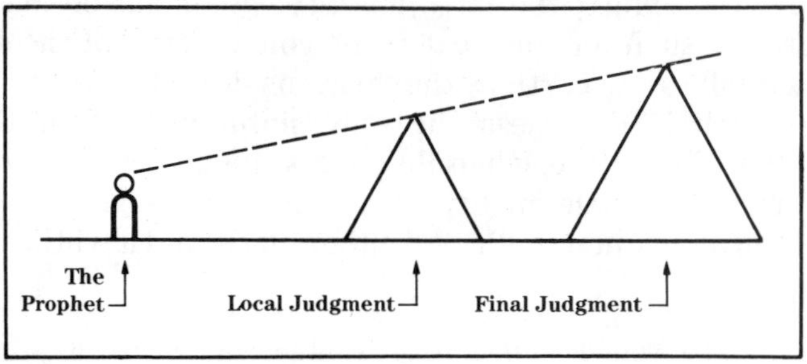

Examples: Isaiah 13:6, 9 (see entire chapter); Joel 1:15; 2:1 (judgment of locusts); Joel 2:11, 31; 3:14 (final judgment at the second coming, before New Heaven and New Earth, projected from local events); Zephaniah 1:7, 14; 2:2, 3; 3:8 (final judgment projected from local events); Zechariah 14:1 (see pp. 170-173.)

Conclusion: "The day of the Lord," used often of local judgments, always anticipates the final "great and notable" day of the destruction of this earth at the second coming of Christ.

(destroyed) and the stars fall. And now we find in 2 Peter a description of the day of the Lord in which the heavens are *dissolved*, and *pass away* with a great noise, and the *elements melt* with fervent heat.

Peter refers to "the elements" to describe the most basic form of matter, which we would indeed call *elements*. Now an element is the most fundamental state to which any substance may be reduced by chemical means. An element exists at the atomic level and can never be further subdivided by any chemical process, by chemical fires, explosions, or other chemical means. The elements themselves disintegrate only into subatomic matter. They break down into subatomic particles by means of nuclear reactions. The only continuously sustained nuclear reactions known in nature are the sun and stars. The temperatures required to sustain such nuclear chain reactions are incredibly high, on the order of twenty-million degrees (Kelvin).[7] Therefore, if a vast nuclear reaction such as a star should come into close proximity with other materials such as this earth, it also, because of the intensive "fervent" heat, will become involved in a nuclear reaction. The elements will literally "melt" or "dissolve" with a *fervent* heat.

Now, remembering the other passages where stars are said to be falling to the earth, it is an easy conclusion that the source of such fervent heat is the convergence of the stars which fall to the earth as the "heavens depart."

Earth is doubtless the only sinful planet[8] in God's universe. Therefore, when He purges the universe of sin, He will bring all those mighty, atomic furnaces together. They will converge upon this little "dot" in space, and it will literally

---

[7] David K. McDaniels, *The Sun* (New York: John Wiley & Sons, 1979;), p. 95.

[8] It is difficult to believe that the redemptive work of God could extend to more than one planet or race. And while God has no legal requirement to redeem any sinful race, His love would doubtless lead Him to seek a way. I would speculate then if there are other races on other planets, they would be pure, unfallen creatures to be received unto God when the universe implodes upon earth.

explode into a fervent heat energy or what we might call a subatomic "plasma." It is likely, then, that from this "plasma" God will reconstruct the new heavens and new earth (2 Pet. 3:13; Rev. 21:1) at "the times of restitution of all things" (Acts 3:21) after the millennium and after the general Judgment (cf. Rev. 20; 21; 22). All these things take place when or shortly after the Lord Jesus Christ returns to earth to receive His people. Therefore, this first rigorous propositional truth is established firmly with these Scriptures and others; and we must conclude that *the destruction of all material things will occur when the Lord Jesus comes at His revelation.*

A corollary to this proposition that the heavens and earth will be destroyed at the revelation of Christ is also the similar proposition that all of the saved will be raptured at His coming, and all of the lost are to be destroyed. Now in the book of 2 Thessalonians (1:6, 7), Paul is writing to church-age Christians — those who are in Thessalonica. He says, "Since it is a righteous thing with God to repay with tribulation those who trouble you, And to give you who are troubled rest[9] with us when the Lord Jesus is *revealed* from heaven with His mighty angels" (NKJV). Now we have here the exact same event that we had in Matthew 24. I know, because both passages describe the *revelation* of Christ with His angels. He shall be "revealed" (2 Thess. 1:7) — not a secret coming; there is no secret coming. There are several clues here which identify this occasion with Matthew 24, Revelation 6, and 2 Peter 3. He will be *revealed* from heaven with His *mighty angels.* And it was also said in the book of Matthew that it was the angels He sent out to catch up the elect.

Paul further describes this: "In *flaming fire* taking

---

[9] That *rest* is used in the original language as a noun is not readily apparent to most of us in the English translation of this verse, but Glenn Kerr, a skilled linguist, has observed, "The original in these verses shows that Jesus will recompense *two* things when He is revealed. This idea is not as clear in the English as it might be. He will recompense tribulation to those who trouble the saints, and He will recompense rest to the saints who are troubled. The same event, His revelation from heaven, will accomplish both" (from unpublished notes).

vengeance on them that know not God, and that obey not the gospel of our Lord Jesus Christ" (1:8). Here is destruction by fire which is to be poured out in vengeance. Such things can only happen once. Doubtless then, this is the conflagration kindled by the convergence of the stars upon this earth. Those who are wicked will be left here to die in that holocaust (Matt. 24:40, 41): "Who shall be punished with everlasting destruction from the presence of the Lord, and from the glory of his power" (2 Thess. 1:9). They will go straight from this holocaust through death to judgment and into the eternal chambers of perdition when Christ returns at the revelation.

Now this proposition emerges: all those who are saved will be raptured at the revelation of Christ; all those who are not saved will die and go into perdition at the revelation of Christ. Now it seems elementary, but that accounts for *all* the people on earth. There are no more. There will be no people left here on earth — natural "flesh and blood" people — to go into a millennium if there were still an earth. But this present earth will not exist to have a millennium on if there were any people left. The earth with the wicked will be destroyed; the saints will be caught up and changed in the twinkling of an eye, no more to reproduce natural flesh-and-blood men. And the wicked will be destroyed with the brightness of His coming (2 Thess. 1:8; Matt. 24:40, 41; 2 Thess. 2:8-12).

Simply taking these passages at face value, *we have now established an order of things — a framework for eschatology.* The order then is a matter of simple but rigorous scriptural logic. These events of universal destruction will occur when Christ is *revealed* from heaven *immediately after the tribulation.* If the world and the universe are to be destroyed immediately after the tribulation, this order means that the tribulation is the last earthly event and will have to occur before Christ comes. Since there will be no earth, nor any people left upon the earth alive, this fact means also that if there is a millennium on this present earth (and there is — see p. 10) it has to occur prior to the termination of the earth. Since the earth is terminated immediately after the tribulation, the millennium, therefore, has to precede the tribulation. Now that is simple logic from what is positively established so far by the Scriptures, with no forcing, no preconditioning of the Scriptures — no tampering with the meaning of them. We know now that when God shakes the heavens, that shaking means the destruction of the material universe. We will have to accept that biblical truth.

Now a summary of the order or sequence so far established:

1. The universe is terminated at the *revelation* of Jesus Christ.

2. The catastrophic events that terminate the universe occur *immediately* after the great tribulation.

3. Therefore, the last event to transpire in the course of human history on earth is the great *tribulation.*

4. These facts mean that if there is a *millennium* on this present earth (and there is: Rev. 20:1-6; Isa. 2:2-4; 11:5-12:6) it must occur *before* the great tribulation. The same sequence — the millennium (a thousand years), then the tribulation ("a little season"; see Rev. 20:3, also Rev. 20:7-9a), then the final destruction (with fire; Rev. 20:9b), and then final judgment (Rev. 20:10-15) — is clearly delineated *in sequence* in the twentieth chapter of Revelation.

5. We therefore rigorously conclude that the second coming of Christ — the *revelation* — occurs *after the millennium.*

For a graphic illustration of this order of events, see page 31.

Thus we have established a postmillennial framework for the return of Christ, and a postmillennial, post-tribulation rapture. That is just the way it works out. I had no reason to *seek* this conclusion, and I have no reason to retain it except that the Scriptures have forced it upon me. But I do now love this conclusion, for God's Word has established it. I have no right to despise the course of events ordained according to the eternal purpose of God. It is ours now to joyfully comply with this schedule.

I have no obligation to try to establish or explain these things in any other way than the way they are simply stated by Scripture. As we shall later see, there is no other reason in any of the other Scripture passages in all of the Bible that would suggest a reason to change the face-value interpretation of these strong, vivid passages that I have just discussed. To the contrary, the Scriptures from Genesis to Revelation are infinitely easier to harmonize with this framework than with any other, once the mind is ready to let the Scripture shape its understanding.

One of the criticisms I received when I first advanced this simple outline of events was that it was too brief and that conclusions were reached on too small a sampling of Scripture. Except for the rigor of those passages, I would agree. But any categorical statement of Scripture, if only one, is compatible with all others. Still we need to be, and will be, thorough. But we should remember that it is easier to establish truth with fewer words and less paper than it is to establish error. Error must be braced up with tomes of elaborate and complex arguments, but truth stands alone.

In a few pages, I have established a firm and cogent framework of eschatology by analyzing a number of major passages from Scripture dealing with the second coming of Christ. I submit this conclusion to the judgment of God's people and the test of time. Of course, the substance of this conclusion is not unique or original with me, only the form in which it appears here. I recognize, however, that it is definitely a minority position. And before I committed it to writing, I inquired diligently of many knowledgeable brethren to see if I had erred in my interpretation of these passages. Some were persuaded by these arguments and changed their position on eschatology. Others were not persuaded, but no one so far who has attempted an answer has been willing to deal analytically and exegetically with these specific passages to demonstrate a serious error in my analysis of them. They have merely brushed them aside saying they are figurative or symbolic passages.

So now we press on to a more complete treatment of many other passages of Scripture to corroborate and strengthen these conclusions.

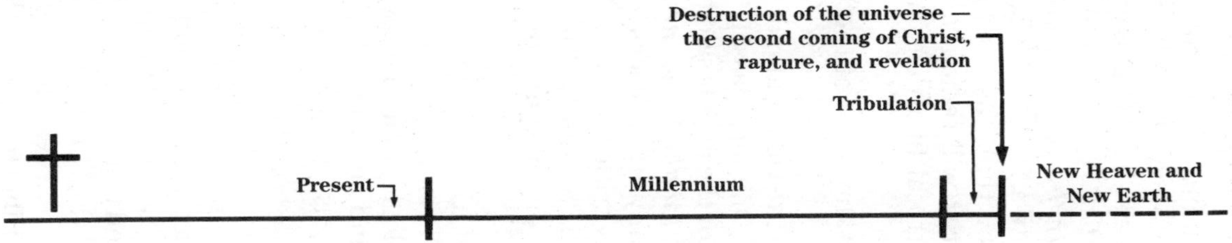

1. Starting with the termination of the universe at the revelation of Christ, a benchmark established unequivocally by Hebrews 12:26, 27; Matthew 24:29-31; Revelation 6:12-17; 2 Peter 3:10-13; 2 Thessalonians 1:6-10; we may now work backward in a sequence.

2. Since the destruction of the universe is said to occur "immediately after" the tribulation (Matt. 24:29), the last event of history on this earth is the tribulation.

3. The millennium then must occur prior to the tribulation or else it cannot occur at all on this present earth.

4. The above order of events correlates exactly with the sequence established in Revelation 20:1-15. The order is as follows: a) Satan bound (v. 2); b) the millennium (vs. 3-6); c) tribulation — Satan loosed a "little season" (vs. 3, 7); d) the gathering of the nations to battle (vs. 8, 9a); e) the termination of the universe (vs. 9b, 11).

5. The order thus established is corroborated by many rigorous Scripture passages, allowed by all Scripture passages, and contradicted by no Scripture passage. It unequivocally puts the second coming of Christ after or *post* to the millennium. Hence the framework of eschatology is postmillennial.

The Framework of Eschatology

The Second Rigorous Propositional Truth

I turn now to the second of five rigorous propositional truths which will further establish, solidify, and corroborate a postmillennial framework of eschatology. The second of these propositions concerns the office of Christ that is called His Session: *that Christ is now "seated" in heaven at the "right hand" of God and will remain in this Session until all His enemies become His footstool.* Now a footstool is something that is under foot — something that has been subjugated, defeated. And therefore Christ will remain at the right hand of God until the time for the total, final defeat of all His enemies.

Psalm 110 is the most quoted Psalm in all of the New Testament, with verse one being the most quoted verse. That Psalm places Christ in the heavens at the right hand of God until His enemies become His footstool. One such passage is in Hebrews (1:13). It says, "But to which of the angels said he at any time, *Sit on my right hand, until I make thine enemies thy footstool?*" Psalm 110 is quoted many other places in the Scriptures; it seems to represent a very critical issue for New Testament writers. Christ will be in His Session at the right hand of God until the time when His enemies are all to be conquered.

Now we need to look briefly at the concept of the "seating" or work of the resurrected Christ in heaven at "the right hand of God." This is known theologically as the *Session* of Christ, and it refers to the work and situation of Christ after His ascension into heaven until His return to earth to defeat the final enemy, death (Heb. 10:12, 13; 1 Cor. 15:25, 26).

The term "right hand of God" is an anthropomorphic expression (ascribing man-like characteristics to God; e.g., God's "right hand," the "eyes," "mouth," "nostrils" of God, etc.), and it is not necessarily to be understood that God the Father sits in a physical body on a throne and that Christ, who does have a body, sits beside Him. The Bible teaches that God is a Spirit (John 4:24). However, since the Bible freely uses these expressions for our understanding, I will freely use the same expressions to denote the work of Christ from the time of His *ascension* until the end of the universe at His *revelation.*

Peter makes it positively clear that the Session of Christ at God's right hand is a situation of honor, dominion, and glory, after His ascension, used to distinguish the *heavenly* regal and intercessory work of Christ from his *earthly* work. A review of Peter's sermon (Acts 2) makes this clear: "Therefore being by the right hand of God *exalted*" (v. 33). "David is not *ascended* . . . but he saith himself, the Lord said unto my Lord, sit thou *on my right hand, until* I make thy foes thy footstool" (vs. 34, 35). This puts clear boundaries on the Session, namely from the ascension to the very end when death is "conquered." This work is confined to heaven in clear contradistinction to earth. No part of the Session takes place on earth (see Acts 3:21).

In the New Testament there are approximately twenty passages where reference is made to the Session of Christ as taught in Psalm 110. Of these passages not one teaches that a part of that Session is to be accomplished on earth, but at least eight of these passages positively teach that the Session is in heaven. Furthermore, it is certain that the writers of the New Testament so regarded it, and upon this principle is based their theology for the course of this age: from the ascension to the destruction of the heavens and the earth.

The New Testament writers thought of the Session of Christ as a heavenly Session to be distinguished from His work on earth. As proof, I submit the following Scripture passages:

1. "So then after the Lord had spoken unto them, he was *received up into heaven*, and sat on the right hand of God" (Mark 16:19).

2. "Therefore being by the right hand of God *exalted* . . ." (Acts 2:33, 34).

3. "It is Christ that died, yea rather, that is *risen again, who is even at the right hand of God*, who also maketh intercession for us" (Rom. 8:34).

4. ". . . When he *raised him from the dead*, and set him at his

own right hand in the *heavenly places, far above* all principality, and power, and might, and dominion . . ." (Eph. 1:20, 21).

5. " . . . seek those things *which are above, where Christ sitteth* on the right hand of God" (Col. 3:1).

6. ". . . when he had by himself purged our sins, sat down on the right hand of the majesty *on high*" (Heb. 1:3).

7. "We have such an high priest, who is set on the right hand of the throne of the Majesty *in the heavens* . . . " (Heb. 8:1).

8. ". . . After he had offered one sacrifice for sins for ever, sat down on the right hand of God; *from henceforth* expecting till his enemies be made his footstool" (Heb. 10:12, 13).

9. ". . . who for the joy that was set before him endured the cross, despising the shame, and is set down at the right hand of *the throne of God*" (Heb. 12:2).

10. "It is expedient for you that I go away . . . " (John 16:7; cf. 14:16).

Some premillennialists, seeing the problem these teachings create for their doctrine, have wanted this Session to include the rapture, the revelation, and a thousand-year physical reign on earth after the second coming. But this would be a serious affront to the inspired New Testament writers; and upon what authority would one presume to do such a thing when it is nowhere taught? Scripture boxes the Session into heaven entirely. Starting at the ascension, Peter says of Christ: "Whom the heavens must receive until the time of restitution of *all things* . . . " (Acts 3:21).

The "restitution of all things" can only mean the destruction of this present heaven and earth and the establishment of the new heaven and new earth (Rev. 21:1). "Behold, I make *all things* new" (21:5). The millennium, wonderful though it may be, is not a full restitution — not a renewing of "all things." Some things may be restored but this present earth will never be restored to the sinless condition of its pristine purity before it was cursed (Gen. 3:17). As long as sin and death exist, "all things" have not been restored. This universe is scheduled for destruction; and when God "makes all things new," only then will total perfection, peace, righteousness, and tranquility be restored. "Nevertheless we, according to his promise, look for new heavens and a new earth, wherein dwelleth righteousness" (2 Pet. 3:13).

Moreover, the work of Christ as a resident of this earth is finished. The only thing He could not do from heaven was to be born of a woman, to live as a man under the law, and die in atonement for our sins. All else may be and will be done from His position of exaltation in heaven (excepting a momentary return to earth for His saints which is no residency). His work of ruling and reigning over the affairs of this earth is done from heaven (we will discuss this thoroughly in a later chapter).

In John 17 we learn: 1) He has "finished" His earthly work (v. 4). 2) Christ was glorified after His earthly sojourn as He was before He came (v. 5). 3) He is to be "no more" in the world (v. 11). 4) He said, "I come to [the Father]" (v. 13). His next visit to the earth will not be for residency, but a mere touch-down to receive His saints and to destroy the universe with all His enemies (Matt. 24:29-31).

The point of so many quotations of Psalm 110:1 in the New Testament is to distinguish firmly the heavenly residency and rule of Christ on the throne of His father David (See Peter's interpretation, Acts 2:30-35, to be discussed more fully later) from His former and only earthly residency.

According to Psalm 110, it is from His vantage point at the right hand of God that Christ executes the providential affairs of history wherein He will have victory over His enemies: "The Lord shall send the rod of thy strength out of Zion, i.e., ["Sion . . . the heavenly Jerusalem . . . " (Heb. 12:22)], rule thou in the *midst* of thine enemies" (v. 2). The Lord "in our midst" does not always indicate physical presence: " . . . yet thou, O Lord, art in the *midst* of us, and we are called by thy name" (Jer. 14:9; cf. Matt. 18:20). "The Lord *at thy right hand* shall strike through kings . . . " (Psalm 110:5). "The Lord hath prepared his throne in the heavens; and his Kingdom ruleth over all" (Psalm 103:19). "The Lord is in his holy temple, the Lord's throne is in heaven . . . " (Psalm 11:4).

No king sits on the throne today except by the providential purpose of Him who sits at God's right hand. "All power is given unto me in heaven and in earth . . . " (Matt. 28:18). No army marches, no ship sails, no breeze blows, no baby cries but by His providential will, oversight, or permission.

From this high throne, He rules the affairs of His kingdom. He guides His people — His churches — to finally accomplish His "eternal purpose" (see Eph. 3:10, 11) through the church. He is "in the *midst* of the seven candlesticks" (churches, Rev. 1:13, 20). He has repaired the "tabernacle of David" (Acts 15:13-18), i.e. the House of God,[10] now the church, "That the residue of men might seek after the Lord, and all the Gentiles . . . ." From His throne in heaven He is prosecuting this great purpose through His new covenant people both Jew and Gentile in the church (Eph. 2:17-22).

From His throne in heaven, Christ is "head over all things" in behalf of His church according to His eternal purpose (Eph. 1:19-23; 3:10, 11; Psalm 110:1f).

He is also a "priest for ever after the order of Melchizedek" (Psalm 110:4; Heb. 7:21-26), attentive to the cry of the penitent soul as thousands of His enemies are conquered by the Gospel of grace. But for those who will have none of His grace, "The Lord *at thy right hand* shall strike through kings in the day of his wrath" (v. 5). He shall judge among the

---

[10] The premillennial position makes the "tabernacle of David" like the "throne of David" to be an aspect of an earthly reign of Christ on this present earth. But James says that the prophecy of Amos (9:11, 12) agrees with God's purpose to take out of the Gentiles a people for His name (Acts 15:14-16). According to James this work, which they were in process of doing, was contingent upon fulfillment of Amos' prophecy to build the tabernacle of David. Some have been confused by the phrase "I will return," thinking it refers to the second coming of Christ. But it has nothing to do with the second coming; James paraphrases Amos according to James' own time-frame and says simply, "after this" (after the "day" of which Amos spoke, i.e., during the first advent of Christ). It should read: "I will turn back (bring back or restore), even build again, the tabernacle of David . . ." etc. James cited this verse to confirm the validity of what they were doing at that time through the church. If Amos' prophecy is fulfilled only after the second coming, it did not confirm the work they were doing and had no relevancy to their problem.

heathen and slay His enemies — all from the right hand of God until the day He returns for the sudden, total, and final defeat of His last enemy. No wonder Psalm 110:1 was the central theme of New Testament eschatology.

Moreover, Paul quotes this great Psalm in the fifteenth chapter of 1 Corinthians:

> For as in Adam all die, even so in Christ shall all be made alive. But every man in his own order: Christ the firstfruits; afterward they that are Christ's *at his coming.* Then cometh *the end,* when he shall have delivered up the kingdom to God, even the Father; *when he shall have put down all rule and all authority and power.* For *he must reign* [and here is the quotation from Psalm 110], till he hath put all enemies under his feet. *The last enemy that shall be destroyed is death* (1 Cor. 15:22-26).

He is now reigning, and the position of His reign is from heaven at the right hand of God until the time that all of His enemies are under His feet. Now there is one last enemy that will not be destroyed until the stars fall and the elements melt with fervent heat. "The last enemy that shall be destroyed is *death*" (v. 26).

Now according to the premillennial pretribulation rapture view, Christ leaves heaven and comes the second time to rapture the saints. But His enemies remain — including much death. Then seven years later He comes a third time at the revelation of Christ, but death remains. And contrary to what Jesus says, instead of the heavens and earth perishing in the great "shaking," this view says life goes on, the natural, sinful, descendants of Adam continue to be born, to marry, to give birth, to sin, and to die. Christ establishes a throne located on this sin-cursed earth, and according to this view He sits on this earthly throne and "rules" over natural flesh-and-blood men reproducing in the normal way; sinful men, dying men, sons of Adam.

Children are born during the millennium; they are born after Adam. The curse is upon *all* Adam's children. "It is appointed unto men once to die" (Heb. 9:27). They sin, and they die. Though longevity increases, still there is death during the millennium (Isa. 65:19-25). Furthermore, there is death following the millennium — a lot of it. Satan is an enemy — the archenemy, and he is loosed from the bottomless pit *after* the millennium. Satan leads other enemies, Gog of Magog, out upon the face of the earth to deceive the nations and to fight and to kill (see Rev. 20; cf. Rev. 12:9-17; 9:1, 2f; 11:7f). Then fire comes down from God out of heaven destroying those that are wicked. So there is death during the millennium; there is death after the millennium. It is a most unreasonable claim that Christ reigns at the right hand of God until His last enemy is defeated in a premillennial configuration. Practically the whole world is filled with enemies after the millennium!

Therefore, Christ must remain in heaven at the right hand of God until after the millennium and after the tribulation, for His enemies will remain until then and finally be destroyed with the "brightness of His coming" (2 Thess. 2:8); "Whom the heavens must receive until the time of the restitution of *all things*, which God hath spoken by the mouth of all his holy prophets since the world began" (Acts 3:21).

In no way can we consistently say that all the enemies of Christ are put under foot at the time He leaves the heavens in a premillennial framework of eschatology. He presently reigns at the right hand of God in that position putting many of His enemies under foot daily; then He puts all remaining enemies under foot at once, at His coming (2 Thess. 1:7-9; 2:8), never to rise again. No sinner shall ever be born after His coming; Satan shall never again rise up to deceive; no death shall ever again mar the domain of God nor grieve the heart of a mother.

Death will be utterly destroyed "at his coming" (1 Cor. 15:23). Therefore, His coming is after the millennium, after the tribulation — at the end of the world. This order of events establishes the period of time Christ will remain in heaven. This proposition is very simple, biblically logical, and sound. There has been no tampering with the Scripture. This conclusion is based upon the teachings of the Bible in numerous places. In no place does the Bible teach that after the return of Christ half the major prophecies of Scripture are yet to be fulfilled but only those that pertain to the new heaven and new earth.

Now I turn again to the third chapter of the book of Acts to further corroborate this truth that Christ will remain in heaven at the right hand of God until all things are put under His feet, terminated, ended. Here we read:

> But those things, which God before had shewed by the mouth of all his prophets, that Christ should suffer, he hath so fulfilled. Repent ye therefore, and be converted, that your sins may be blotted out, when the times of refreshing shall come from the presence of the Lord; And he shall send Jesus Christ, which before was preached unto you; *Whom the heaven must receive* [that is, retain or contain, in the sense that He will remain in the heavens] until the times of *restitution of all things, which God hath spoken by the mouth of all his holy prophets since the world began* (Acts 3:18-21).

That statement includes *all* prophecy. All of the prophecy that pertains to earthly human life, human history, the history of the world, and the existence of the present universe must be fulfilled as the heavens yield up the Lord Jesus Christ — as God sends Him back to earth in the revelation.

The emphasis is on *all* things spoken by *all* prophets of *all* times: the heaven must receive him until the "times of restitution of *all* things, which God hath spoken by the mouth of *all* his holy prophets *since the world began.*" In this place *all* means *all*; we know by the repetition and by the boundaries placed on the prophecies. Now there are yet many prophecies to be fulfilled in this environment of death: Ezekiel 38, 39 has yet to be fulfilled. The millennial prophecies have yet to be fulfilled. The tribulation prophecies have yet to be fulfilled. It is both a logical and scriptural incongruity to suppose that any prophecy pertaining to this present world system could be fulfilled after Christ is "revealed from heaven with His mighty angels, in flaming fire taking vengeance on them that know not God . . . " (2 Thess. 1:7, 8) when all enemies are put down and the saints are at home with God.

When "this mortal shall have put on immortality, then

shall be brought to pass the saying that is written, Death is swallowed up in victory.... The sting of death is sin" (1 Cor. 15:54, 56). As long as men are born after Adam, sin remains; as long as sin remains, the curse remains; as long as the curse remains, death remains; as long as death remains, all things have not been restored to their pristine purity. "Nevertheless we, according to the promise, look for new heavens and a new earth, wherein dwelleth righteousness" (2 Pet. 3:13). The "restitution of all things" must wait for the new heaven and new earth after this present earth is "passed away" (Rev. 21:1). "And there shall be no more curse" (Rev. 22:3); only then will Jesus come.

So the second propositional truth is that *Christ will remain in heaven, reigning at the right hand of God, until the time when His last enemy is to be made His footstool; and the last enemy to be destroyed is death.* Once again we have an order: 1) We have the Lord Jesus Christ ascending to heaven, continuing at the right hand of God until it is time for the destruction of all the final enemies of God; then 2) He will return to finalize the destruction of this universe, of all His enemies, all the wicked, Satan, and finally death itself. Therefore, 3) if there is to be a millennium, it must occur before that. After He comes, all His enemies will be destroyed; no more sons of Adam will ever be born; no sinner shall arise; and no defiant voice shall disturb the tranquility of the universe ever again forever. Therefore, once again His coming proves to be postmillennial and post-tribulational.

The Third Rigorous Propositional Truth

Now I take up the third rigorous propositional truth which further establishes and corroborates a postmillennial framework of eschatology. It is this: *when Christ returns, there will be a general resurrection event in which both the just and the unjust are resurrected in the same general time-frame.* The Bible teaches this fact plainly and clearly if there is no preconditioning or tampering with the Scriptures. The first passage I want to bring in proof of this truth is from the book of Daniel:

> And at that time shall Michael stand up, the great prince which standeth for the children of thy people: and there shall be a time of trouble, such as never was since there was a nation even to that same time: and at *that time* thy people shall be delivered, every one that shall be found written in the book. And many of them that sleep in the dust of the earth shall awake, *some to everlasting life*, and *some to shame and everlasting contempt* (Daniel 12:1, 2).

Now you notice that this event is at the time when the greatest of all the times of trouble is upon the earth — the great tribulation. It is so compatible with the other passages we have read that "immediately after the tribulation" Christ will come back; He will "gather together his elect" (Matt. 24:29-31), and it is the same sequence here in Daniel.

Then in this connection Daniel speaks of the resurrection: "And many of them that sleep in the dust of the earth shall awake, some to *everlasting life*, and some to shame and *everlasting contempt*" (12:2). The event before us is the resurrection of the righteous and wicked, both essentially at the same time. The phrase "at that time" puts the resurrection of both classes in the same general time-frame, not a thousand years apart. Furthermore, this text shows a time of rewarding the saints: "And they that be wise shall shine as the brightness of the firmament; and they that turn many to righteousness as the stars for ever and ever" (12:3). We see here then an example of Scripture that simply states that the resurrection of the just and the unjust will occur within the same time-frame. The resurrection is at the time of the second coming of Christ (1 Cor. 15:52; 1 Thess. 4:16) which, as Daniel indicates, is at the time of the tribulation period. This is very compatible with all other Scripture.

Premillennial interpreters arbitrarily attempt to insert a thousand years between those who arise to life, and those who arise to shame. Not only is it an artificial interpretation not required by any principle of Scripture, but the language of the text cannot bear this at all, because it ties the resurrection of both classes to the time-frame of the great tribulation. The use of the word "many" (v. 2) has been thought to show that a general resurrection is not in view here, but since the subject of the passage is "the children of thy people" (v. 1), namely natural Israel, the term "many" is appropriate and does not at all imply a partial resurrection. When we consider the subject of the passage, "the children of thy people," two things are said about them: 1) some of them (a few) will be delivered, i.e., those "written in the book," and 2) "many of them," i.e., the many of "the children of thy people" who "sleep in the dust" (the many who have died, in contrast to the few who are then living) "shall awake." Of this "many" who are dead, some are resurrected to everlasting life and some to everlasting contempt. The living remnant, the few, who are alive and "written in the book" will be delivered without dying.

Keil and Delitzsch summarize their linguistic analysis of this passage by saying:

> The word "many" is accordingly used only with reference to the small number of those who shall then be living, and not with reference either to the universality of the resurrection of the dead or to a portion only of the dead . . ."[11]

Regardless of this, the language is unequivocal that the "many who awake" are comprised of both classes. They arise together, and no passage teaches or even implies a thousand-year separation between them; that is sheer invention. There must be a compelling reason for the insertion of a foreign thought of a thousand years between the two classes, but there is no reason at all. Of the "many" who rise at that time, some arise to life and some arise to everlasting contempt, and that is not compatible with the premillennial concept.

Continuing then, with this same thought, I turn to the Gospel of Matthew where Jesus is speaking to the Scribes and Pharisees concerning the condemnation of that generation. There He says to those Pharisees: "The men of Nineveh *will rise* in the judgment *with this generation* and condemn it, because they repented at the preaching of Jonah; and indeed a greater than Jonah is here" (Matt. 12:41, NKJV).

Now what did Jesus mean by this statement? He meant

---

[11] C. F. Keil and F. Delitzsch, *Commentary on the Old Testament* (Wm. B. Eerdmans Publishing Company, Grand Rapids) Vol. 9, p. 482.

those saved people who repented when Jonah preached in Nineveh would *rise* in *the* judgment with this condemned generation. The article *the* precedes *judgment* in verse 41 of the NKJV the same as in verse 42 showing that the great final judgment is in view here, not merely an abstract principle. Some have argued that *rise* in this passage is a generalized usage and does not refer to resurrection. The interpretation cannot be made on the basis of the word *rise*; it is frequently used in both ways. But the rigor of this passage inheres in the fact that *the judgment* occurs after the resurrection of all men (Rev. 20:13), and the wicked "rise" to judgment in a resurrection and in this passage the righteous "rise with" them. If anyone complains that this interpretation is not rigorous, let it not be the person who arbitrarily inserts a thousand years into the passage.

A simple and guileless interpretation of the passage must conclude that there would be a resurrection of the *saved* men of Nineveh, and the *lost* people to whom Christ was speaking — both at the same time ("with this generation").

Notice further, in verse 42: "The queen of the south shall *rise up* in *the judgment with this generation*, and shall condemn it: for she came from the uttermost parts of the earth to hear the wisdom of Solomon; and, behold, a greater than Solomon is here." So we find, in this passage, the wicked and the righteous rising together. This is *normal* Scripture language showing that the writers of Scripture, and even Jesus Himself, normally thought that way.

I turn now to the Gospel of John:

> Marvel not at this: for *the hour* is coming, in the which *all that are in the graves* shall hear his voice, And shall come forth; they that have done good, unto *the resurrection of life;* and they that have done evil, unto *the resurrection of damnation* (John 5:28, 29).

Both classes are in the graves. Both classes will hear His resurrection voice uttered only on this one occasion. It is one voice — the same "hour" (this refers to the same general time-frame, not necessarily 60 minutes). "For the Lord himself shall descend from heaven with a *shout*, with the *voice* of the archangel, and with the *trump of God*" (1 Thess. 4:16). Again we read: "In a moment, in the twinkling of an eye, at the *last trump*: for *the trumpet shall sound*, and the dead shall be raised incorruptible . . . " (1 Cor. 15:52). And again: "And he shall send his angels with *a great sound of a trumpet*, and they shall gather together his elect from the four winds . . . " (Matt. 24:31; see also Mark 13:27).

The "voice" or "shout" of Christ is mentioned in two passages (John 5:28, 1 Thess. 4:16). Now we must ask, how many times does the Lord utter the resurrection "voice" or "shout." John mentions it once only and both classes come forth. Paul mentions the "shout" in conjunction with the resurrection of the righteous and the "trump of God" (1 Thess. 4:16) which is the same as the "last trump" (1 Cor. 15:52).

These therefore must all be different references to the same event. The burden of proof that there is a second uttering of the resurrection voice of Christ a thousand years after the first is upon the premillennialist.

But as we consider this matter of the trumpet sound in conjunction with the resurrection, the problem of defending a thousand-year separation becomes even more arbitrary and difficult.

I used to have a difficult time preconditioning these trumpet passages. The "last trump" sounded, obviously, at the *rapture* (1 Cor. 15:52) which I then thought was before the tribulation. But then I found that at the *revelation* of Christ (Matt. 24:31) there was another trumpet seven years after the "last" one! One of my colleagues suggested maybe that was the "last trump" before the final one. . . . Well? Maybe. But the problem disappeared completely when I changed my position instead of the Scriptures. God's impeccable logic will guide those who are willing to change to the truth, if we notice His little clues. There was great satisfaction when I yielded to what all the evidence was forcing upon me: that the rapture (1 Cor. 15:52) and the revelation (Matt. 24:31) were one and the same event and that both followed the millennium.

Even the one Scripture that is most often cited as a "secret" rapture (1 Thess. 4:14-17), separate from the resurrection of the wicked, contains its own evidence that this is not the case. First, the word "coming" (v. 15) means the *presence* of one coming and connotes an obvious, known, visible presence — not a hidden act. Second, if it is to be a secret, it is a great mystery why the Lord would "shout," why the archangel would sound his voice, and why the very "trump of God" would sound. When God sounded a trumpet on Sinai, it was no secret (Ex. 19:16). No, a person has to "doctor" this passage to make it a secret coming. There is no problem when we acknowledge the "shout" of 1 Thessalonians 4:16 to be the identical "voice" of John 5:28. Also the "trump of God" of 1 Thessalonians 4:16, the "last trump" of 1 Corinthians 15:52, the "great sound of a trumpet" (Matt. 24:31), and the "seventh angel sounded" (Rev. 11:15-18, which also shows both classes together) are one and the same trumpet sound and one and the same occasion.

Now, I used to have to modify these passages, but I do not have to do that anymore. It is a good feeling just to let them say what they will. In the same hour, John teaches, at the voice of the Son of God, both classes come forth. There is no hint here, or in any of these passages, that the resurrection of the just and unjust is separated by a thousand years. That concept did not come from the words of Scripture. It had to be extrapolated from another source and inserted or added to these texts, and I am unwilling to force this concept upon Scripture.

Again, in the book of Acts Paul says:

> But this I confess unto thee, that after the way which they call heresy, so worship I the God of my fathers, believing all things which are written in the law and in the prophets: And have hope toward God, which they themselves also allow, that there shall be *a resurrection* of the dead, *both of the just and unjust* (Acts 24:14, 15).

Here, again, there is *a* (single) resurrection of both classes. On the face of these obvious Scriptures then, we have a general resurrection of both the just and the unjust at the coming of the Lord Jesus Christ when there is not mentioned anywhere a thousand years of separation between the resurrections of these two classes.

There is yet another passage wherein Jesus Himself taught that the final disposition of the wicked and righteous would be accomplished in the same time-frame:

> So shall it be at the end of the world: the angels shall come forth, and sever the wicked from among the just, and shall cast them into the furnace of fire . . . (Matt. 13:49, 50).

Although the word *resurrection* is not mentioned in this passage, the only way the angels could "sever the wicked from among the just" at the end of the age is if both classes were resurrected and stood together in judgment (just as we read of the Ninevites). The scenario is conclusively resurrection, for in verses 37-43 the resurrection passage from Daniel is quoted when the "righteous shall shine forth," etc. (cf. Dan. 12:3).

Jesus taught His disciples that the wheat and the tares were to "grow together until *the* harvest" (v. 30, 38-42). Some premillennial interpreters attempt to make an issue that the end of the "age," is not "the end of the world." But it would not help their cause even if it were true. If the harvest is prior to the millennium, they lose because the wicked are not cast into the furnace of fire at that time — only at the final judgment (Rev. 20:14, 15). If the harvest is after the millennium, they lose because the righteous continue to grow along with the wicked through the millennium until the one and only harvest — there is no separation until *the harvest* (a single occasion).

We ought to stop playing games with the simple direct words of God. Jesus teaches here that at the final event —and only then — there will be separation and disposition of both the just and the unjust, and this has to involve resurrection even as Daniel, Matthew, John, and Paul also consistently teach. We must give up the unwarranted and presumptuous attempt of trying to wedge a thousand years between the resurrection of the just and the unjust.

Now there is one mention of what is called a "first

resurrection" (see Rev. 20:4-6). But this is not a passage that is cleared up by merely saying the rapture is before the millennium and the wicked are raised after the millennium. This theory creates problems with dozens of Scriptures in a poor attempt to solve one. Most cults or heresies have arisen by misinterpreting one obscure or difficult passage in such a way that the rest of the whole Bible has to be reinterpreted. That is the basic problem with pretribulation rapturism, which arose in mysterious circumstances[12] around 1827-30 and was formalized and popularized by J. N. Darby. It was later put on the same pages with the Scripture by C. I. Scofield as an ubiquitous guide to thousands of unsuspecting Christians in reinterpreting the rest of the Scripture in the light of that error. That is where, as a young Christian, I got most of my erroneous presuppositions about prophecy.

Now we will interpret Revelation 20:4-6 at its face value. Our conclusion must be compatible with the passages discussed above and all other Scripture. Relying then on light from this and other Scriptures, God's impeccable precision in inspiration will guide to an accurate answer if we are patient.

First we must get the facts before us. From Revelation 20 we learn: 1) John saw thrones. 2) The location of the thrones is not specified. 3) John saw the souls of a special group of saints. 4) They were all martyrs for Christ and the Word. They were otherwise distinguished as having resisted the "beast." In view of their faithfulness unto death, these were definitely not casual, moss-backed Christians saved "yet so as by fire" (1 Cor. 3:15). These are the spiritually elite as God sees them. So upon the face of this Scripture the theory that this is a general rapture of the saints, or the so-called universal, invisible church, prior to the millennium is ruled out. Not one tenth of one percent would qualify, and fewer than that are martyrs.

Now we know what it is *not*; then what *is* this first resurrection group? We recall the mention of the souls of

---

[12] For a complete account of these mysterious circumstances see: Dave MacPherson, *The Incredible Cover-up* (Plainfield, N. J.: Logos International, 1975) and John L. Bray, *The Origin of the Pre-Tribulation Rapture Teaching* (Lakeland, Fla.: John L. Bray Ministries, Inc., 1982).

martyred saints in another passage under the fifth seal (Rev. 6:9-11) before the group was complete. They were told to wait a while. This is the same group, at least in part, because they are the martyrs, probably from the time of "righteous Abel" to the millennium.

It is a sad thought that those faithful martyrs gave their all in a time when it seemed that Satan had won the victory. They did not have five thousand in Sunday school; the Lord did not seem to be "blessing" their ministries. They had raw faith to sustain them, and the cause they loved more than life itself seemed to be essentially lost in the flourishing power of kings and high churchmen — "the beast" surmounted by the "mother of harlots" (see the interpretation of Rev. 13:1-4; 17:1-6, pp. 77-82, 228-230).

But now, during the millennium, the cause they preserved with their lives is about to flourish. The fruits of their labors are to ripen into a harvest surpassing their every hope, and righteousness is to cover the earth as the waters cover the sea. Then will God have nothing special for them? Are these who were last in everything never to be first in anything? But God remembers!

These, the choicest of servants, are about to receive a special, unique reward. They are, I believe, described at two other places in the book of Revelation. I would not be dogmatic on this, for the same rigor does not attach to these passages as to some others. But I think this is sound. In Revelation chapter 14 they are in heaven before the throne singing a new song known only to them. This is a special elite group in God's eyes. "These are they which follow the Lamb whithersoever he goeth" (Rev. 14:4, 5; cf. 6:9-11; 7:4-8; 20:4-6). They are singled out for special treatment and special reward, " . . . redeemed from among men, being the *firstfruits* unto God and to the Lamb" (Rev. 14:4). They are a hundred forty-four thousand (Rev. 14:1, 3; cf. 7:4).[13] "Firstfruits unto God" is the same thought and concept as "first

---

[13] Although the hundred forty-four thousand are said to be of Israel (Rev. 7:4-8), it is not uncommon for this title to be applied to any of God's people for special honor (see Gal. 6:16; Rom. 2:28, 29; 9:6; John 1:47). This honorary title would therefore be especially appropriate for this group.

resurrection," and this is strong evidence that these passages refer to the same group.

Those who were *last* will now be *first* in something. They will share a special honor with Christ who is Himself the "*firstfruits* of them that slept" (1 Cor. 15:20). As Christ is *the* firstfruits of the resurrection, so these hundred forty-four thousand (a perfect symbolic number — 12^2 x 1000) will be the "*firstfruits* unto God and to the Lamb" and will share with Christ as part of the *first yield* of the resurrection harvest or the "first resurrection." According to Hebrews 11:35, martyrdom results in a "better resurrection." Unless this is a correct assessment of the martyr's reward, I cannot see how martyrdom could provide a "better resurrection" than that of other Christians. Yet the writer of Hebrews says " . . . others were tortured, not accepting deliverance; that they might obtain a *better resurrection*." There will be special resurrection treatment. As the millennium begins they will "live again" and be "before his throne" and will "reign with Christ" (cf. Rev. 14:3; 20:4) during the millennium. If Revelation 7 and 14 have no connection with the group of Revelation 20, it makes no difference as to the interpretation of the "first resurrection." It definitely is a martyr's resurrection.

But the millennium is *their* day. It is the time when their labors will be vindicated from the days of their humble gatherings, when the few were scorned and persecuted by all the throngs whom the Lord *seemed* to be "blessing." Now these are blessed; they are resurrected to a special celebration in heaven with Christ for this special thousand-year period. This time is the vindication on earth of the Gospel for which Christ and these faithful martyrs died in the true "fellowship of his suffering." How fitting then that they should share with Christ as firstfruits of the resurrection and join His reign in heaven (Rev. 14:3) while victories are won on earth and enemies are conquered by the Gospel. This is the "first resurrection," and it changes in no way the uniform teachings of the Scripture concerning the massive general resurrection when the "rest of the dead" (Rev. 20:5), including the righteous and wicked, shall live again at the revelation of Christ.

The Fourth Rigorous Propositional Truth

Now the fourth of these rigorous propositional truths is this: *When Christ returns, there will be a judgment of both classes together.* Just as there is a general resurrection, so there is to be a general judgment wherein both classes will be judged at once. Although this has been the uniform view of Christians for many past centuries, in the last century or so this truth has been scorned by many. And yet, it remains true.

The theological significance of "the judgment" is such that only a vast generalized gathering of all intelligent beings, both righteous and wicked, would serve the purpose. We must think for a moment of the purpose of the judgment. It is not to give God an opportunity to find out who is guilty or not — who should go to heaven or not. He already knows that. But rather, it is to demonstrate to the satisfaction of all beings, both men and angels, wicked and righteous, that God's decrees are just and right. It is to vindicate His work of redemption through Jesus Christ and to receive the acknowledgment of His preeminence and the righteousness of His final sentences and eternal consignments. In the awesome setting of this universal gathering when some are committed to life everlasting and some to everlasting destruction, *everyone* will say amen. This judgment will settle for eternity the enmity in the creation: "That at the name of Jesus every knee should bow, of things in heaven, and things in earth, and things under the earth; And that every tongue should confess that Jesus Christ is Lord, to the glory of God the Father" (Phil. 2:10, 11).

By the display of the redeemed and the mercy of God through the blood of the cross, He will "reconcile all things to himself," and the creation will be at peace regarding who is Lord. "And, having made peace through the blood of his cross, by him to reconcile all things unto himself; by him, I say, whether they be things in earth, or things in heaven" (Col. 1:20).

This great final judgment will establish truth before all beings in such an awesome way that every voice will be silenced and that even the devils and the most wicked of men will grudgingly acknowledge it. They will bow the knee and bitterly admit that they are justly consigned to the flames of hell, while the redeemed will for the first time truly recognize the awesome severity of God's justice and truly appreciate the raw mercy in their own redemption. Every intelligent created being will be awe-struck and speechless, and a profound silence will pervade the universe in that awful moment of truth. "And when he had opened the seventh seal, there was silence in heaven about the space of half an hour" (Rev. 8:1). Definitely, there will be a general judgment.

In proof of this, I turn again to Matthew: "The men of Nineveh will rise *in the judgment with this generation* . . . " (12:41, NKJV). There is to be a general judgment as well as a general resurrection. "The queen of the south will rise up *in the judgment with this generation* and condemn it . . . " (v. 42). These statements establish the judgment of both the wicked and the righteous together for the very purpose of vindicating the righteousness of God and of the redeemed.

Then turn the page in Matthew and review the Lord's interpretation of the parable of the sowers and the harvest at the end of the world. It is usually not appropriate to establish doctrine from parables, but we can establish doctrine from the interpretation of parables when the Lord is the interpreter. And He said: "The enemy that sowed them [speaking of the tares among the wheat] is the devil; the harvest is the end of the world . . . " (13:39). As we have said, our premillennial brethren make a point that *world* here means *age*. It does, but the world ends when the age ends. In any case, world or age, we have both the righteous and the wicked being judged together. The passage continues:

> As therefore the tares are gathered and burned in the fire; so shall it be in the end of this world. The Son of man shall send forth his angels [there again are the angels, just as in Matthew 24 and other places], and they shall gather out of his kingdom all things that offend, and them which do iniquity; And shall cast them into a furnace of fire: there shall be wailing and gnashing of teeth (Matt. 13:40-42).

This is one of the few places in Scripture where we have any detail on how God handles the wicked at the end, and we might wish there were more. But this is the judgment of the wicked — the resurrected dead who are wicked — cast into the furnace of fire. And then Matthew continues with almost the same words, certainly the same thought, as expressed in Daniel: "*Then shall the righteous shine forth* as the sun in the kingdom of their Father . . . " (Matt. 13:43). Now the "kingdom of their Father" is the kingdom of God, and the Bible says "that flesh and blood cannot inherit the kingdom of God" (1 Cor. 15:50). Therefore, this is not an earthly kingdom with Christ upon a throne of this world ruling over the sons of Adam in their natural, sinful state. These then are resurrected, glorified saints that are going into the eternal kingdom of their Father — not people going into a millennial reign on earth. This passage certainly establishes that in the last events there will be a judgment of both classes together.

A rather elaborate system of presuppositions has been built up by premillennial writers (to avoid the face-value implications of these parables and other passages) to enable the insertion of a period of a thousand years between the resurrection and judgment of the righteous and wicked.

But looking further, we read: "For the Son of man shall come in the glory of his Father with his angels; and *then* he shall reward *every man* according to his works" (Matt. 16:27). Here, when Jesus comes, the rewarding of "every man" is a judgment, and "every man" includes both classes. This is the simple teaching of the Scriptures.

We turn now to a passage that is wholly conclusive on this matter:

> When the Son of man shall come in his glory, and all the holy angels with him, then shall he sit upon the throne of his glory: And before him shall be gathered all nations: and he shall separate them one from another, as a shepherd divideth his sheep from the goats (Matt. 25:31, 32).

Now here is a passage that I had to precondition unreasonably before it could bear a premillennial interpretation. I was taught to call this a judgment of *nations as national entities*; I had been told that individual souls were not in view here — only nationalities. I had been shown how to use certain presuppositions which destroyed the face-value message of this passage and made it of "none effect." And yet what a tremendous affront to the uniform theology of the Bible from Genesis to Revelation, to suppose that God judges the eternal destiny of men nationally! There is only the judgment of nations in terms of individuals as is made very clear from the verses right in this same passage. Christ separates them *one* (individual) from *another* (individual) as a shepherd divides his (individual) sheep from the (individual) goats. The picture is of a flock where individual animals (sheep and goats, like wheat and tares) are mixed together (they "grow together," Matt. 13:30). They must be separated one by one. This is not a picture of several homogeneous flocks, several flocks of sheep and several flocks of goats, to be separated flock from flock. If they are in flocks, they are already separated. The normal meaning of such language conveys the picture of a mixed flock to be segregated.

The external reason given for this separation is based upon deeds of kindness. These are fruits of righteousness characteristic of the saved. These fruits of salvation form the foundation of the judgment (cf. Rev. 20:12, 13). This does not teach a works salvation, but a vindication by fruits of those saved by grace. "By their fruits ye shall know them." Those having characteristics that are peculiar to the redeemed go into "life eternal," but the others (the wicked) go away into "everlasting punishment."

Eternal destinies are established in this passage; the eternal states of both the righteous and of the wicked are fixed. But there has never been, and never will be, anything like a *national* salvation. Surely a nation, as such, cannot be kind; a nation, as such, cannot take in a stranger; a nation, as such, cannot visit the sick and imprisoned. It cannot repent; it cannot believe. These things are done only by individuals. And to suppose that there should ever be nationalities upon earth with one hundred percent saved and others with one hundred percent lost is a travesty upon both Scripture and reason. We cannot accept that rationale. When we read

Revelation 21:24, we do not suppose it to mean some nations are all saved and others lost. We rightly read it as a reference to individuals of the nations. Why should Matthew 25:32f be different?

On the face of this passage there is to be the separation of the righteous from the wicked; and the eternal destiny of all is established in this judgment. The occasion described is "When the Son of man shall *come in his glory, and all the holy angels with him*" (Matt. 25:31). This occasion is categorically described in Matthew 24:30. This is obviously an extension or elaboration of that judgment which follows Matthew 24:29-31 — the revelation of Christ. In His great Olivet discourse on future things, Christ paused in His description of the main event — His revelation and the ensuing judgment — to give some instructive parables and comments from Matthew 24:32 through 25:30. There He picks up again the continuity of the main event of His second coming (25:31) and continues to describe what happens after the holocaust which destroys the physical universe. There is the gathering of all nations by the resurrection of all the dead and the rapture of the living saints. They are assembled for the judgment. Then Christ gives us a simple, direct account of this one great general judgment that fixes forever the destiny of all individual souls. One reading this passage with no preconceived notions could reach no other conclusion.

Now the only difficult thing about it is how to precondition this passage in such a way as to make it teach that these are plain flesh-and-blood men present who are to remain on this earth — after the stars have fallen, the sun has been darkened and the powers of the heavens shaken (destroyed) — to intermingle with glorified saints as the subjects of Jesus who now assumes an earthly throne over sinful men in a kingdom of this present world. Pentecost, while admitting individual judgment, makes these to be living Gentile persons remaining as normal, reproducing, flesh-and-blood people on earth. Having survived the shaking of the heavens and the falling of the stars after the revelation of Christ, it is, biologically speaking, more or less business as usual. Pentecost says, "The one group [on the right] is taken into the kingdom [he means an earthly kingdom] to become subjects of the King . . . "[13]

Pentecost furthermore makes the "kingdom prepared for you from the foundation of the world" (Matt. 25:34) to be an earthly "theocratic" millennial kingdom here on this present earth. Yet, Matthew could only mean the much broader eternal kingdom of God (used interchangeably with the kingdom of Heaven) which "flesh and blood cannot inherit" (1 Cor. 15:50). Luke expressly calls it the "kingdom of God" (Luke 21:31). When Jesus comes in "power and great glory," Luke identifies this as the kingdom of God (see Luke 21:25-33; cf. Matt. 24:29-35; 25:31-34). The premillennial presuppositions that must be brought to all these passages make it wholly impossible to exegete accurately these simple passages of Scripture. These are very serious blindspots. We need to go openly to God's Word believing its plain statements.

Because there is only one judgment determining destiny, the scene of this judgment is before the great white throne (as in Rev. 20:11). The earth and heavens have been "shaken" (Matt. 24:29), "removed" (Heb. 12:27), "dissolved," "melt [ed]" (2 Pet. 3:10-12); have "departed" (Rev. 6:14), "fled away" (Rev. 20:11), "passed away" (Rev. 21:1). This is the final general judgment of the righteous and wicked together.

Turning now to another example of the general judgment, we see again the same principle:

> And the nations [i.e., the individuals in the nations] were angry, and thy wrath is come, and *the time of the dead, that they should be judged*, and that thou shouldest give *reward unto thy servants* the prophets, and to the saints, and them that fear thy name, small and great; and *shouldest destroy them which destroy the earth* (Rev. 11:18).

Once again here is a passage that describes the revelation of Christ, because Christ is coming at the "last" (1 Cor. 15:52), the seventh, trump (Rev. 11:15). It is called the "time of the dead, that they should be judged" (v. 18). Now this is all of the dead, "small and great." This is a phrase that includes *all*; the

[13] J. Dwight Pentecost, *Things to Come* (Findlay, Ohio: Dunham Publishing Co., 1958), p. 422.

same phrase is used of the great white throne judgment (Rev. 20:12). The rewards (of righteousness) are given to God's servants, the prophets; and to those who hate the Lord are given the reward of destruction. He rewards His servants and destroys them which destroy the earth. Now this is an account of the judgment of both classes, specifically and categorically said to be the time when both classes are judged together.

Some will ask, "How can this be the judgment in the 11th chapter of Revelation when chapters 4-19 treat the great tribulation?" That question arises from the presuppositions one must bring to the Scriptures to maintain a premillennial interpretation. The proper key to understanding the book of Revelation is *parallel* interpretation. We do not have here a series of serial events from chapters four through nineteen. These are independent visions that John saw and are to be interpreted, for the most part, as individual parallel units. They give different aspects of parallel events. We saw the end of the world in chapter six, and here we see another account of the end. This is repetition, giving different detailed information in parallel visions. There is in chapter 11 both a rapture of saints (v. 12) and the destruction of the wicked (vs. 13, 18). We will deal more fully with the interpretation of Revelation later.

Now there are other passages in the Bible that we could certainly call to witness to this principle of general judgment, but this is sufficient to show that the resurrection of both classes and the judgment of both classes are together at the second coming, the revelation, of Christ. They occur essentially together at the end. The fourth propositional truth then is established: *when Christ returns there will be a general judgment of all, both classes together*. This is truth on the face of Scripture.

It is a very satisfying thing to be able to have a view of eschatology that does not have to be supported by strange and unnatural interpretations of those things which the Bible says plainly upon its face. How unfortunate to be laden with a theology which makes it necessary to try and wedge a thousand years of time between the resurrection and judgment of church-age saints and the wicked dead in every one of these direct, simple, rigorous, and coherent Scripture passages.

Now the premillennial view of eschatology can only be true if all four of these major propositions are false. You have seen the Scriptures. Now you must judge. I pray that we all may be able to say with Paul that we "have renounced the hidden things of dishonesty, not walking in craftiness, nor handling the word of God deceitfully; but by manifestation of the truth commending ourselves to every man's conscience in the sight of God" (2 Cor. 4:2).

To learn the truth, you must be bold enough to trust the face of Scripture and humble enough to say, "I was wrong," even to people who have trusted you in your error. If you do, those who really love the truth will only trust you more as they see your honesty and as you together evaluate these things anew. It is not easy to say, "I was wrong" — I know. But I would rather be right, for His name's sake, than popular.

The Fifth Rigorous Propositional Truth

There is yet another serious misuse of Scripture, connected with the pretribulation rapture view of eschatology, which needs to be treated, and that is the theory that the second coming of Christ is in two phases: 1) a coming secretly in the clouds "for His saints," a *rapture* prior to the tribulation and 2) a coming to earth "with His saints," the *revelation*, seven years later after the tribulation.

The fifth rigorous propositional truth is this: *The Bible teaches only one coming, appearing, revelation, of Christ. It does not distinguish a rapture from a revelation by a time difference.*

In an effort to discern if there were two phases of the second coming, without bringing any presuppositions to the Scriptures to color my thinking, I reasoned that if this were so, God would reveal it on the face of the Scriptures dealing with the respective events. If it were true, He would want us to know it. He would include information that would distinguish one occasion from another for us. If we found no such distinction, we would have no moral right to hold it as a doctrine, much less to demand that others believe it as a ground of fellowship as some have done.

Now to search this out, I pored over every passage in the Bible relating to the second coming for its peculiar and particular characteristics to see if I could discriminate and differentiate between these two different events if they existed. I intended to catalog the passages and place one group in one category — i.e., the rapture at the beginning of the tribulation — and the other group in another category, i.e., the revelation at the end of the tribulation. I made a chart of the characteristics mentioned (see page 59) in each passage, and when finished I found no such distinction. On the face of each and every one of them there are simple statements that really signify that there is just one event. Just as the book of Hebrews says, "yet *once* more" God shakes the heavens and the earth, there is *one* "second" coming.

Some cite 1 Thessalonians 4:15-17 as the rapture, and yet the characteristics there are very much like the others. True, there are no falling stars mentioned. But there is enough mentioned, such as the voice of the archangel, the trump of God, and so on, that we know it is the same event as the revelation. It would be ludicrous for us to expect God to make a complete, identical listing of each characteristic in every place the second coming is mentioned; He lists only those features appropriate to the purpose of each passage. But the characteristics are all similar, both for passages emphasizing rapture and for passages emphasizing revelation. No real distinction is discernable. Study carefully the passages listed in the chart, and you will know. There is only one phase of the second coming of Christ.

If you will study these things with the intent just to let the Bible speak, you will see how marvelously easy it is to interpret the prophecies of Scripture in this light. I understand from experience, though, that when one has been trained in a system of thought, it is difficult to break out of that system, to shake off the presuppositions, and to give yourself a chance to think objectively in another framework. But with resolve to follow Scripture it can be done.

Characteristics of the *One* Second Coming

	Clouds	Trumpet	Angels	Saints, elect	Rapture, gather	Visible — not secret	Catastrophe	Voice, shout	Judgment, reward	Jud., both classes	Resurrection	Res., both classes	Throne(s), reign	Power/glory	Revealed	Sun, moon, stars
Rev. 20:11-15						•	•		•	•	•	•	•	•		
Rev. 19:11-21				•			•		•					•		
Rev. 16:14-21			•				•	•					•			
Rev. 14:14-20	•		•			•	•	•	•							
Rev. 11:15-19		•	•	•		•	•	•	•	•			•	•		
Rev. 6:12-17						•	•						•			•
Rev. 1:7	•					•										
Jude 14				•					•	•						
2 Pet. 3:4-13						•	•		•							
1 Pet. 1:13									•						•	
Heb. 12:26, 27							•									
2 Tim. 4:1						•			•	•						
2 Thess. 2:1-12					•	•	•									
2 Thess. 1:5-10			•	•		•	•		•					•	•	
1 Thess. 4:14-17	•	•	•	•	•			•			•					
1 Thess. 3:13				•												
1 Cor. 15:22-24, 52		•									•					
1 Cor. 1:7						•									•	
Acts 24:15											•	•				
Acts 1:9, 11	•					•										
John 14:3					•						•					
John 5:28								•	•	•	•	•				
Luke 21:25-28	•					•	•							•		•
Luke 17:29, 30						•	•								•	
Luke 14:14									•		•					
Mark 13:24-27	•		•		•	•	•							•		•
Mark 8:38			•											•		
Matt. 26:64	•					•										
Matt. 25:31-46			•		•				•	•			•	•		
Matt. 24:26-31	•	•	•	•	•	•	•							•		•
Matt. 19:28-30									•				•	•		
Matt. 16:27			•						•	•				•		
Matt. 13:30, 39-43			•		•		•									
Matt. 12:41, 42									•	•	•	•				

Premillennialism Negatively Considered 3

We have seen that on the face of the major prophetic passages of the New Testament, the premillennial position is not readily discernible. This is obviously an understatement. Actually we have seen that it cannot even be preserved without modifying, by a multitude of presuppositions, the direct, ordinary sense in which other New Testament language is normally understood. In this chapter I want to examine the basis for these presuppositions. I want to discover the foundations which cause the well-meaning persons who hold the premillennial position to feel the necessity to press these presuppositions against the simple declarations of Scripture, particularly of New Testament prophecy.

A Way that Seemeth Right But is Not

I think perhaps the best way to illustrate how good and honorable men come to hold a belief that is so problematic in terms of what is so positively stated in New Testament prophecy is to examine the work of a typical premillennial writer.

As we read the writings of men, the development of a thesis in a book or a sermon, we all usually proceed by laying a foundation for some premise and then building conclusions upon that premise. Now if that basic premise is unsound but still can be made to seem feasible, one still may build some very logical conclusions upon the basis of a false thesis, and sometimes, as we forget or fail to recognize the false premise, such conclusions may appear to be very true.

I think I was a victim of this problem when I went to the eschatological books, failing to carefully test them against the Bible, many years ago. Sometimes we are prone to read along in a book; we see a Scripture reference, and someone makes a few comments, not necessarily about that passage of Scripture, and we say, "Well, that seems right and he cited Scripture." But the Scripture passage itself may not at all teach or support the thesis that was to be ultimately established. And yet often we do not notice it. Then we are led along unawares as the author proceeds to build an entire body of doctrine upon that erroneous premise. It seems logical based upon the original thesis, but we failed to notice the original thesis was not established by the words of any passage of Scripture. In this vein, I urge all who read my works, or those of others, to check the Scriptures cited to see if the actual words and sentences of the passage support the premise.

Now I want to select a standard premillennial work to examine in order to illustrate how the position is established. I might select any of a dozen writers; but I want one who takes a serious approach to scholarship, who has treated the subject fairly thoroughly, who has been rather widely read, and who holds the popular premillennial, pretribulation rapture view of the subject.

A writer who meets these criteria is J. Dwight Pentecost[1] in his book, *Things to Come*. The first 64 pages of the book deal with issues of interpretation. While this is a relevant issue, it is not wholly the determining factor for establishing a framework of eschatology. In general, I agree with the

---

[1] J. Dwight Pentecost, *Things to Come* (Findlay, Ohio: Dunham Publishing Company, 1958). This choice of Pentecost's work does not imply personal criticism. To the contrary, his is among the best works on the subject — hence the choice.

"literal" approach to interpreting Scripture[2] as anyone can see from the foregoing discussion. But a literal approach evidently does not always lead to the same conclusions, and Pentecost implies that a literal interpretation will invariably lead to a premillennial conclusion (pages 1-64). And on page 392 he erroneously states: "The literal method of interpreting the Scriptures, as previously set forth, makes necessary a premillennial coming of the Lord."

That premise categorically stated is in error; consequently, all the conclusions he builds upon it are in error. It is easy to see that I have dealt more literally with the passages considered than it is possible for anyone holding a premillennial view to do. Indeed it is the literal meaning of the words of New Testament prophecy that drives the interpreter to a postmillennial position.

Thus *it is a false premise that a literal interpretation will lead to premillennial conclusions.*

The reason this premise sounds reasonable to a reader is because it is generally cast over against amillennialism, or perhaps against the evolutionary approach to postmillennialism: in which case we may forebear it as an inexactitude arising from the fact that these views do not properly test Pentecost's premise. What Pentecost should have said is that a literal interpretation will prevent one from reaching an amillennial conclusion.

Pentecost's main premise for a premillennial framework of eschatology, however, is developed in sixty-three pages (pp. 65-128) under a lengthy discussion of the biblical covenants. He deals with four covenants. I list the references for these covenants for your convenience. You see if the words and sentences of any of these covenants, taken literally, actually establish a premillennial return of Christ:

1. The Abrahamic covenant — Genesis 12:1-3, 7; 13:14-17;

---

[2] Actually Pentecost and other premillennialists do not always practice literal interpretation of the words of Scripture. They hold what would be more accurately called an earthly philosophy of interpretation. When a conflict arises, this philosophy takes precedence over the words (e.g., Matt. 24:29, 30; Luke 1:33; John 5:28, 29; Acts 3:21; Rev. 6:12f).

15:1-21; 17:1-21; 22:15-18

2. The Palestinian covenant — Deuteronomy 30:3-5

3. The Davidic covenant — 2 Samuel 7:12-29; Jeremiah 33:19-22

4. The New covenant — Jeremiah 31:31-33.

After introducing these covenants Pentecost comments:

> Thus it may be said that the land promises of the Abrahamic covenant are developed in the Palestinian covenant, the seed promises are developed in the Davidic covenant, and the blessing promises are developed in the new covenant. This covenant, then, determines the whole future program for the nation Israel and is a major factor in Biblical Eschatology (p. 72).

As a generalization I would take only minor issue with that statement, but still I say that none of these covenants even treat, much less justify, a conclusion that the return of Christ is before the millennium. The notion that the Old Testament covenants require a premillennial return of Christ is a "venerable" sacred cow, and it has never occurred to many otherwise scholarly and godly men to check and see. Furthermore, a postmillennial return of Christ is at least no less compatible with any of the words and sentences of these covenants than a premillennial return. But it is infinitely more compatible with the plain and voluminous data of the New Testament. *Therefore, Pentecost's main premise, that these covenants establish a premillennial eschatology, is in error; and so also are all the conclusions built upon this premise.*

At this point I want to lay down a sound principle for reaching accurate doctrinal conclusions, especially concerning the framework of eschatology. We have all heard the little truism that "the Old Testament is the New Testament concealed, and the New Testament is the Old Testament revealed." The best principle for reaching accurate doctrinal conclusions is to start with what is *revealed* instead of what is *concealed*. That which is apparent is a better guide than that which is the shadow. If we drew our major premises for the doctrine of salvation from the Old Testament, the shadow, and interpreted the New Testament in the light of it, it would be infinitely more difficult to avoid the pitfall of legalism. So it is with eschatology, the millennium, and the second advent of Christ. The New Testament is plain; the Old Testament is shadowy.

But Pentecost's big stand on the millennial question is taken on the Davidic covenant, and all the premillennial framework of eschatology hangs on the one question: Does Christ sit on an earthly throne during the millennium or on a throne in heaven? One may search these covenants exhaustively, and not one of them answers this question. But the question is settled clearly by other prophecies (see "The Second Rigorous Propositional Truth," pp. 32-40). Therefore, over against the rigorous ***biblical statements*** in many places, as I have shown, that Christ will reign in heaven at God's right hand until the "restoration of all things" and death itself is conquered, you have a mere philosophical *assumption* that He will reign on earth with no such *statement* at all.

The Root of the Matter — A Kingdom of This World

Now we have located the basis for the premillennial presuppositions brought to the New Testament passages. It is a philosophical assumption as to the location of the reign of Christ. The New Testament passages must be *prepared* or *preconditioned* to allow an *earthly* reign of Christ. For after the discussion of the Davidic covenant Pentecost says:

> According to the established principles of interpretation the Davidic covenant demands a literal fulfillment. This means that Christ must reign on David's throne *on the earth* over David's people *forever* (p. 112 — italics mine).

The strength of that statement hangs not upon Scripture, as we shall show, but upon a philosophical assumption. The assumption is that because David himself was an earthly king that his prophetic Son, God incarnate, must also be an earthly king. The Bible nowhere establishes that assumption, but in many places refutes it (John 18:36, 37; 16:7, 10; 6:15, 62,

63; Matt. 22:44; 1 Cor. 15:25, 26; Acts 3:21). Christ has *finished* His work on earth (John 17:4) and is now glorified with the glory He had with the Father before the world began (John 17:5). What an anti-climax it would be for such a One who rules over men from the heavens with the power and glory of the Father (Psalms 11:4; 89:2-4, 29; 103:19; 145:13; Heb. 1:8) to seek to rule again on this earth, His footstool, among sinful men. Kings do not reign from their footstools.

Yet Larkin said that Christ has been trying to set up a visible kingdom on earth ever since creation![3] Pentecost said that Christ proclaimed an earthly kingdom during His first advent and the Jews rejected it, so Christ "postponed" it![4] In reality Christ came proclaiming a heavenly kingdom (Luke 17:20, 21) while the Jews proclaimed an earthly kingdom (John 6:15), and Christ rejected them. Premillennialism is upside down to Scripture. It makes precisely the same mistake the Jews made; because, as we will later show, it was derived from "Jewish fables" — not Scripture. In fact, the Jewish argument to this day is that Christ cannot be the Messiah because He rejected an earthly kingship. This proves two things: 1) that the Gospels make it plain for anyone to see that Christ rejected the notion of an earthly reign, and 2) that the first-century Jews, being earthly minded, never did understand the nature of the messianic kingship. The Bible makes one thing clear: Messiahship was never predicated on earthly kingship — ever.

And so in premillennial writing, almost imperceptibly the impression is thrust upon the unwary reader that these covenants establish a thesis that there will be a premillennial return of Christ and a bodily reign of Christ upon this sin-cursed earth over natural, sinful, flesh-and-blood men. *Yet none of these covenants, anywhere at any time, teaches such a thesis.* It is sheer invention.

But once such a false premise is accepted, then comes

---

[3] Clarence Larkin, *Dispensational Truth* (Philadelphia: Author, 1920), p. 85.

[4] Pentecost, p. 142.

the task of restructuring the simple order of the plain New Testament Scriptures in order to support this false premise. This philosophical assumption that Christ's throne must be on earth is a dangerously thin thread to support the weight of such a complex and unwieldy network of doctrines as premillennialism is. It is bound to crash. If not by the reinvestigation of God's people, it will eventually crash of its own weight. As history develops, the sheer weight of future events will bring it down — probably in less than three decades.

Now I want to turn to the seventh chapter of 2 Samuel where the Davidic covenant is first and most fully expressed. We will simply look at the pages, and look at the sentences, and look at the words to see if they do indeed teach that Jesus will reign over sinful men from a position upon this earth on an earthly throne.

Here we read:

> And when thy days be fulfilled, and thou shalt sleep with thy fathers, I will set up thy seed after thee, which shall proceed out of thy bowels, and I will establish his kingdom. He shall build an house for my name, and I will establish *the throne of his kingdom for ever*. I will be his father, and he shall be my son. If he commit iniquity, I will chasten him with the rod of men, and with the stripes of the children of men: But my mercy shall not depart away from him, as I took it from Saul, whom I put away before thee (2 Sam. 7:12-15).

Now here is the heart of the Davidic covenant; notice carefully:

> And thine house and thy kingdom shall be *established for ever* before thee: *thy throne shall be established for ever* (2 Sam. 7:16).

Observe carefully, none of these words deals with location. They deal with duration, but not with location. None of them teaches that this eternal throne is to be located on this earth. You be the judge.

Obviously a part of this prophecy refers to the merely human descent of David as early as Solomon. Doubtless Solomon and other descendants are referred to in this passage. But it also refers to a much greater and more extensive fulfillment of this promise of the throne of David. It is to be established beyond the boundaries of earth or of earth-time. It is established not for a thousand years, not merely for the term of life on this earth; it is to be established "*for ever*." And that is the *Messianic* aspect of the Davidic covenant — the "forever" throne. The term *for ever* in the Old Testament does not always mean eternality; but in this case it must, for Christ's eternal Sonship makes Him heir to an eternal throne. To limit that by an earthly location is to strip the glory from this great Messianic truth.

Now this covenant is repeated in essence in a number of other passages in Scripture, but none of these passages ever says that the location of this Messianic throne is on the earth. I will give you a few locations of other passages so you can look them up for yourself. They are Isaiah 9:6, 7; Jeremiah 23:5, 6; 30:8, 9; 33:14-17, 21, 22. There are yet other passages in the Bible that touch on this issue, but none of them requires the location of the Messianic throne of David to be an earthly throne.

Rather, now, let us go to the Davidic covenant and consider a truly *literal*, instead of an earthly, interpretation of this passage: "And thine house and thy kingdom shall be *established for ever* before thee: thy *throne* shall be established for ever" (2 Sam. 7:16). We will be careful to be literal, which means we must determine the literal meaning (not apply an earthly philosophy) of the words used. The words literally compel us to think of the throne of David as extending beyond Solomon and his mere human descendants, beyond earth, beyond the temporal — as being eternal, not temporal. There is no possibility that this passage could be fulfilled by merely a thousand-year reign from the city of Jerusalem over flesh-and-blood men on this earth by Jesus or any other of David's seed. This earth, as we have already thoroughly demonstrated from Scripture, is not eternal. Flesh-and-blood men are not going to last *forever*; marriage and reproduction are not eternal elements of God's plan for the human race (Matt. 22:29, 30). And if we take the words written in a literal sense, our interpretation of these passages requires that the throne be forever — a *forever* throne.

I am aware that the Hebrew word translated "forever" does not always demand an interpretation of eternality. This can easily be seen in Solomon's statement, "the earth abideth for ever" [i.e., indefinitely] (Eccl. 1:4, see chart p. 19). But when we compare this statement with the consistent teachings of the New Testament, e.g., "the first heaven and the first earth were *passed away*" (Rev. 21:1; see also Matt. 24:35; 2 Pet. 3:10-12; Rev. 6:12-14, etc.) it is certain that Solomon did not intend to ascribe eternality to this present physical earth with its perpetual cycle of generations born after Adam. The real sense of the Old Testament word translated "for ever" is to be without boundaries, of indefinite duration. Sometimes it does denote eternality, but the context or other Scriptural data must determine the interpretation. When it is used of deity, eternality is certain. The Messianic heritage is eternal. Jesus will eternally be the Son of David. Since Jesus will be the living Son of David eternally, He will eternally hold heirship to David's throne. The context requires an interpretation of eternality. Of one thing we may be certain, the meaning of the Old Testament word *forever*, i.e., indefinite duration, rules out a period with definite boundaries such as a thousand years. A period of a thousand years is neither indefinite nor eternal.

But we have this matter rigorously settled for us by God's own interpretation. The angel who announced the birth of Jesus to Mary (Luke 1:32, 33), interpreted the Davidic kingship of the Messiah for us; he unequivocally put it in terms of eternality. There is no hint of an earthly throne in this angel's expression of the Davidic covenant. Furthermore, this reference to the Davidic throne settles completely the question of the eternality of Christ's reign upon it: He shall reign "for ever; and of his kingdom there shall be *no end*" (*οὐκ ἔσται τέλοσ*).

This is the Holy Spirit's interpretation of 2 Sam. 7:16; the matter is settled.

Therefore, the Messianic throne of David cannot be identified by its location. The passage itself does not speak of location; it does not treat the subject. We are not even required to consider by these passages that the localization of the Messianic throne is ever on this earth. Nowhere do these passages teach this notion. They do require that we think of the throne as eternal, and this thought requires an extra-terrestrial throne unless we are prepared to accept this present earth as eternal. I assume that the throne is literal, because Jesus Christ is literal. Heaven is literal. Christ literally arose from the grave. He literally, I assume, sits in heaven. These interpretations are as literal as anyone can interpret the Scripture.

The premillennial idea of *literal* interpretation is not literal. No literal words deal with location. This mode of interpretation would better be called *natural* or *earthly*. Premillennial interpreters do not actually give a *literal* interpretation to the meaning of the words in these Davidic passages. This problem is especially serious when applied to the rigorous New Testament passages as we have seen. This *earthly* philosophy of interpretation colors the analysis of every clear New Testament passage by numerous presuppositions.

The philosophy is based on a value judgment of the situation. It grows out of an earthly or natural mind-set which was the main problem with the Jews of Christ's day. It is not an interpretation of the meaning intended by the words, but an assessment of human circumstance that because David's rule was earthly, so must Christ's be.

This is philosophy, not exegesis.

But the location of the throne is not in view in that prophecy. To the contrary, it is not even possible to have a literal fulfillment of these words by a location on earth, because this earth is not going to last long enough to satisfy the divine aspects of the prophecy. And if most of the prophecy *must* be fulfilled in a heavenly location, all of it *could* be. Therefore, we should reject any philosophy which acts to obscure and confuse the direct meaning of the words of both the Old and New Testament Scriptures.

Rather, the weakness in the premillennial view is its failure to realize that it is not the *location* of the throne that defines it as David's throne; it is the *person* who sits on the throne. The Son of David, wherever He sits, sits on David's throne. When Franklin D. Roosevelt was president, he used to visit Hot Springs, Georgia. They called that the "Georgia White House." When Nixon was president he visited San Clemente, and when he did, they called that the "San Clemente White House." It is the presence of the king that defines the throne, not the location of the throne that defines the king. The person defines the throne. Whenever Jesus, David's Son, sits upon a throne, that is David's throne. Why? Because He is the legal heir — the Son of David. The Georgia White House was called the White House because the president stayed there. San Clemente was called the White House because the president was there, not because they were respectively in Georgia or in San Clemente. And the throne of David is in heaven today, because David's Son is there today, sitting at the right hand of God; and He will so remain until all of His enemies — including death — are made His footstool.

Now we can tell that David did not understand this Messianic promise to mean an earthly throne. David's response to God's great promise was long-range: "And this was yet a small thing in thy sight, O Lord God; but thou hast spoken also of thy servant's house for a great while to come. *And is this the manner of man*, O Lord God?" (2 Sam. 7:19). He knew that this was not the "manner of man," a merely human situation. He understood it to refer to deity (cf. Matt. 22:42-46; Psalm 110:1). David knew it transcended the earth. How else could he have written the hundred and tenth Psalm? And he says further: "For thou hast confirmed to thyself thy people Israel to be a people unto thee *for ever*: and thou, Lord, art become their God" (2 Sam. 7:24). And in verse 29: "Therefore now let it please thee to bless the house of thy servant, that it may *continue for ever before thee:* for thou, O Lord God, hast spoken it: and with thy blessing *let the house of thy servant be blessed for ever.*" So David understood the eternal nature of this thing, and he knew that this Messianic promise had no earthly boundaries.

Jesus certainly did not understand His kingship as earthly. Neither did Peter understand it that way, because on the day of Pentecost Peter preached that great sermon concerning David and David's Son:

> Therefore being a prophet [speaking here of David], and knowing that God had sworn with an oath to him, that of the fruit of his loins, according to the flesh, he would *raise up Christ to sit on his throne; He seeing this* before *spoke of the resurrection of Christ,* that his soul was not left in hell, neither his flesh did see corruption. This Jesus hath God raised up, whereof we all are witnesses. *Therefore being by the right hand of God exalted,* and having received of the Father the promise of the Holy Ghost, he hath shed forth this, which ye now see and hear. For *David is not ascended into the heavens:* but he saith himself [and now here is the quotation from Psalm 110 again], The Lord said unto my Lord, *Sit thou on my right hand, Until I make thy foes thy footstool.* Therefore let all the house of Israel know assuredly, that God hath made that same Jesus, whom ye have crucified, both Lord and *Christ* [*Christ* here distinguishes Him as the heir of David to the throne He now occupies] (Acts 2:30-36).

It is significant that Peter, on this important and unique occasion, answered the question "what meaneth this?" (Acts 2:12) by the joint interpretation of the Davidic covenant and Psalm 110. In setting the Davidic covenant in this relationship to Psalm 110, Peter positively makes the point that the Session of Christ at the right hand of God is in fulfillment of the promise that God "would raise up Christ to sit on his throne." Otherwise he made no point at all. It would be senseless to bring up the issue of the throne of David and not mention the act of Christ which fulfills the prophecy. It is clear, therefore, that Peter was making the point that David's Son, in sitting at the right hand of God, was sitting on David's throne.

Though we have obviously not treated all of the issues in the premillennial view, yet the kernel of the issue in the premillenial view is this: is the Messianic throne of David an earthly throne, or is the Messianic throne of David a heavenly throne? Because that question, in the premillennial view, has been answered erroneously, the whole complex and elaborate system of premillennialism has been built to support it. If the throne of David is a heavenly throne, then the need to bring presuppositions to the interpretation of the plain-language New Testament passages vanishes away.

If there ever was One who could have made and established an earthly throne, it was the Lord Jesus Christ. On one occasion the people tried to take Him by force and make Him an earthly king (John 6:14, 15). If Larking and Pentecost were right that Jesus wanted to be an earthly king, He had the perfect opportunity. But they were wrong, and Christ rejected the offer of the Jews because He refused to be a king on this earth in this world. Now the premillennialists want to do the same thing again. They want to make Him an earthly king. Christ told Pilate, "My kingdom is not of this world" (John 18:36). There could be no plainer language than that. Jesus repudiated an earthly kingship. It is high time that men quit trying to force an earthly kingship upon the Incarnate God.

It is literally possible for God to be the king of earth from a throne in heaven. That is made very clear by a passage in 1 Samuel 12. When the children of Israel asked for an earthly king, the Lord rebuked them. He told Samuel to protest solemnly. He did not want them to have an earthly king, but He gave them one anyway. And then Samuel said:

> And when ye saw that Nahash the king of the children of Ammon came against you, ye said unto me, Nay; but a king shall reign over us: *when the Lord your God was your king* (1 Sam. 12:12).

Now God said *He* was the king; yet He was in heaven. So there is no necessity for God to be located on earth or for Christ to be located on earth to be the king and reign over His people on earth. God in heaven was the king of the Jews before they ever had an earthly king.

Furthermore, if the Davidic covenant cannot be satisfied from the throne in heaven, then there has been no king on David's throne for the past nineteen centuries, and God's promise to David is found false (Jer. 33:19-21). That wonderful and mysterious prophecy from the lips of Jacob confirmed the sceptre until Christ's first advent:

> The sceptre shall not depart from Judah, nor a lawgiver from

> between his feet, until Shiloh come; and unto him shall the gathering of the people be (Gen. 49:10).

Then Jesus Himself perpetuated that sceptre from His first advent forward. There has always been a sceptre in Judah.

So I deny that the words and sentences in the plain and literal meaning of these passages pertaining to the throne of David permit, much less demand, an earthly location of His throne. David did not think so; Peter did not think so; and Jesus Himself categorically denied it. Yet this proposition is what Pentecost and all other premillennial writers use to lay the foundation of the premillennial view. He first assumes premillennialism from the Davidic covenant, and then he builds all of the other interpretations upon it. All those complex and unnatural reinterpretations of New Testament truth would not have ever been generated except for this one assumption.

Now we have not dealt with all the issues of premillennialism, but we have gone to the heart of it. We have struck the jugular vein. When a sword pierces the heart or severs the jugular vein, the body dies. There is no need to attack and pierce the arms and legs and every toe and finger. When the theory of the earthly reign of Christ dies, premillennialism dies. And all the words that might be spoken and all the tomes of books that might be written, and have been written, on this subject can never remove the fact that the heart of the issue is simply: Does Jesus reign from an earthly throne over sinful flesh-and-blood men for a thousand years, or does He reign from heaven until His enemies are made His footstool? The Bible denies the first and establishes the last.

Next on the Horizon 4

Now we need to consider what is ahead for this and the next few generations so that we may chart a safe course through the troublesome times just ahead. It may seem incongruous to some that a postmillennarian would be talking about troublesome times ahead. One brother questioned the fact that I was dissatisfied with the status quo in Christendom today as being incompatible with my eschatology.

As I have said, I do not think things are going to get *gradually* better, but rather the world will go through a terrible convulsion and then things will get suddenly better. This change will be discussed later. But the proper understanding of the framework of eschatology is essential for God's people to chart their course safely through this convulsion and to emerge on the other side with sound churches which will then carry out the great commission as they have never done before — not even in the unified church of the first century.

The Shape of the Future

Many things must change before the coming convulsion has run its course. I will first list these major changes without Scripture reference for clarity and conciseness, and then I will develop the scriptural proofs that something very near this chain of events will actually transpire:

1. Through ecumenical activity, mergers, and compromises, the

Catholic Church will probably receive back her Protestant daughters and other Protestant-minded movements. Even some Baptists who historically have never been Protestants will doubtless be taken in. If this does not occur, the Protestant and interdenominational world will continue to apostatize until there is no real resemblance to the biblical faith.

2. Satan will make his strongest effort to date to rise to world supremacy and enthrone an antichrist world leader. He has made this effort several times before and failed, e.g., Cain, Nimrod, Pharoah, Nebuchadnezzar-Belshazzar, Antiochus Epiphanes — who desecrated the temple and offered a sow on the altar and who is perhaps the most typical prototype of the final antichrist (see Dan. 8:16-25; 11:2-45; cf. 1 Maccabees i:1-vi:33). Then finally came the Roman Caesars and their descendants. But this next effort, like the others, will fall short of the level of power and deceit that Satan will achieve in the final antichrist, or Man of Sin (2 Thess. 2:3-8), in the great tribulation after the millennium.

3. These apostate churches (above, point 1) or a great ecumenical apostate church (formed by denominational mergers which will include some true Christians, perhaps many) will suddenly and permanently be destroyed (as institutions) by those political powers involved with the would-be antichrist. Hence these "venerable" Catholic and Protestant denominations, that are so much a part of the familiar historical heritage of the western world and of our social and religious environment today and seem to make up the very fiber of it, will be no more.

4. There will be left only the true churches[1] of Jesus Christ —baptistic in kind but not necessarily in name — with no conventions or para-church organizations.

5. There will be a third great world war, instigated by the would-be antichrist, with Israel at its center. Israel will be

---

[1] For a biblical analysis of the nature of the church see: William C. Hawkins and Willard A. Ramsey, *The House of God* (Simpsonville, S.C.: Hallmark Baptist Church, 1980).

victorious; and if there be any other nation with her, they too will be victorious. Yet, God will deliver in such a way that all the world will know He has done these things.

6. Out of this conflagration the Jews will be converted. They will be baptized into these baptistic churches and go over the earth preaching the Gospel of their pierced Messiah, their blood Brother, and their King, as there has never been preaching before.

7. The world will respond as the Holy Spirit honors this preaching, while Satan will be bound for a thousand years.

8. Then the task of reconstruction from war will give way to "Zion's Glad Morning," a golden age where for the first time ever the fruits of righteousness will be demonstrated in human society to the glory of God.

These events, I believe, are on the near horizon, and many living today may live to see them. One of the most grievous errors made by the premillennial doctrine is that it counts the church of Jesus Christ as a failure.[2] No wonder such a gloomy pessimism has gripped the whole world today. Christendom is splintered into a thousand denominations ranging from the liberal pacifists to the fighting fundamentalists. There is no time, they say, to resolve the strife and division scripturally — no need to purge the sin, the moral and doctrinal corruption, from the swollen church rolls. The church is finished anyway, because Christ is coming any minute. And if not Christ, then the seven-year tribulation wherein antichrist, not the church, will have the upper hand. Leave the corruption alone; just snatch a few more brands

---

[2] I want to acknowledge that there are a few premillennialists who hold a very sound doctrine of the church, including discipline, discipleship, biblical succession, etc., until it comes to "the eternal purpose" of God in Christ — the victorious church through the Gospel as expressed in Ephesians 3:10, 11, 20, 21. Inherent in the premillennialist's doctrine is that the church will not be God's instrument for the salvation of the world and that it will essentially be overwhelmed by antichrist and rescued by Christ at His coming, never having made a serious impact on the unbelieving majority in the world.

from the burning — bus them in, count them, and forget them. No time, they say, to make disciples or to discipline those members who will not be disciples.

The view is one of desperate pessimism. There remains no confidence in the power of God through His churches. They have embraced an eschatology of pessimism: the world is going to hell and Christ must come to rapture out a whimpering failure of a church. But this is not the picture the Bible paints. The eschatology of the Bible is one of hope. The world can and will, generally, through the agency of the church be saved. We turn now to the Scripture to see how God will accomplish the things listed above.

Biblical Analysis of Future World Powers

Now I want to begin a biblical analysis of the events that are now on the horizon. Awesome events loom ahead that we may indeed see occurring in our lifetimes in fulfillment of the prophecies of Scripture. In order to make this discussion clear, we will have to study one phenomenon of biblical prophecy that has perhaps the greatest bearing on near future events. This phenomenon is called "the beast."

To introduce this "beast" I will turn to the book of Revelation, and there we find these words:

> And I stood upon the sand of the sea, and saw a *beast* rise up out of the sea, having seven heads and ten horns, and upon his horns ten crowns, and upon his heads the name of blasphemy. And *the beast* which I saw was like unto a leopard, and his feet were as the feet of a bear, and his mouth as the mouth of a lion: and the dragon gave him his power, and his seat, and great authority. And I saw one of his heads as it were wounded to death; and his deadly wound was healed: and all the world wondered after the beast. And they worshipped the dragon which gave power unto the beast: and they worshipped the beast, saying, Who is like unto the beast? who is able to make war with him? (Rev. 13:1-4).

In the days ahead this phenomenon presented under the image of a *beast* is going to play a significant part in what is on the horizon for us. To understand this beast, we have to study and understand at least five different chapters in the Bible. These chapters are Revelation 13 and 17; Daniel 2, 7, and 8.

We must begin the study with Daniel. In Daniel chapter 2 we find that Nebuchadnezzar had had a dream of a great image, and Daniel was to interpret Nebuchadnezzar's dream concerning the image. This image was divided into four sections: the head, the breast and arm section, the belly and thigh section, and finally the legs and toes. We are told in this passage that the head represents the king of Babylon; Nebuchadnezzar himself was the head. So we get the first clue right away, from this passage, that we are dealing with four great, world-wide kingdoms. We will return to this vision later when we have gathered other data from the other chapters.

In chapter 7 we see the image of four beasts: a lion, a bear, a leopard, and then a fierce — a very special — beast different from the rest. And we are told there by the Bible's own interpretation, and I think no one really disagrees, that these beasts represent, again, four great kings, rulers of the world-wide kingdoms, which were also represented by the image of chapter 2.

Then in chapter 8 of the book of Daniel we find a vision of a ram and a he-goat. And we are told specifically in this passage that these represent respectively the Medo-Persian and the Greek empires. Everyone knows the Greek empire under Alexander the Great conquered the Medo-Persian empire. So it is confirmed that we are dealing with great national, world-wide kingdoms and with great rulers.

Now we will summarize the information gained so far from these three chapters: by the Bible's own interpretation the head of the image is Babylon, the ram is the Medes and Persians, and the rough goat is Greece. It is an easy step then to name the four empires represented in chapters 2 and 7. They are *Babylon*, the *Medes and Persians*, *Greece*, and then *Rome*, with her divided western and eastern divisions (the legs) and the remnants of the western world (the toes). Rome is also represented by the fierce beast that is different from all the others. These four sections of the image of the great statue, that Nebuchadnezzar saw in his dream, and the four beasts really speak of the same four kingdoms. All three of these chapters present, in fact, parallel visions (the same scheme primarily employed in Revelation), each giving certain details relating to the dominion of world empires.

Now applying these principles to the 13th chapter of Revelation, we notice some similarities; but the image is of a different sort. This is a single beast, but he has seven heads. And yet this beast has characteristics of those same four beasts in Daniel. He rises out of the sea, as do Daniel's beasts, and has similar features: "the beast which I saw was like unto a leopard, and his feet were as the feet of a bear, and his mouth as the mouth of a lion . . . ." And so we easily recognize characteristics of those beasts in Daniel, the identity of which we are easily led to understand.

But here in Revelation chapter 13, we see that one of the seven heads was wounded unto death. This was not told us in Daniel; this is new data. We begin to see then that the Revelation beast represents an expanded expression of Daniel's account. Daniel's beasts only go as far as Rome. But the seven-headed beast, we would expect, should tell the whole story since seven is the number of completion. Therefore if we can unravel the mystery of this beast, it should open up great insight into both the past and future.

The wounded head implies there will be a time when this beast dies, essentially, during the period that is represented by one of his heads. Now if we can understand what this means — the wounding to death of one of his heads — then it will give us a key to unlock the door of understanding of the future course of events now on the horizon for us possibly within the next few decades.

We turn then to Revelation 17 to further analyze this beast and to see if we can understand what is meant by the head wounded to death. In this chapter (17) we see the image of the same seven-headed beast, and this seven-headed beast is surmounted by what the Bible calls a "great whore," otherwise called "Mystery, Babylon the Great, the mother of harlots and abominations of the earth." A woman drunken with the blood of the saints is mounted upon this beast. We will consider the woman later, but for now we must concentrate on the beast.

Now an angel appeared to John and began to explain the vision:

> And the angel said unto me, Wherefore didst thou marvel? I will tell thee the mystery of the woman, *and of the beast* that carrieth her, which hath the seven heads and ten horns. The beast that thou sawest *was, and is not; and shall ascend out of the bottomless pit, and go into perdition:* and they that dwell on the earth shall wonder, whose names were not written in the book of life from the foundation of the world, when they behold the beast that *was, and is not, and yet is* (Rev. 17:7, 8).

We must carefully follow these sequences to learn the true nature of the beast: 1) There is a time when the beast has an existence, "was"; 2) there is a time when it is not in existence, "is not," or dead; and 3) there is a time when it is revived (from the bottomless pit) and is alive again; and then 4) finally it is permanently destroyed — "perdition." This order is categorically stated in Revelation 17:7, 8 and is implied in the 13th chapter where one of the heads was wounded unto death and the people marvelled because it came alive again.

Now chapter 17 tells us more: "And here is the mind which hath wisdom. The seven heads are seven mountains, on which the woman sitteth" (Rev. 17:9). Forget the notion that the seven mountains are the seven hills of Rome, as so many people say; there is no connection at all. Verse 10 says: "And there are seven kings . . . ." So then there are seven heads; there are seven mountains; but there are also seven kings, which Rome's seven hills do not have. Now a mountain in the Scripture is sometimes used in a symbolic way as a kingdom, and we have been told that Daniel's beasts are kings. So there are seven heads, seven kings, and seven kingdoms.

It all becomes clear; the seven mountains are seven kingdoms. This beast then, like Daniel's visions, is comprised of world-wide kingdoms. We must conclude that this seven-headed (seven being the number of completion) beast represents all of the world-power kingdoms that have ever been or will ever be with their great kings.

Now notice what is said of these kingdoms: "... five are fallen, and one is, and the other is not yet come ..." (v. 10). At the writing of the book of Revelation, there were five that had already arisen and fallen, and there was one then in existence. And that one in existence everyone knows to be Rome. It was the last one that was symbolized in the book of Daniel. So we have a good correlation there — a good tie point. And then there is one yet to come, "... and when he cometh, he must continue a *short space.* And the beast *that was, and is not, even he is the eighth,* and is of the seven, and goeth into perdition" (Rev. 17:10, 11). Now that may sound like double talk, but actually it is not difficult.

Let us see if we can name these kingdoms. Starting with Rome as a benchmark, which existed at the time of John's writing, we will work backwards. We run into the world-wide kingdom of Alexander the Great, the *Greek* kingdom, then beyond that the *Medes and Persians;* then beyond that the *Babylonian* kingdom; then beyond that the *Assyrian* kingdom; then beyond that the *Egyptian* kingdom. These are at least five world-wide kingdoms that have fallen. Now we can illustrate:

1. Egypt 2. Assyria 3. Babylon 4. Medes and Persians 5. Greek Empire	The first five kingdoms are fallen.

6. The sixth was in existence at the time John wrote. This is Rome.

7. The seventh has not yet come. But soon now (within decades, I believe) it will begin its rise; yet it will never reach full power. During its rise to power this "head" ("was, and is not" — 17:8) is wounded to death to revive later from the bottomless pit.

8. The eighth is the seventh revived. It has a short vicious career, and is destroyed. "... even he is the eighth, and is of [the same nature as] the seven" (17:11). (See page 93 for Cluster Study 6 with a graphic illustration.)

Most people believe the kingdom that is to come is a revival of the remnants of the divided Roman empire, to be revived under a world ruler. Yet in no way can a case be made, as some try to do, that the fall of the Roman empire represents the head wounded unto death. The beast in its "diverse" (Dan. 7:7; 2:33) form has been very alive for the past two thousand years though it has had no complete world dominion. It has continued on in the kings of the western world (ten horns) that have survived from the remnants of Rome, from the days of Constantine until now, still surmounted by the great whore — the Roman church and her apostate Protestant daughters and perhaps many false cults. But a reuniting and strengthening of the political remnants of Rome under some strong leader, will be the "seventh head" and is doubtless on the horizon of the future. This is the head that will be wounded unto death.

Now things are becoming clearer. The beast that was, and is not, shall later ascend out of the bottomless pit, be revived for a short space, then be fully destroyed by the Lord's return. This order parallels the career of Satan. Satan is definitely not in the bottomless pit at the present time. Likewise the remnants of Rome, the seventh head, in its divided, "diverse" ten-horn form is also very much alive. But there is coming a time when this seventh head will start to gain power.

Satan energizes the beast (Rev. 13:2, 4). Without Satan, the beast is dead. But Satan will be bound some day in the bottomless pit where he can no longer give "power" to the beast, and that will occur only during the millennium. Then after the millennium he will "ascend out of the bottomless pit" (Rev. 17:8), continue for a short space (17:10), then be destroyed (17:11; cf. Rev. 20:7-10). So it is obvious that the beast follows exactly the same career as Satan.

We would expect that, since Satan is the energizer of the beast. The head wounded unto death is doubtless that seventh head which will soon start to arise. There will be a time when the beast "is not" because Satan is in the bottomless pit. That time will be the millennium, the days when the Gospel of Christ will have power all over the earth.

That is a very clear, coherent, and satisfactory interpretation of these truths. I have taken these Scriptures at face value; there has been no modification of the plain sense of the words and sentences. I have introduced no theory not suggested in the text. I feel confident, therefore, that it must be accurate.[3]

Biblical Analysis of Future World Wars

Now I want to uncover a bit more detail concerning the immediate future, but again we must start at a known point near the end and work backwards:

> . . . when the thousand years are expired, Satan shall be loosed out of his prison [his prison is the bottomless pit], And shall go out to deceive the nations which are in the four quarters of the earth, *Gog and Magog*, to gather them together to battle: the number of whom is as the sand of the sea. And they went up on the breadth of the earth, and compassed the camp of the saints about, and the beloved city: and fire came down from God out of heaven, and devoured them (Rev. 20:7-9).

Here is a revival of the beast under Satan. There will be the continuation of the beast a short time after the millennium — after he has been wounded to death and revived; but that will be only for a short time, and then he will be totally and finally destroyed never to rise again (Rev. 20:10).

Now we notice a new term: "Gog and Magog" (Rev. 20:8). There are two other places in the Scripture where these names are mentioned in this way: the 38th and 39th chapters of Ezekiel. We want to turn there to see if we can discover more detail about these names and the events relating to them.

The natural thing to do would be to start with Ezekiel 38 since it contains the first mention of Gog and Magog. When we do, we find a remarkable thing. We find that this chapter assumes that Israel had been dwelling for a long time in

---

[3] I will not at this time treat the passage from Revelation 13:4 to the end of the chapter, because it relates to the period after the millennium, and my present purpose is to analyze the events on the more immediate horizon.

peace. Then Gog comes against her, and God terminates that action with a great "shaking" and by fire from heaven. The parallel is strikingly similar to what happens in Revelation 20:7-9. I must believe then that this is a prophecy of the same occasion, and for now we will assume it is and will return to it later for a more careful analysis.

However, as we move on to Ezekiel 39, we would expect a continuation of this discussion, but we actually find something quite different. We read:

> Therefore, thou son of man, prophesy against Gog, and say, Thus saith the Lord God; Behold, I am against thee, O Gog, the chief prince of Meshech and Tubal: And I will turn thee back, and leave but the sixth part of thee, and will cause thee to come up from the north parts, and will bring thee upon the mountains of Israel: And I will smite thy bow out of thy left hand, and will cause thine arrows to fall out of thy right hand. Thou shalt fall upon the mountains of Israel . . . (Ezk. 39:1f).

Now in this passage we find Gog, the prince of Magog, coming upon Israel, but he is not completely devoured by fire as in chapter 38. He lives in the northern parts. And I think most everyone agrees that the people described as "Gog, the land of Magog" (cf. Ezk. 38:2; Gen. 10:2) are those who settled in the territory north of the Black Sea. Magog is one of the sons of Japheth (Gen. 10:2). Josephus says that the Magogites are the same as those called Scythians by the Greeks (*Antiquities*, I, VI, 1). The Scythians inhabited the territory north of the Black and the Caspian Seas[4]. That area today is Russia.[5]

---

[4] H. Porter, "Scythians," *International Standard Bible Encyclopedia* (1937), IV, 2706.

[5] Israel is bisected by longitude 35 E which runs due north equal distance between Tel Aviv and Jerusalem and passes almost directly through Haifa. Then it continues north across Turkey, almost bisecting the Black Sea, then through the central populous area of Western Russia within less than a hundred miles of Moscow to the east and Leningrad to the west. The only lands due north of Israel are Turkey and Russia. Yet the name Magog is not associated with Turkey (which lies south of the Black Sea) but with the Scythians in the territory that is now Russia, north of the Black Sea and the Caucasus Mountains.

Then Russia, and doubtless many of her satellites (Ezk. 39:4), are coming upon the mountains of Israel, and Israel will have a great victory over them (Ezk. 39:1-8). After the war, Israel will begin a reconstruction and clean-up period that will last for a number of years (Ezk. 39:9-16). The greatest result, however, of this massive threat to Israel will be their complete regathering and conversion to Christ (Ezk. 39:21-29). This war and the subsequent conversion of Israel are described also in Zechariah 12. Although Gog is not named, the occasion and result are the same.

Now the events of Ezekiel 39 result finally in victory for Israel (vs. 3-5), in the completion of the regathering of Israel from among the nations among which many today are still scattered, and finally in their conversion (v. 29). As we reflect upon the situation of Israel and the world today, the stage appears to be peculiarly set for the events of Ezekiel 39 to begin. We should be forewarned then that these are the next major prophetic events upon the horizon of the future for us. How is this all discernible? We can tell by the way these chapters (Ezk. 39; Zech. 12) begin and end. They begin with a great conflagration of war involving those hordes of the north (Russia and other nations — Ezk. 39:4; Zech. 12:3).

With the advent of *Glastnos* and *Peristroika* under Mikhail Gorbachev it might appear to the naive that Magog is changing for the better. However, human nature never changes fundamentally except by the power of God. Although Magog may at times exhibit a temporary improvement, the prophecies of God's word will stand firm and be fulfilled in their time.

The final result of these events will be a *complete* regathering of Israel and their conversion to Christ (Ezk. 39:22-29; Zech. 12:10-14; Rom. 11:26). The conversion of Israel signals, I believe, the onset of the millennium. We read:

> *Then shall they know that I am the Lord their God*, which caused them to be led into captivity among the heathen: but *I have gathered them unto their own land*, and have left none of them any more there. Neither will I hide my face any more from them: for *I have poured out my spirit upon the house of Israel*, saith the Lord God (Ezk. 39:28, 29).

So this prophecy begins with a war and ends in the conversion of Israel. Both Jew and Gentile will be made to understand the meaning of the past centuries of Israel's suffering:

> So *the house of Israel shall know* that I am the Lord their God from that day and forward. *And the heathen* [the Gentiles] *shall know* that the house of Israel went into captivity for their iniquity: because they trespassed against me, therefore hid I my face from them, and gave them into the hand of their enemies: so fell they all by the sword (Ezk. 39:22, 23; cf. Luke 21:24).

The Jews, everyone knows, have been scattered throughout all the nations since the conquering of Israel by the Roman armies in 70 A.D. In 1948 they were reestablished as a national entity. Since then a regathering has been proceeding, and God is continuing to gather them together even now. They are now threatened by the very enemies of Ezekiel 39. War is almost certain to erupt sooner or later. Before the events of Ezekiel 39 could become imminent, it was necessary that Israel be back in their homeland as a national entity. People of all the nations are watching the development of these affairs on their television sets. A great battle appears even now to be shaping up in the Middle East. Russia may begin her involvement in the Middle East with overtures of peace, but she will come down upon the nation of Israel sooner or later. It is just a matter of time, and the events will proceed just as Ezekiel has written.

Now when that happens, the Jews will have no way to look but up. God will give them a great victory against overwhelming odds, and they will be converted to their Messiah. They will then acknowledge that they have crucified their Messiah, and will weep for Him and for their sins (Zech. 12:10-14). The rest of the world will be astonished at these events and will say, "Surely the Lord, He is God."

These events will cause people to focus attention on the Gospel which will bring salvation not only to the Jews, but to many thousands all over the earth. And then the Jews are going to preach the Gospel as only a converted Jew can. The whole world will see the power of God in these events as He reveals His power in all these affairs. With the Jews converted, and with the Gospel they will preach, there will be the repentance of people everywhere and the millennium will ensue. Coincident with these events, the seventh head of the beast will be wounded unto death, and Satan will be bound for a thousand years (Rev. 13; 17; 20). These are the events that mark the onset of the millennium.

The time of the coming of these affairs can only be determined by watching the development of world events as they unfold in the light of these prophecies. The Jews have been reestablished in their homeland as of 1948, and partially regathered. They regained possession of the city of Jerusalem in 1967 for the first time since 70 A.D. This event is significant in the light of Luke's prophecy that Jerusalem will be trodden down by Gentiles until the time of the Gentiles be fulfilled (Luke 21:24). Since Gentiles remain in Jerusalem and a Moslem shrine is on or near the temple site and Israel still remains blinded to the Gospel, perhaps we should not suppose the time of the Gentiles is yet fulfilled. However, these matters could well be resolved at any time because events can take shape in that direction rapidly. All the very nations of Ezekiel 39 are poised, and any act of war could bring these events to a climax.

Concerning the way in which a future leader could become the seventh head of the "beast," to be wounded unto death, I would like to borrow a very revealing snapshot from contemporary history which I wrote for *The Pillar* (Winter 1988). I am neither suggesting nor ruling out the possibility that the two characters in this excerpt will be the very persons involved in the seventh-head drama, but the phenomena described here are the types of phenomena that I believe must be employed to give world stature to a leader who might make a serious bid for future world leadership. To be successful, he must, at least, not have the opposition of apostate religion, "the mother of harlots" (Rev. 17:5, we will examine this phenomenon in detail later).

But in this snapshot from the past, we can readily see how such a leader might gain the favor of the people of the world necessary to become truly a world-class power:

Babylon, Magog, and the People

The year 1987 was remarkable for many things, but two events occurred that may be more significant than most of us realize. This country was touched by two remarkable personalities, and the masses of people were favorably moved by both of them. These two personalities were both leaders of great multitudes of people very diverse in kind, and yet they have something highly significant in common. They are both representative, I believe, of phenomena identified by God in Scripture. The two personalities to which I refer are Pope John Paul II, the head of the Roman Catholic Church, and Mikhail Gorbachev, General Secretary of the Soviet Union.

Pope John Paul visited the USA in September of 1987. His visit enthralled not only the Catholic faithful, but Protestants, media personnel, and apparently even our own president who was at the Miami airport to greet the Pope. Among the Pope's first words were, "I come as a pilgrim . . . in the cause of justice and peace and human solidarity, striving to build up the one human family."

He flew from Miami to Columbia, South Carolina, for an ecumenical meeting with 27 Protestant leaders after which a massive ecumenical service was convened in the stadium at the University of South Carolina. His itinerary across the country to California and back to Detroit was covered by the media in intimate detail as powerful lenses zoomed in close to pick up the facial expressions, lip movements, the countenance in speech, in prayer, and in personal contact with the masses of people that crowded in to touch him. His assumed role as the ultimate in piety, the father of the "one human family," the vicar of Christ, came across unmistakably; and it pleased the people well.

The December 1987 visit of Mikhail Gorbachev was no less impressive. Seldom has there been a more urbane figure — self-confident, persuasive, intelligent, energetic — coming in the name of peace. The close eye of the video camera again captured the intensity of his countenance, the persuasiveness of his expressions — and the people marveled.

They wanted to believe.

But does the USSR really want peace? Or is Gorbachev's

warm, disarming personality calculated to lull the Western World into complacent disarmament while the Russians lay a colossal trap for the world?

I will make no judgment as to the personal motives of either of these men as individuals; God will attend to that. But it is ours to realize, as forewarned by Scripture, that they each are heads of institutions which will never be peacemakers. To the contrary, Scripture portrays them as the enemies of peace — as institutions of persecution and war against truth, righteousness, and the saints of God.

In Revelation 17 we are informed of a phenomenon portrayed as a woman called "Mystery, Babylon the Great, the mother of harlots and abominations of the earth" (17:5). How can we identify this phenomenon? It is not difficult, for we are told: "the woman [was] drunken with the blood of the saints, and with the blood of the martyrs of Jesus" (17:6). Now all we need to do is to identify those who have consistently been the religious martyrs in history and those who have consistently been their persecutors. As a class the consistently persecuted saints (from the third through the eighteenth centuries) have been the Donatist-Waldensian-Anabaptist-Baptist peoples. And as a class the consistent persecutors of them (for the same period of time) have been the Catholic-Protestant peoples. Babylon the Great represents the aggregate of the counterfeit churches. The Catholic churches (Roman and Eastern) do not alone comprise this Babylon; there are the Protestant daughters who, as their Catholic mother, were born as persecuting state churches. Moreover the interdenominational fundamentalists and evangelicals, who would have nothing to do with Catholics, are essentially one with the Protestants and have not concerned themselves to identify with the true biblical churches that stood fast in the dark ages of Catholic, and later Protestant, state-church oppression. Though many saved people are in all these movements, including the Catholics, God pleads with them: "Come out of her, my people" (Rev. 18:4), because the entire system is to be destroyed (Rev. 17:16-18:24).

But now the papal world-figure, with overtures of peace and his regal-humble father-image, seems the most likely candidate to bring them all back to his fold, eventually, before these institutions perish together.

Concerning the institution of which Gorbachev is presently the head, there are three significant passages in Scripture that help us to identify Russia also as a consistent enemy of peace (except in the millennial period). The first is Revelation 20:8. After the millennial period Satan stirs up "Gog and Magog" who go to battle against God's people. God terminates this action by fire from heaven which terminates this present earth as well (see Rev. 20:7-15). The second mention of "Gog, the land of Magog" is in Ezekiel 38. The Jews are "dwelling safely" (v. 11); Gog comes upon them and fire comes down, as in Revelation 20, terminating the action and the whole earth. These are therefore parallel prophecies.

However, one other mention of the war-mongering character of Magog is in Ezekiel 39 (a distinctly separate prophecy from Ezk. 38). In this chapter Gog of Magog comes upon Israel, is defeated but not totally destroyed. The chapter describes war, victory, and reconstruction for Israel (39:1-20). It continues with the complete regathering and conversion of the Jews (39:21-29). This signals the onset of the millennium (cf. Rom. 11:26; Isa. 11:1-12:6).

Now, who is Magog? Josephus says the descendents of Magog (a son of Japheth, Gen. 10:2) are the same as the Scythians. The Scythians lived north of the Black and Caspian Seas, which today is Russia. Magog comes upon Israel from the "north parts" (Ezk. 39:2). Looking due north, the 35th meridian (east) bisects Israel, passes directly through Haifa, bisects the Black Sea, and passes across the populous landmass of Western Russia midway between Moscow and Leningrad. Thus Gorbachev is presently Gog (prince) of Magog (Russia). He may not be the one who invades Israel (Ezk. 39). But who knows? He is a young, shrewd, ambitious, Magogite who doesn't want to take on the USA with its arsenal of atomic weapons. Can he charm us out of them and then fulfill Ezekiel's prophecy? I do not mean to say we should never have signed the INF Treaty; it may be a temporary advantage. But both God and history agree that war runs in Magog's blood, and we should always negotiate with that in mind. Gorbachev himself appears to be really interested in *perestroika* (restructuring) and *glasnost* (openness). But if we believed, and our leaders would be advised from Scripture, that Russia will one day lead an assault on Israel, what an advantage this would be in future negotiations.

But the scary part is, our country has been visited, moved,

> and favorably influenced in 1987 by two agents of institutions identified by God as the enemies of truth and peace — and the people knew it not![6]

It is reasonable to believe also that the wave of unrest for more democratic government that seems to have started in the late 1980's involving such unlikely peoples as Russia, China, Poland, and many other countries around the world, may be just the sentiment that can be exploited by a cunning leader to gain world dominion. If there is an individual alive today who has the right philosophy and all the characteristics necessary to become such a leader, and toward whom the grass-roots sentiment is rapidly drifting, it is Mikhail Gorbachev. Can we believe it is only a coincidence that this man is also a Magogite who despises Israel? World affairs are inexorably moving on a collision course with the conflagration of Ezekiel 39 and Zechariah 12 involving Magog, Israel, and most of the other nations of the world. On the horizon, therefore, there is bad news and good news. The bad news is that there will be death and suffering in this conflict. The good news is that the people of Israel will turn to their Messiah, and there will begin the time when righteousness will cover the earth as the waters cover the sea.

It is time now to discuss the contrasting events of Ezekiel 38. For years I had read Ezekiel chapters 38 and 39 as one prophecy essentially to be fulfilled in serial fashion just as I had been taught to view the prophecies of Revelation. But it always troubled me to find in the last part of chapter 38 great catastrophic events — the mountains thrown down, great hailstones, fire, and brimstone — indeed a great "shaking" at "my presence." All this to finally put down Gog, and yet in the first part of chapter 39 we find him coming against Israel *again* just as if nothing serious had happened.

But after I found that the book of Revelation could not consistently be interpreted serially, I asked the obvious question: Is Ezekiel 38 and 39 one serial prophecy or two distinct prophecies whose relative positions in the Bible have

---

[6] Willard A. Ramsey, "Babylon, Magog, and the People," *The Pillar*, Winter 1988, 10-11.

nothing to do with their interpretation? I then looked at each as a unit and considered the specific setting and the final result of each chapter. At once it was apparent what their respective messages were.

Ezekiel 38 finds the Jews already regathered in their homeland, not in the process of *being* regathered as in chapter 39. Chapter 38 names Gog as a leader, but it also names Persia, Ethiopia, and Libya (NKJV), with others gathered together. Then a very significant statement in verses 6 and 7 strongly implies that this gathering is a *second* attempt on the part of Gog and his allies to conquer Israel:

> Prepare yourself and be ready, you and all your companies that are gathered about you; and be a guard for them. *After many days you will be visited.* In the *latter years* you will come into the land of those *brought back from the sword and gathered from many people* on the mountains of Israel, which had long been desolate; *they were brought out of the nations*, and *now all of them dwell safely* (Ezk. 38:7, 8, NKJV).

This scene is wholly different from that of chapter 39. There Israel was in the process of being regathered (39:25-28). After the war of chapter 39 there was a reconstruction period, Israel was converted, and life went on with the promise that God would not hide His face from them again (39:29). There is no indication of catastrophic events; no earthquakes, fire and brimstone — only peaceful reconstruction. In view of many other biblical passages regarding the conversion of Israel, it is certain that this event occurs prior to the millennium.

In chapter 38, however, Gog comes again, and the reaction of God is swift with total destruction paralleling exactly the action of Revelation 20:7-9.

The evidence is overwhelming that chapter 39 is prior to the millennium, and chapter 38 follows — "after many days" — when Gog is revisited. The same characters, Gog of Magog, will come down upon Israel; this will be a *second* time. But this time they find Israel in the land of "unwalled villages" (v. 11) — dwelling safely, at rest, and not thinking of war at all. This condition certainly is not a picture of Israel today. It will,

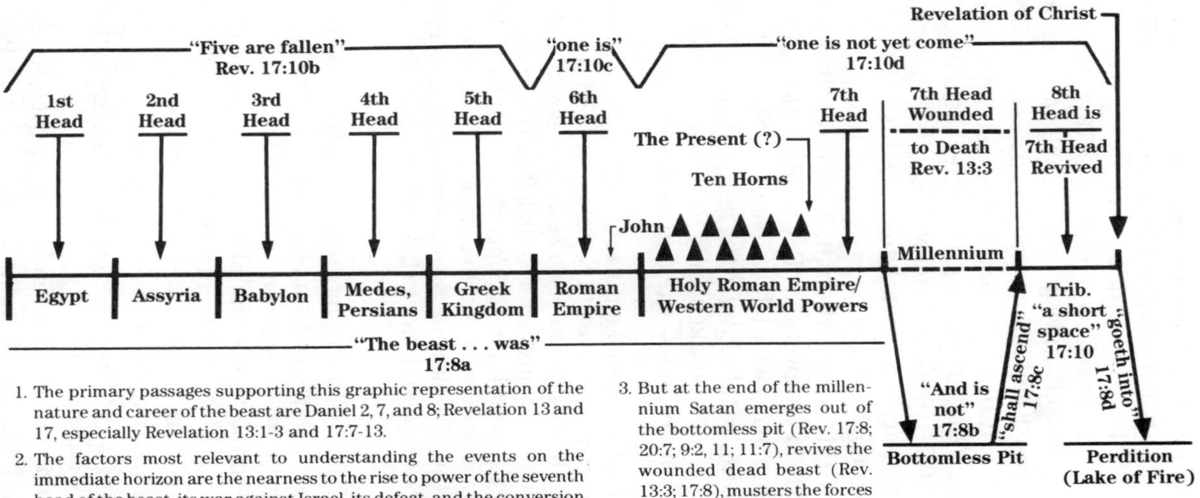

1. The primary passages supporting this graphic representation of the nature and career of the beast are Daniel 2, 7, and 8; Revelation 13 and 17, especially Revelation 13:1-3 and 17:7-13.

2. The factors most relevant to understanding the events on the immediate horizon are the nearness to the rise to power of the seventh head of the beast, its war against Israel, its defeat, and the conversion of Israel to Christ (see Ezk. 39; Zech. 12), and the "wounding unto death" of the beast's seventh head during the millennial period (Rev. 13:3; 17:8), as Satan who gives the beast his power (Rev. 13:2, 4) is bound in the bottomless pit (Rev. 17:8; 20:3, 7; cf. 9:2, 11; 11:7). During the millennium the world is free, for the first time since the flood, of the phenomenon of satanically controlled governmental systems.

3. But at the end of the millennium Satan emerges out of the bottomless pit (Rev. 17:8; 20:7; 9:2, 11; 11:7), revives the wounded dead beast (Rev. 13:3; 17:8), musters the forces of the world to build the most powerful and cruel empire ever known and makes one last desperate attempt at world dominion (Rev. 9; 11; 19:19-21; 20:7-10; 2 Thess. 2:3-12) — finally to be committed to perdition at the second advent of Christ (2 Thess. 2:8, 9; Rev. 17:8; 20:9, 10).

The Long Cruel Career of the Beast

however, be a picture of Israel in the millennium, after the millennium has gone on for several centuries. Toward the end of the millennium when Israel will be at peace, tranquility and prosperity shall have been the norm for centuries. They will be "unwalled," unarmed, not even thinking about an attack. Some will probably have grown carnal, careless, and spiritually dull — the "great falling away" (2 Thess. 2:3). Then Satan will be released from the bottomless pit, and he will deceive the nations, "Gog and Magog, to gather them together to battle" (Rev. 20:7-10). Gog then will again fight against Israel for the final time. It is remarkable how history repeats itself in the same people.

The result of this battle, though, is different from the result of the battle in chapter 39: "For in my jealousy," God says, "and in the fire of my wrath have I spoken, Surely in that day there shall be a *great shaking* in the land . . . " (Ezk. 38:19). Remember, the earth is shaken only *once more,* and this speaks of great catastrophe — the end of the world:

> . . . there shall be a great shaking in the land of Israel . . . and *all men* that are upon the face of the earth, shall shake *at my presence,* and the *mountains shall be thrown down,* and the steep places shall fall, and every wall shall fall to the ground . . . . And I will plead against him with pestilence and with blood; and I will rain upon him, and upon his bands, and upon the many people that are with him, an overflowing rain, and *great hailstones, fire, and brimstone* (Ezk. 38:20, 22; cf. Rev. 20:9, 10).

There is at this time a complete wipeout of the hordes of Gog and Magog, just as there is in the 20th chapter of Revelation. There can be no reasonable question that these two passages both describe the terminal event. The same characters are present; the same events occur. There is also a great *shaking* of the earth, which means the end of time as we know it (Heb. 12:25, 26) at the second coming of the Lord (see Matt. 24:29-31) and the destruction of both the wicked and the earth with the entire universe.

Ezekiel 38 then finds the Jews in Israel at peace, wealthy, unarmed toward the end of the millennium, and it ends with the destruction of the world and all God's enemies. Ezekiel chapter 39 finds them still partially scattered, being regathered, very much on the defensive, armed, not in "unwalled villages"; it ends with their conversion as they enter into the millennium. Now I know the chronology of the events of these prophecies is reversed relative to the numerical order of the chapter divisions in the Bible, but that is true of many prophecies of both the Old and New Testaments. Most prophecies came to the prophets one at a time, often separated by years, and their location in Scripture is of relatively little importance compared to the contents. These prophecies are generally stand-alone units of information, and the books of the major prophets do not have the coherency of, say, the Pauline epistles. Hence, the order or sequence of the prophetic units cannot be made the primary criterion for their interpretation.

A Narrative Description Extrapolated from the Biblical Analysis

The contents of these two prophecies then, in conjunction with the nature, the course and career of the beast, very broadly outline what is upon the horizon for the remainder of the time the earth will exist. I believe the 39th chapter of Ezekiel (see also Zech. 12 for a parallel account) very clearly outlines what will be upon the horizon possibly within the next twenty-five to one hundred years. And many living today may live to see these things.

Now I will relate in narrative form what I have established by the careful analysis of the Scripture concerning the beast and concerning the wars of Gog of the land of Magog against Israel.

The beast, from a few centuries after the time of the writing of John in Revelation, has been represented by the old Roman empire in its decayed state. Everyone knows this powerful empire, weakened by the corruption within, became easy prey for the barbaric hordes from the "uncivilized" tribes of northern Europe and fell before them. But the remnants of Rome survived through the influence of the Roman church.

The "Holy Roman Empire" surmounted by the Roman Catholic Church, e.g., Charlemagne and other European kings subservient to the Roman church, carried "civilization" and "Christianity" back to the barbarians.

The Roman church had incredible power over the European kings through the awesome threat of papal interdict, an act of the pope to cut off all confessions or other rituals by which the people thought to gain salvation. Such an act threw the superstitious people into a severe panic. They thought they were doomed to hell without the church rituals. No king could successfully oppose the pope with this weapon. The great harlot upon the backs of the political powers (see Rev. 17:1-6) drove them mercilessly anywhere she pleased.

For example, Henry IV of Germany, Holy Roman Emperor, opposed Pope Gregory VII in what was called the "investiture" struggle. The pope excommunicated him, threatened to put the Holy Roman Empire under interdict, and Henry had a revolt on his hands. He went to see the pope and was kept waiting barefoot in the snow for three days. Henry gave in.

John of England attempted to prevent the flow of English money out of the country into the Roman coffers. He was excommunicated by Pope Innocent III; England was placed under interdict. John capitulated. He gave England to the pope and received it back as a *fief* (a feudal holding). It was left to Philip IV of France to resist a pope with arms. He, too, was concerned about the exodus of money from France to the pope. The pope, Boniface VIII, excommunicated him, and Philip promptly took an army and captured Pope Boniface and put him in prison for three days. A month later Boniface died. The "Holy See" was later moved to Avignon where it remained in a state of confusion for several years. But the papacy ultimately prevailed in France, and the "great harlot" remained on the back of the beast.

Although there has never been an affectionate relationship between the beast and the harlot, there has been a certain strange symbiosis. They need each other; they use each other. Together they have kept the essence of Rome alive in the Western world. Its Latin influence pervades

Western civilization. As Noel Smith (a great old premillennial preacher and a powerful writer) said: "Take all the Latin out of our law books and you couldn't try a Tennessee bootlegger before a county judge."

Western civilization is deeply characterized by the Roman. There is the preoccupation with the games and sports, the political corruption, the moral declension. In the last days of the Roman Empire the social order rotted from within; the literature, the music, and the public entertainment were characterized by sex, violence, and homosexuality. And modern Western civilization is right on cue.

Once the people of Rome departed from the principles of their ancient democratic republic, they traded their freedom to big government for economic security. The Caesars rose to a position of world power. Worshipped as gods, they became early prototypes of Paul's "man of sin" (2 Thess. 2:3). Satan was earnestly trying to gain complete ascendency through them, but he fell short.

Now as the Western world yields up the principles of liberty, seeking peace and economic security, some man will be standing by to "accommodate" her. He will have a sharp rise to power, and as the Caesars before him used pagan religion and then overthrew it for political reasons, this new ground swell for world dominion will first use the apostate "Christian" denominations, the great harlot, as long as they are useful; then they too will be overthrown (see Rev. 17:1-6, 16-18; 18:1-24).

Therefore, on the horizon, we will eventually see the sudden demise of the giant "venerable Christian" denominations in which today many of God's people carelessly remain, contrary to God's will (see Rev. 18:4). This demise will probably be brought about politically and economically because this "great whore" has always been on the backs of the political systems like a parasite sucking the wealth from them. The "beast" and the "harlot," i.e., the counterfeit church and the state, have not loved each other, but have been tolerant because they are useful to each other. This strange symbiosis has been characteristic of all the ancient states and religions, e.g., Babel, Egypt, Babylon, etc.

Both the Catholic Church and her Protestant daughters have always tried to be state churches. From the days of Constantine until the nineteenth century, this has been so. Luther followed Rome and set up a state church in Germany. Henry VIII did the same in England, Calvin in Geneva, John Knox and the Presbyterians in Scotland. The Puritans did likewise in Massachusetts, and the Episcopalians in the colony of Virginia. The only ancient Christian movement that has historically and consistently repudiated the very thought of the church-state union, with the church riding on the back of the beast, is the Donatist-Waldensian-Anabaptist-Baptist succession.

The symbiotic relationship of state and church accounts for the bloodshed of Donatists, Waldensians, Anabaptists, and Baptists under both Catholic and Protestant influence through the civil powers from the fourth until the 19th century (cf. Rev. 17:6). The "church" judged the "heretics," and the state executed the sentence.[7]

Now the ancient character of these institutions will probably again be asserted as they are reunited in an ecumenical union and as opportunity arises. And opportunity will probably arise temporarily as the new bid for world dominion gathers momentum.

It should be remembered that the sword of persecution was not surrendered voluntarily by the Catholic and Protestant denominations who used it, even in the American colonies. But they were forced by the American Constitution and the Bill of Rights to give it up. There has been no official

---

[7] This principle is the true essence of the symbiosis suggested by the image of the "great whore" (apostate religion) riding upon the seven-headed beast (the civil powers) and "drunken with the blood of the saints" (Rev. 17:1-6). Leonard Verduin, in his excellent book, *The Reformers and Their Stepchildren* (Grand Rapids: Baker Book House, 1980), treats in detail this relationship of church and state. He says, "The horrible idea that the Church of Christ may move the wrist of the hand that holds the sword was, of course, carefully stated in the jurisprudence of the Middle Ages. None put it more succinctly that [sic] did a jurist of the early sixteenth century, Philips Wieland, who taught that 'Heresy is punished by fire; the spiritual judge tries the case and the secular judge performs the execution'" (p. 44).

repudiation of — no institutional repentance nor open confession of — the former sin of persecution by the Protestant and Catholic denominations. The symbiotic principle of condemnation of "heretics" by the church and prosecution by the civil powers still remains in the official church canons and ancient confessions without official and public condemnation of these principles.[8]

Now as the opportunity arises for the "mother of harlots" and her daughters to again seize this power, will they not again revive the practice according to their ancient principles? I would therefore warn the people of God first to "come out of her," and second to stand prepared for a possible revival of persecution under the symbiotic relationship of the apostate church and state as the seventh-head leader begins its rise to power prior to the millennium.[9]

This relationship need not be an official union. But the state, ordinarily blind to spiritual matters, will always take the word of the prominent and powerful denomination as

---

[8] For example, in the decrees of the Catholic Fourth Lateran Council, 1215, Article 3, the principle is expressed: "Convicted heretics shall be handed over for due punishment to their secular superiors. . . ." Again, even in the Westminster Confession of the Presbyterians, who were perhaps the mildest of the early reformers (notwithstanding Calvin's instigation of the burning of Servetus by the civil powers), we find the principle: " . . . they [heretics] may be called to account, and proceeded against by the censures of the Church and by the powers of the civil magistrate" (Article XX).

[9] Should persecution in the Western nations continue to rise beyond the simple denial of tax exempt status as the state attempts to control religious truth, we would expect it to be a bit more sophisticated than burning at the stake. A "heretic" will probably be "psychologically deranged" and will need "care" in some state institution. Or perhaps churches that consider homosexuality a sin must be penalized for discrimination; or churches that will not ordain women as pastors may be prosecuted for sexual discrimination; or biblical church discipline (see Matt. 18:15-17; 1 Cor. 5) for any sin may be judged as defamation of character. In all these things, however, the state will appeal to the apostate church leaders to testify as "experts" in these matters, and their opinions, not those of the true churches, will be considered authoritative. In some countries this kind of thing exists today. Only since c. 1987, have signs of softening been seen in Russia. The beast and harlot still use each other.

official over the individual or the local congregation in court proceedings. Hence, the "beast" may possibly attempt to enforce allegiance to him by imposing his "mark" upon the true churches even prior to the millennium in the next effort to gain world dominion. Churches must indeed, under the command of Scripture (1 Cor. 5:1-13; Matt. 18:17, 18; Rom. 16:17; 1 Thess. 5:14; 1 Tim. 5:20, 21; 6:3-5; Titus 3:10) purge themselves of heretics by withdrawing fellowship from them. But there the principle stops. The church may not scripturally instigate nor condone corporal punishment of a religious heretic by the civil powers! Any church which has participated in that grievous sin is no church of Jesus Christ.

Nevertheless, let us be forewarned that as the lines are drawn between truth and righteousness in the struggle on the horizon just before the millennium, God's churches may again face persecution.

However, as events proceed, the new would-be "antichrist" and some of the "ten horns" with him will first *use* and then *destroy* this parasitic harlot (Rev. 17:16-18:24), and the world will be free of her until after the millennium. Only the true churches will remain, because the gates of hell shall not prevail against them. But they may again, as in the past, suffer temporary persecution.

Then as the ground-swell for a world ruler gains momentum and he, as the seventh head of the beast (probably Gog of the land of Magog), moves with all his allies — almost the whole world — against the Jews (Ezk. 39; Zech. 12:2-14), the odds against Israel will be tremendous. Then the people of Israel will remember the accounts of the awful sufferings of times past when again and again they have been at the mercy of the nations. There was Egypt, Assyria, Babylon, the horrible destruction of Jerusalem by Titus in 70 A.D., and finally two millenniums of suffering without a country climaxed by Auschwitz and the German holocaust. They will have no more of it.

They will cry out — No!

Never again!

Out of desperation they will look to Him Whom they have pierced (Zech. 12:10), and He will hear them:

> Then they shall know that I am the Lord their God, who sent them into captivity among the nations, but also brought them back to their own land, and left none of them captive any longer. And I will not hide My face from them anymore; for I shall have poured out My Spirit on the house of Israel, says the Lord God (Ezk. 39:28, 29, NKJV).

All the people of the world, watching these affairs through the media, will be astonished, awe-struck, and Israel likewise. They will read Ezekiel and other prophecies and will be smitten with a deep conviction of their sins. The remaining faithful Gentile churches will be pressing the Gospel hard upon the Jews (Rom. 11:25-31).

Then God will pour out upon Israel "the spirit of grace and of supplication; and they shall look unto me whom they have pierced; and they shall mourn for him, as one mourneth for his only son . . . " (Zech. 12:10, ASV). "And so all Israel shall be saved . . . " (Rom. 11:26). God will then give such an astonishing victory that the forces of the beast will be severely beaten (Ezk. 39:2f).

With the would-be antichrist defeated and Satan bound in the bottomless pit (Rev. 20:1-3), the seventh head of the beast is thus wounded unto death (Rev. 13:3; 17:8). The world population will be diminished and disillusioned by war. People of all nations will be shocked by the defeat of their great world leaders; and as the awesome evidence that the Bible has been true all the time (Ezk. 39:21-23) dawns upon the world, people everywhere will be looking for answers.

The faithful Gentile churches will baptize the new Jewish converts, just as the first Jewish church baptized the Gentile converts long ago (Acts 10:47). Their ranks will swell as the Jews become the real firebrands that spark the greatest revival the world has ever known — far outdoing Pentecost — and the millennium will rapidly become a reality. God received the "early rain" at Pentecost. Now He has been waiting, and He will receive the "latter rain" for the next thousand years:

> Be *patient* therefore, brethren, unto the coming of the Lord. Behold, *the husbandman waiteth* for the precious fruit of the

> earth, *and hath long patience for it, until he receive the early and latter rain.* Be ye also patient; stablish your hearts: for the coming of the Lord draweth nigh (James 5:7, 8).

Now we can be patient, our hearts stablished. We can settle down patiently as the "husbandman" is patient until he gains from earth the fruits of the latter rain. We must "account that the longsuffering of our Lord is salvation" (2 Pet. 3:15) to this sin-battered world. Meanwhile, we look for the victories of the latter rain when Zion's glad morning breaks and shouts of salvation rend the sky.

Zion's Glad Morning 5

The title of this book and of this particular chapter has been deliberately chosen to highlight the hope and gladness that should and would accrue to the churches if they could again see the prospect of the great harvest of souls to be reaped as the millennium dawns. If the premillennial view is correct and if the world is on an irreversible course of ever deepening sin, degradation, and apostasy until Jesus comes again, this can only mean that at least 4,000,000,000 souls — by any reasonable conservative estimate of the number of unbelievers on earth today who have been exposed to the Gospel — will be instantly consigned to the flames of hell (2 Thess. 1:7-9; 2:8-12). If the premillennial theory is true we must give them up as beyond hope, or else resort to the unscriptural proposition that they will have a second chance after Christ returns, as is claimed by the false interpretation of Matthew 25:31-46.

However, the proposition of a second chance is directly contrary to Scripture: Romans 1:20 teaches that everyone who has the witness of creation is "without excuse." Moreover, Jesus comes "in flaming fire taking vengeance on them that know not God, and that obey not the gospel of our Lord Jesus Christ" (2 Thess. 1:8). He will destroy everyone who "received not the love of the truth, that they might be saved. And for this cause God shall send them strong delusion, that they should believe a lie: that they *all* might be damned who believed not the truth . . . " (2:10-12).

Scripture leaves us no options at all; if these billions are to be saved, they must be saved by the proclamation of the Gospel through the church, the agency God has ordained for this purpose (Eph. 3:10, 11), before Jesus comes. But unless we purge this false eschatology, which has blanketed the churches with a pall of weakness and a doctrine of futility before the task, there will be no serious inroads made toward seeing the four billion souls saved, try as we may.

It is absolutely imperative that we return to a scriptural eschatology. The power of the doctrine of the "latter day glory" must arise again.

An Eschatology of Gladness

Any Christian who understands and loves the purpose for which Christ has established His church would find his greatest joy in the success of that purpose. The heartbeat of the true disciple, though it may cost him great suffering, is to see his Master's name exalted and His purposes rolling on to a victorious climax through His ordained means.

From a selfish point of view, nothing could be more pleasant to me personally than, in the twinkling of an eye, to be raptured free from the toil, sorrows and infirmities of the present world and to find myself in the presence of the Lord. But if this bliss must be at the expense of four to five billion unsaved souls on earth who must just as suddenly be eternally consigned to the flames of hell, I would gladly forbear. This fact is the very reason given for the long-suffering and forbearance (2 Pet. 3:15) of God as He waits patiently for the "precious fruit of the earth" (James 5:7).

It has become fashionable to long for the "soon-coming" of Christ. To "love his appearing" does not mean that we should despise His long-suffering, patience and determination to reap the "fruit of the earth." Far from being a badge of spirituality to desire the Lord's coming right now, it is rather a badge of thoughtlessness, shortsightedness, and perhaps selfishness.

The joy of the unselfish disciple therefore is to see his Master have this fruit. We are to "account that the long-suffering of our Lord is salvation. . . " (2 Pet. 3:15). He is waiting for a purpose that means salvation, not for the population to continue to mushroom in order to abandon it to antichrist and sweep it into hell.

What greater joy could we have than to be the instruments used of our Lord to see the whole circumstance and course of this world turned to salvation and true righteousness? He who has sustained His churches against incredible odds and awful suffering for these many centuries has sustained them for the purpose of victory and not for failure. This great truth concerning the church has been obscured by the extreme dispensationalism of the past century. This error has held the church, to which Christ committed the earthly affairs of His kingdom (Matt. 16:18, 19), and which He commissioned to disciple all nations (Matt. 28:19, 20), to be a contemptible failure.

Calvin Goodspeed illustrated this selfish premillennial abandonment of God's instrument of harvest by citing the following example:

> Here is an authoritative statement of the view, as given by Canon Ryle, and published in the Introduction of the "Pre-millennial Essays" of the great Prophetic Conference of 1879: "I believe, finally, that it is for the safety, happiness and comfort of all true Christians to *expect as little as possible from churches* [emphasis added] and governments under the present dispensation . . . and to expect their good things only from Christ's second Advent."[1]

With this attitude of abandonment and subtle contempt for the work of the only institution Christ established to spread the Gospel, the churches have either gone into cold, dead frustration, or they have turned to every kind of carnal drum-beating expedient imaginable to sustain the numbers. Those of the former type are about to fold up, and those of the

---

[1] Calvin Goodspeed, *Christ's Second Advent* (Toronto: William Briggs, 1900), p. 274.

latter type are like pithy, overgrown mushrooms which arise in the moist night and dissipate with a stench in the noonday sun.

The human psyche has been made by its Creator to respond to the expectation of victory. It is impossible to motivate soldiers to fight a battle they know they cannot win. They may go through the motions, stand on the right side, and die for the right cause, but there is a certain irony in it — a certain cynicism. The older premillennialists used to use the term from Matthew (24:14) — preaching the Gospel "for a *witness*" — in just such a cynical way. They did not expect it to really do much good; they merely put it out as a "witness," as a duty, to leave the world without excuse.

Goodspeed further observes that the postmillennialists on the other hand:

> . . . will organize their work, and settle down for the long and conquering campaign of the ages. While they will wish to reach all men with the Gospel, they will also study to occupy the ground as they go on to the ends of the earth, and entrench themselves for the long hand-to-hand struggle. Expecting triumph through the present agencies, they will make the most of them, trusting God to fill them with His own effectual power.[2]

Now either that is the appropriate outlook, or it is not. We must turn then to an analysis of Scripture to see if God has determined that the Gospel will indeed be victorious in this world through His ordained agency, the church.

We have seen that just beyond the conflicts of war and the social, religious, and political convulsions that are now developing on the near horizon, is that glorious time known in Scripture as the millennium. It will indeed be a glad morning; but it will be a time, at least in the beginning, of relentless work — training, teaching, and grounding millions of babes in Christ, sorting out values, and searching out truth. It therefore behooves us to learn the nature of the millennium and what to expect when it arrives. But first some blind spots must be removed.

---

[2] Goodspeed, p. 275.

The Issue of Spiritual vs. National Israel

Neither of the two most widely held views of eschatology have given appropriate treatment to the interpretation of the Old Testament prophecies pertaining to Israel. One school of thought, usually identified with the amillennial position, holds that all the covenants or prophecies that pertain to national Israel — especially regarding the land and the natural seed of Abraham — have either been fulfilled or were conditional and will never be fulfilled. Hence, they say, beyond New Testament times national Israel or the natural seed of Abraham have no place in any prophecy. All such references are thought to refer to the spiritual seed of Abraham. The result is that national Israel is wholly negated in future prophecy.

On the other hand the premillennial position is dominated by a naturalistic or earthly principle of interpretation which we have previously discussed. Consequently, national Israel and a presumed earthly theocracy is grossly out of proportion in their prophetic picture. The church is only tolerated as an intercalation, a sort of time-filling expedient which resulted from Israel's rejection of Christ's first "offer" of the earthly theocracy. The church as an agency, destined for failure, is of relatively little importance in God's program and hence in its present New Testament form will have no existence or function during the millennium. God will revert to the Old Testament theocracy, national Israel, and His "rod of iron" for the millennial harvest after Jesus returns.

Neither of these majority views is the result of a literal or direct interpretation of the words and sentences of Scripture. The first applies the philosophy of spiritualization so completely that national Israel is negated in millennial prophecy. The second applies the earthly mind-set so uniformly that the New Testament church is negated in millennial prophecy.

Surely, we do not have to be confined to these two extreme polar views of biblical interpretation. If we allow the Scriptures to speak, and if we are careful to formulate our views by the literal meaning of the words written, we will soon see that there is indeed a spiritual seed of Abraham, a spiritual Zion, and true spiritual applications of Old Testament prophecy. Then we will see also many prophecies that clearly refer to the future national Israel. These two doctrines are both true; they are not mutually exclusive but complementary.

The Millennial Existence of National Israel

The demonstration of the survival and final restoration of a national Israel is inherent in the words of many prophecies. We have already considered two such prophecies: Ezekiel 38 and 39. It would be unreasonable to try to "spiritualize" the Israel of these prophecies or to relegate them to past fulfillment:

1. Israel as a nation is clearly distinguished from the Gentile nations.
2. In Ezekiel 39, they are seen at the first in unbelief; then at the end, they are converted. They begin the chapter as natural Israel and end up as both natural and spiritual Israel. Being spiritual Israel does not negate their natural lineage nor alter their nationality.
3. This passage could not have had former fulfillment because 1) they have never before confronted Gog, and 2) they have never been predominantly converted before. If they had been, they still would be: "Neither will I hide my face *any more* from them . . ." (Ezk. 39:29).

These are only a few of many passages which clearly refer to national Israel of the future. Though they become believers and are such throughout chapter 38, they are still the natural seed and in national form. [Lest anyone should misunderstand, when Israel is converted it will be individual by individual, "every family apart" (Zech. 12:12-14).]

Other prophecies teaching the national regathering and conversion of Israel are Ezekiel 36; 37; Jeremiah 30; 31. But I will cite one more which is a very positive proof of Israel's final regathering of which we have already seen the beginning:

> And in that day there shall be a root of Jesse, which shall stand

> for an ensign of the people; to it shall the Gentiles seek: and his rest shall be glorious. And it shall come to pass in that day, that the Lord shall set his hand *again the second time* to recover the remnant of his people, which shall be left, from Assyria, and from Egypt, and from Pathros, and from Cush, and from Elam, and from Shinar, and from Hamath, and *from the islands of the sea*. And he shall set up an ensign for the nations, and shall assemble the outcasts of Israel, and gather together the dispersed of Judah *from the four corners of the earth* (Isa. 11:10-12).

There are some definite clues that this refers to a regathering of national Israel, not from Babylon but from the present dispersion:

1. It will be in the days *after* the "root of Jesse" arises, which is Christ (v. 10).
2. It will be after the Gentiles have responded to Him (v. 10).
3. Israel will be recovered "the second time" (v. 11). The Babylonian captivity was the first.
4. It will be a regathering of a dispersion "from the four corners of the earth" (v. 12), and there had never been such a wide dispersion before.

Now we need not further belabor the fact that there is a future for national Israel, the natural seed of Abraham. The Abrahamic and Palestinian covenants, while they do not conclusively prove this, are in agreement with such a future national occupation of the land. Contemporary history is in full agreement with the prophecies of Scripture that national Israel will be a very central entity on the millennial scene. The older scholars, who lived prior to 1948 when the modern state of Israel was founded, and particularly those who lived prior to 1917 when the Balfour Agreement opened the door for Jewish migration back to the land of the Palestinian covenant — these older scholars may be forgiven if they had difficulty seeing a revival of national Israel. Those, however, who held the doctrine of the "Latter Day Glory" saw it. It is an amazing feat of the providence of God. But today none should have a problem seeing the development of current history as the providential preliminaries to the prophecies of Israel's millennial and final blessings on earth.

The Millennial Existence of Spiritual Israel

Now I will treat the concept of a spiritual seed, or spiritual Israel which includes also the idea of a spiritual Zion or a spiritual Jerusalem. As in most other theological matters, the clearest and most direct discussions tend to be in the New Testament Scriptures since they are largely an open revelation of truth sometimes veiled or shadowed in the Old Testament. Paul therefore explains:

> For he is not a Jew, which is one outwardly; neither is that circumcision, which is outward in the flesh: But he is a Jew, which is one inwardly; and circumcision is that of the heart, in the spirit, and not in the letter; whose praise is not of men, but of God (Rom. 2:28, 29).

In this passage Paul has clearly expressed the idea of a spiritual Jew defined by the spiritual condition of the heart. Then without a break, Paul speaks in the next verse (Rom. 3:1) of the natural Jew. The implication is clear that the concepts of a spiritual Jew and a natural Jew are not mutually exclusive. Even a Gentile *may* be a "spiritual Jew," and a natural Jew *may* be also a "spiritual Jew." But this much is certain; there is a spiritual Jew that has nothing to do with natural Israel or with nationality. Therefore the concept of spiritual Israel is biblical. Either a natural Jew or a Gentile may be a spiritual Jew.

With this much established, I move on to other passages: "For they are not all Israel [spiritual], which are of Israel [natural] . . . but the children of the promise are counted for the [spiritual] seed" (Rom. 9:6, 8). Again we read: " . . . they which are of faith, the same are the children of Abraham" (Gal. 3:7). And Paul comments further that God preached the Gospel to Abraham in the covenant "saying, In thee shall all nations be blessed" (Gal. 3:8; see Gen. 12:3). Now this special blessing is conferred by one specific Seed, " . . . to thy seed, which is Christ" (Gal. 3:16). But all believers are also referred to as the children of Abraham, and in their proper relationship to Christ and the church are also involved in "blessing the nations." We cannot negate the concept of "spiritual Israel."

In addition to the spiritual *seed*, there is also a "spiritual" *Jerusalem.* There is the "Jerusalem which now is [earthly], and is in bondage with her children. But Jerusalem which is above [heavenly or spiritual] is free, which is the mother of us all" (Gal. 4:25, 26). Hence, every reference to Jerusalem need not be interpreted as earthly, nor as heavenly. The Bible uses both aspects, and we distinguish by the context. Iain Murray points out that Paul did not hesitate to apply the prophecy of Isaiah to this spiritual Jerusalem of Galatians (4:25-27):

> It is to this spiritual Jerusalem that he [Paul] then proceeds to apply the glorious prediction of Isaiah 54:1. The assertion that prophecies spoken of "Zion" or "Jerusalem" in the Old Testament can only refer to national Israel is untenable.[3]

There is also reference to a "spiritual" *Zion* and *Jerusalem* in Hebrews: "But ye are come unto mount *Sion*, and unto the city of the living God, the *heavenly Jerusalem* . . . " (12:22). Then in Revelation we find the term "holy city, new *Jerusalem*" (Rev. 21:2), and the "holy *Jerusalem*" (Rev. 21:10). Zion and Jerusalem are used synonymously in these passages. They designate the abode or "city" of God.

The earthly Zion has come to mean the "house of God," the official representative of God's name on earth. The term "house of God" was conceptualized first in the Old Testament (Gen. 12:8; 28:17) in the experience of Abraham and Jacob. It was institutionalized in the tabernacle (Ex. 40:34, 35), then in the temple and the associated worship (cf. 1 Sam. 1:24; 2 Chron. 7:2; Psalm 122:1). Then in the New Testament the Scripture "spiritualizes" the term "Zion" in clear references to the church which superseded the temple as the temple did the tabernacle. Hence Peter, under inspiration, refers to what can only be the church as *Zion*:

> Ye also, as lively stones, are built up a *spiritual house*, an holy

---

[3] Iain Murray, *The Puritan Hope* (Carlisle, PA.: The Banner of Truth Trust, 1975), p. 73.

priesthood, to offer up spiritual sacrifices, acceptable to God by Jesus Christ. Wherefore also it is contained in the scripture, Behold, I lay in *Sion* a chief corner stone, elect, precious: and he that believeth on him shall not be confounded (1 Pet. 2:5, 6).

Peter freely applies the "Zion" from Isaiah's prophecy (28:16) to the building of a "spiritual house." This could only have reference to the church. Likewise, in Ephesians Christ is called the "chief cornerstone" of a "building fitly framed together . . . for an *habitation* [or house] of God through the Spirit" (Eph. 2:20-22). Then Paul calls the church "the house of God" (1 Tim. 3:15) answering to the same idea as the Old Testament Zion, the temple, which was superseded by the church. Zion then has come to refer to the earthly institution where God has put His name. Furthermore, Paul quotes the same "Zion" passage (Rom. 9:33) in the context of Israel's blindness after the temple had been left to them "desolate" (Matt. 23:38). If there was a "Zion" of which the Messiah was "the chief cornerstone," it had to be the church. The New Testament writers obviously considered the "Zion" of Isaiah (28:16) to refer to the church, not national Israel.

Now these are "spiritualizations" made for us by the words of Scripture. The literal interpretation of the words of these passages requires a spiritual meaning: e.g., a "Jew inwardly," "Jerusalem above," Zion a "spiritual house" as the church. These are New Testament applications of Old Testament prophecies and concepts. We *must* recognize and use them or there will be a gaping hole in our theology.

If we have no room in our theology of future things for a national Israel on the one hand or for a spiritual Israel or Zion on the other, then we had better expand our theology to include both.

Israel and the Millennial Church

I cannot help feeling a certain sadness, in a way, knowing that the title of the above sub-heading will seem incongruous to the vast majority of Christians in the world today. Our amillennial brethren will say, "What has Israel to do with the millennial church?" But our premillennial brethren will echo, "What has the church to do with millennial Israel?" I trust that the impeccable logic of Scripture will lead us to an answer that will satisfy both questions.

Now I turn to an examination of the biblical data that will clarify the respective roles of national Israel and the millennial church. Please bear in mind that this discussion is not made for the purpose of determining whether the church, in its earthly New Testament form, will continue into the millennium. It has already been rigorously established that there is no rapture until after the millennium and after the tribulation. The following, then, is to see how God's purpose for national Israel and the church is all going to work out.

I am aware that in an analysis of a question concerning which there is so much controversy, any approach I might take is not going to be the way you — those who have studied it — would go about it. Most people who have made a first-hand study of Scripture concerning these matters have an image or picture in their minds, comprised of a combination of Scripture passages and special terminology, which serves them as a vehicle to deliver their particular conceptions and conclusions. Sometimes this image or this "vehicle" may have been given by one person a certain name, or it may be identified by certain biblical or traditional phrases or labels. The same concept may be identified by another individual by a different label or set of phrases. We ought to be careful to try to understand each other's concepts rather than to reject them out of hand because one man's "shibboleth" does not have quite the same accent that is familiar to another. We ought also to be careful not to apply any terms to one concept that the Scriptures reserve for another concept. This creates immense confusion.

Also when we approach a concept that has a multitude of Scripture passages relating to it, it is not likely that any two persons would "put in" at the same passage. Then too, when space for discussion has some practical boundaries, as in this small book, one may be excused for not being wholly exhaustive on a given subject.

My aim, therefore, will be to present this concept as directly and concisely as possible to establish the outline of the picture. I do not want to include so many details that the outline would be obscured.

Now, I have chosen to "put in" to this subject by referring first to the prophecy of Joel:

> And it shall come to pass afterward, that I will pour out my spirit upon all flesh; and your sons and your daughters shall prophesy, your old men shall dream dreams, your young men shall see visions: And also upon the servants and upon the handmaids in those days will I pour out my spirit. And I will shew wonders in the heavens and in the earth, blood, and fire, and pillars of smoke. The sun shall be turned into darkness, and the moon into blood, before the great and the terrible day of the Lord come. And it shall come to pass, that whosoever shall call on the name of the Lord shall be delivered: for in mount *Zion* and in *Jerusalem* shall be deliverance, as the Lord hath said, and in the remnant whom the Lord shall call (Joel 2:28-32).

This will be immediately recognized as the prophecy which Peter quoted (Acts 2:12-21) and applied to the events that were beginning to occur on the day of Pentecost. This was the initial text Peter used in preaching the great sermon so aptly given in answer to the question that was on everyone's lips: "What meaneth this?" (Acts 2:12). In explaining the meaning of the event, Peter used 1) Joel's prophecy of the coming of this special work of the Holy Spirit on the church, and 2) David's prophecy relative to Christ's resurrection to occupy David's throne (Acts 2:30; cf. Psalm 132:11) and of His Session at the right hand of God (Acts 2:34, 35; Psalm 110:1).

By the use of these Scripture passages Peter chose to introduce the inquiring throng to the main features of the church age. Those features are 1) the work of the Holy Spirit in the church on earth, and 2) the overruling authority of Christ from His throne in heaven. From this divine arrangement I draw three significant scriptural observations:

1. All power (or authority) in heaven and earth has been relegated to Christ (Matt. 28:18).

2. The Holy Spirit empowers the church (Acts 1:8) and, according to the will of Christ (John 16:13-15), directs the church as an agency to execute the affairs of God's kingdom on earth (Matt. 16:18, 19; 18:18).

3. Therefore, Christ Himself is the head of the church (Col. 1:18); and beyond that He is the "head over all things to [or in behalf of] the church" (Eph. 1:22).

These three things at least are implied by the divine arrangement described in Peter's sermon; and in this arrangement we are able to see the power, the agencies, and the means by which Christ executes both His providential purposes as expressed in Psalm 110:2, 5-7, and His redemptive purpose as expressed in this same Psalm (vs. 3, 4).

The same broad purposes, the power, and the works of Christ in this age and beyond are vividly expressed in Ephesians:

> The eyes of your understanding being enlightened; that ye may know what is the hope of his calling, and what *the riches of the glory of his inheritance* in the saints, And what is the *exceeding greatness of his power to usward* who believe, according to the working of his mighty power, Which he wrought in Christ, when he raised him from the dead, and *set him at his own right hand* in the heavenly places, Far *above all principality, and power, and might, and dominion*, and every name that is named, not only in this world, but also in that which is to come: And hath put all things under his feet, and *gave him to be the head over all things to the church*, Which is his body, the fulness of him that filleth all in all (1:18-23).

Hence, the subjects addressed by Peter in his sermon introducing the church age or the "last days" (Acts 2:17) are very aptly complemented by Paul's characterization of the church age: 1) the power of Christ 2) exercised above all dominion 3) toward or on behalf of the church for victory 4) from the right hand of God.

Both Joel's prophecy and the passages from Psalms appropriately bracket these "last days" — from the early days of the church (Acts 2:17) to the great and notable "day of the

Lord" (Acts 2:20) when all enemies are put under foot. Joel's prophecy starts with the outpouring of the Holy Spirit (Acts 2:17) and extends to the events of final destruction (v. 20; cf. Matt. 24:29; Rev. 6:12f; 2 Pet. 3:10-12). Between Pentecost and the "day of the Lord," there is no hint of nor any room for an earthly kingdom. Furthermore, the Psalms passages begin with the resurrection of Christ (Acts 2:24) and extend until the last foe has been made Christ's footstool (2:24-35), which likewise occurs at the final event.

This, then, is the general course of this final age — called the "last days" (2:17). The major goal is the redemptive purpose of God through the church in behalf of which the providential works of God are being executed to guarantee final success (cf. Matt. 16:18; Luke 12:32; Eph. 3:10, 11).

Now we go on to an examination of further detail in Peter's sermon. The remarkable thing about this special outpouring of the Holy Spirit is that it includes "all flesh." The Jewish members of the church did not see any uniqueness in the manifestations of the exercise of power and miracle by the Holy Spirit. He had long done those kinds of things on Israel's behalf when the earthly agency in the kingdom of God centered first around the tabernacle (Ex. 40:34), then later around the temple (2 Chron. 5:13, 14). In those days God through the Holy Spirit did many mighty works on their behalf. So the Jewish disciples had no trouble with the idea of God pouring out His Spirit on the church, but the idea of the church being comprised of "all flesh" gave them some problems.

It was difficult for them, as it is for the premillennialist today, to conceive of an institution where the official earthly representatives of the kingdom of God, the covenant people, would not be centered in national Israel but would also include the Gentiles alongside of Jews in a peer relationship. God finally had to convince Peter through a vision (Acts 10:9-16) that He now wanted the Gentiles included in the church. This was a new format for the house of God. It was a new kind of "building" not made of material stone, but of "living stones" comprising a "spiritual house" — the "Zion" of which Jesus Christ is the chief cornerstone.

Peter came to understand the meaning of "all flesh" and of the spiritual nature of this new "house." He learned that being a natural Jew of national Israel was not sufficient of itself to qualify one for membership in this new house (Acts 10:34, 35, 44-48; cf. 11:15-18; 15:7-10, 14-18). He further learned, with some vacillation (Gal. 2:11, 12), that being of a Gentile nationality was not sufficient to exclude one from fellowship in this new house. *Nationality, then, would never again be an issue.* Membership for the Gentile in the church is on the same basis as for the Jew (Acts 2:41).

Peter had known this in theory and had preached:

> For the promise [Joel 2:28] is unto you, and to your children [the natural Jew], and to all that are afar off [the natural Gentile], even as many as the Lord our God shall call (Acts 2:39).

Now the book of Hebrews is dedicated to the proposition that the Old Testament format of the house of God has been permanently superseded, and a new and permanent covenant has been established in its place. The core of this truth is expressed in chapter 10:

> Then said he, Lo, I come to do thy will, O God. He *taketh away the first, that he may establish the second.* By the which will we are sanctified through the offering of the body of Jesus Christ *once for all.* And every priest standeth daily ministering and offering oftentimes the same sacrifices, which can never take away sins: But this man, after he had offered *one sacrifice* for sins *for ever*, sat down on the right hand of God; *From henceforth expecting till his enemies be made his footstool* (Heb. 10:9-13).

I want to make the following observations on this passage:

1. Predicated on the first coming of the Messiah, the old temple sacrificial system was taken away, the new covenant established (10:9).

2. This is a permanent arrangement, because the true sacrifice was offered "once for all . . . for ever" (10:10, 12).

3. The unbelieving Jewish priests continued the old form

which was an exercise in futility (10:11); so it will ever be, though some premillennialists expect to return to the old Jewish format of the house of God (even animal sacrifices) for the real success of God's purposes.

4. Christ has *finished* His work on earth. He offered "one sacrifice for sins for ever." Then He "sat down on the right hand of God" indicating the completion and finality of His work on earth (10:12). The only thing Christ could not do from heaven is to be born of an earthly virgin, to manifest Himself in the flesh, and to die as a sacrifice for our sins. The rest He can and does do from heaven. He intercedes as the high priest. He rules as the king over "all things" (Eph. 1:22). He directs as the head of His church. He executes the providential affairs on earth until He accomplishes His purpose. All of this He can and does do from heaven.

5. Having finished His earthly work and having sat down at God's right hand, He now waits "from *henceforth* [from now on] expecting." There will be no more format changes. "But this Man . . . sat down at the right hand of God, *from that time waiting till His enemies are made His footstool*" (10:12, 13, NKJV).[5]

Therefore, the earthly agency, which had already been established under Christ, will see His purposes through until the last enemy is ready to be destroyed, which is death itself. This earthly agency in charge of the affairs of His kingdom on earth (see Matt. 16:19; 18:17, 18) is the church comprised of both Jew and Gentile. The New Testament utterly negates the Jewish theocracy.

Now this much has been said to show the divine order or arrangement for the duration of these "last days." In the

---

[5] It is quite surprising to see how all-pervasive Psalm 110 is in New Testament theology and with what frequency it appears. It is as if the writers of the Scriptures were intent upon proving that victory over Christ's enemies will be from God's right hand, not from an earthly throne. It is incredible that with this emphasis of the rule and victory of Christ from God's right hand, premillennial doctrine has essentially ignored this truth and looks for an earthly rule — of which the Scripture speaks not a word.

church age, the normal and essential constituency of the church is Jew and Gentile, and this is the only arrangement that will ever be in this world until the end of time.

Now I want to consider the events that will involve the Jews more completely in this church-age order of things. Perhaps the clearest expression of these events is in Romans:

> For I would not, brethren, that ye should be ignorant of this mystery, lest ye should be wise in your own conceits; that blindness in part is happened to Israel, until the *fulness of the Gentiles be come in. And so all Israel shall be saved: as it is written, There shall come out of Sion the Deliverer, and shall turn away ungodliness from Jacob* (Rom. 11:25, 26).

Here is a categorical statement concerning the conversion of Israel at a time identified as the "fulness of the Gentiles." Paul had been reasoning about the troublesome matter of Israel's blindness toward the Gospel (Rom. 9:1-11:36). It is apparent, as we have seen from the book of Acts, that at the beginning the church was predominantly Jewish. But things changed. We can see it happening in Paul's ministry. For example, at Antioch of Pisidia he went first to the Jews and preached that Jesus was the Messiah:

> And when the Jews were gone out of the synagogue, *the Gentiles besought that these words might be preached to them* the next sabbath . . . . And the next sabbath day came almost the whole city together to hear the word of God. But when the Jews saw the multitudes, they were filled with envy, and spake against those things which were spoken by Paul, contradicting and blaspheming. Then Paul and Barnabas waxed bold, and said, It was necessary that the word of God should *first have been spoken to you*: but seeing ye put it from you, and judge yourselves unworthy of everlasting life, *lo, we turn to the Gentiles* (Acts 13:42, 44-46).

The Jews had been so accustomed to being thought of as God's people, they could not bear the implications in the Gospel that they, too, were sinners and needed forgiveness; whereas the Gentiles, however, knew they were in need. They sensed a great privilege in the Gospel and wanted it "preached to them the next sabbath." But the Jews resisted it, and Paul said "lo, we turn to the Gentiles." The same thing occurred in Corinth (Acts 18:4-6). Since those days the Jews have had only limited participation in the church, and the Gentiles have been carrying the major load in the execution of the great commission. But more and more the Gentiles are, like the Jews of old, becoming so accustomed to thinking of themselves as the people of God that they can hardly bear the implications in the Gospel that they, too, are sinners needing forgiveness.

Now according to Romans (11:11, 12) the "fall" of the Jews worked out to the benefit of the Gentiles, for just as God led Paul to "turn to the Gentiles," so has He kept the Gospel before the Gentile nations for these many centuries. Paul makes this analogous to the grafting of wild branches (Gentiles) into an olive tree (Rom. 11:16-24). But he argues that the natural branches (Jews) could more naturally, and will be, "graffed into their own olive tree" (11:24). Then (11:25) he coins a phrase "the fulness of the Gentiles," and claims this will signal the end of Israel's blindness.

We might surmise then that the apparent hardening of the Gentiles against the Gospel would suggest that their "fulness" is at least near; or that "the times of the Gentiles," as Luke put it, is about complete. But we have a more objective means of identifying this event. Luke, in one verse spans all the time from the destruction of Jerusalem (70 A.D.), throughout the long Jewish dispersion, to the time of the fullness of the Gentiles as follows:

> And they shall fall by the edge of the sword, and shall be led away captive into all nations: and *Jerusalem shall be trodden down of the Gentiles, until the times of the Gentiles be fulfilled* (Luke 21:24).

The signal here is that Jerusalem is trodden down of the Gentiles until their time is fulfilled. But this "fullness" doubtless means that they will no longer be the predominant power in the church.

Now we have two clues to identify that this time is approaching: 1) the current hardness of the Gentiles, and 2) the fact that the Jews have control (as of 1967) of the city of

Jerusalem for the first time since the first century. We cannot tell exactly when, in God's mind, the fullness of the Gentiles begins. But the stage is set, and in some connection with the great battle of Ezekiel 39 and Zechariah 12, the Jews will be converted, which event Paul gives as a conclusive sign (Rom. 11:25).

Now the human agency involved in the conversion of the Jews will doubtless be the remaining faithful Gentile churches. For Paul continues, "There shall come out of Sion[6] the Deliverer, and shall turn away ungodliness from Jacob" (Rom. 11:26). Then Paul describes the full-circle phenomenon of the Gospel witness, and it is plain that the Gentile church is the earthly agent in the conversion of Israel:

> For as ye [Gentiles] in times past have not believed God, yet have now obtained mercy through their [the Jews] unbelief: Even so have these also now not believed, that *through your* [Gentile] *mercy they also may obtain mercy* (Rom. 11:30, 31).

We have now gone full circle. The Jewish church of old turned to the Gentile with the Gospel as the Jews hardened themselves. Now the modern Gentile church will turn to the Jews with the Gospel as the Gentiles harden themselves — "through your mercy they also may obtain mercy."

But when the Jews are converted, they will still be the "natural branches," will have a national homeland and a natural heritage; but they will not revert back to the old Mosaic

---

[6] It is of little consequence whether this usage of "Sion" is intended to refer to the Jewish Zion at Christ's first advent or to the church as Zion. The "deliverer," Christ, came to both. He worshipped in God's house, the temple (John 2:17), and built God's house, the church (Matt. 16:18). This gives no credence at all to the Jewish-theocracy idea.

As we compare Joel's wording "Whosoever shall call on the name of the Lord shall be *delivered*: for in Mount *Zion* and in Jerusalem shall be deliverance" (2:32) with Peter's quotation, "Whosoever shall call on the name of the Lord shall be *saved*" (Acts 2:21), we find that Peter applies the quote from Joel to the work of the church. Therefore, the "deliverance" or salvation which is in "Zion" and "Jerusalem" must be in the church since the former "house" (the temple) had been left "desolate" (Matt. 23:38). It is highly likely, therefore, that Paul's quotation (Rom. 11:26) is likewise intended to be the church.

covenant of temple sacrifice. Their natural lineage will no more prevent them from serving through the church than it prevented Peter and Paul. The covenants pertaining to their national homeland will not be "disannulled" by their church relationship. They will be baptized by the Gentile churches, realizing that the "house of God" is with them. The spiritual seed of Cornelius will reciprocate to the spiritual seed of Peter, "Can any man forbid water, that these should not be baptized, which have received the Holy Ghost as well as we?" (Acts 10:47).

Then the Jewish zeal will out-do anything we have ever seen in the history of God's people. For Paul observes:

> Now if the fall of them be the riches of the world, and the diminishing of them the riches of the Gentiles; how much more their fulness? . . . For if the casting away of them be the reconciling of the world, what shall the receiving of them be, but life from the dead? (Rom. 11:12, 15).

According to this passage, the now-hardened Gentiles will be mightily stirred again by the Gospel as these newly converted Jews begin to proclaim Christ as not only their Savior, but as their crucified blood brother. This witness, in conjunction with all the other manifestations of God's power surrounding the victorious deliverance of the Jews from the invasion of Gog (Ezk. 39), will spark the world's greatest revival to date.

The church then, under the banners of the God of Abraham, Isaac, and Jacob, will march to the ends of the earth with both Jew and Gentile unified in the same body. Then will be fulfilled the words of Isaiah:

> And it shall come to pass in the last days, that the mountain of the *Lord's house* shall be established in the top of the mountains, and shall be exalted above the hills; and *all nations shall flow unto it.* And many people shall go and say, Come ye, and let us go up to the mountain of the Lord, *to the house of* the *God* of Jacob; and he will teach us of his ways, and we will walk in his paths: *for out of Zion shall go forth the law, and the word of the Lord from Jerusalem.* And he shall judge among the nations, and shall rebuke many people: and they

> shall beat their swords into plowshares, and their spears into pruninghooks: nation shall not lift up sword against nation, neither shall they learn war any more. O house of Jacob, come ye, and let us walk in the light of the Lord (Isa. 2:2-5).

Righteousness will then prevail over all the earth (Isa. 11:9). Ephraim and Judah shall be one (Isa. 11:13). Israel will occupy the land from the Nile to the Euphrates (Gen. 15:18; Isa. 11:14-16). Natural enemies will be at peace together (Isa. 11:6-9). The candlesticks (the churches) of God will be ablaze from the oil of the "olive tree" (cf. Rom. 11:16-24; Zech. 4:2-6; 11-14; Rev. 1:20; 11:3, 4).

I have not space to develop the implications of all these passages, but you study them. They are in the Bible, and they mean something.

In summary then, national Israel will be mostly converted and prosperous during the millennium. The saved individuals of Israel will be in the church just as they were in the first century. The Gentiles will be by their sides. A great harvest of souls — "the latter rain" will be reaped during this time. The blessings of the Abrahamic covenants will be realized to their fullest extent — those covenants relative both to the natural seed and the spiritual seed, involving material blessings as well as spiritual blessings. Both natural Israel and spiritual Israel will be essentially coextensive during this glorious time.

The Church and the Future

Now the stage is set for God to begin in earnest the final, and by far the most prolific, phase of His "eternal purpose which he purposed in Christ Jesus our Lord" (Eph. 3:11). If the thought of the *eternal purpose* which God has for the incarnation of Himself in Christ — if that thought has any weight of glory, then I am about to cite what could be one of the most significant passages in the Scripture:

> . . . to make all men see what is the fellowship of the mystery, which from the beginning of the world hath been hid in God, who *created all things* by Jesus Christ: *To the intent* that *now* unto the principalities and powers in heavenly places might

be *known by the church* the manifold *wisdom of God, According to the eternal purpose* which he purposed in Christ Jesus our Lord" (Eph. 3:9-11).

To digest the meaning of this great passage, we notice first that God "created all things" for a specific "intent." "To the intent that *now*" designates a specific time frame: the present dispensation, the New Testament or church era. It is significant that God did not expect this final and complete "eternal purpose" in a former age nor in a later age, but *now* in this age. The Old Testament theocratic setting was preparatory in nature, not a suitable institution for this final work. It was never designed as the ideal institution for the final, broad propagation of God's redemptive message. It was designed to foreshadow by types and then to genetically produce the special Messianic Seed of Abraham and David. The work of the Old Testament economy of types is forever finished. It prepared for the first advent of Christ and delivered Him to the world. Henceforth, Israel will be used in the church.

We notice secondly the actual objective: to make known the *manifold wisdom of God* to the *powers and principalities.* Paul elsewhere (Eph. 6:12) elaborates that these powers are the rulers of the darkness of this world. They are men under the influence of satanic spirits in the world everywhere, but these spirits are to be conquered and bound for a thousand years. Millions who were deceived and influenced by them will be released to see God's "manifold wisdom" in the Gospel.

Third, we note the earthly agency, the instrument in God's hand, is not a revival of the Old Testament theocracy or system of types — goats and bullocks. But the agency is the *church*, the "house of God" which in its day of greatest victory will be composed of both Jew and Gentile. This institution has had some victories so far — and some severe suffering at the hand of the spiritual wickedness in high places. But the stage is set for millennial blessing at the time when God's *eternal purpose* for the Gospel through the church will reach a crescendo.

The stage will be set by a number of events. The majority of the Jews will be saved. Satan will be bound. The people of God, Jew and Gentile, will be discipled and will labor side by side in the glow of victory. The churches will be doctrinally and visibly united around Scripture truth. They will be disciplined, pure, kept free from the scandalous immorality that pervades most of them today. It will be a glorious day when the church through the power of God will fulfill the "eternal purpose" for which it was designed.

The success of the church as described in Ephesians (3:10, 11) clearly establishes the church as the most fruitful and the most successful agency God has ordained. It is obvious from many Old Testament passages in addition to Joel's prophecy of the church that some such agency more extensive than the Jewish theocracy was in the final purpose of God. Consider for example:

> So the heathen [Gentile] shall fear the name of the Lord, and *all the kings of the earth* thy glory. *When the Lord shall build up Zion, he shall appear in his glory. He will regard the prayer of the destitute,* and not despise their prayer.... *For he hath looked down from the height of his sanctuary; from heaven* did the Lord behold the earth; *To hear the groaning* of the prisoner; *to loose* those that are appointed to death; *To declare the name of the Lord in Zion, and his praise in Jerusalem;* When *the people* are gathered together, and *the kingdoms,* to serve the Lord (Psalm 102:15-17, 19-22).

If this is not a millennial passage, I would not know when it could ever be fulfilled. But it is "from heaven" that the Lord accomplishes these mighty works "when the people [Jews] are gathered together, and the kingdoms [Gentiles], to serve the Lord." This is all from a base in "Zion" and "Jerusalem" and now the ancient Zion and the "spiritual" Zion (see 1 Pet. 2:6), the church, are one. This is a very strong incidental proof-text that Jesus is in heaven during the millennium.

In view of the fact that we are expressly told that the Lord does these things "from heaven" we cannot consistently interpret the "appear" of verse 16 to mean the second coming of Christ. Certainly in the midst of such glorious revival power, the Lord will "appear" glorious even though He will not be physically present. The word translated "appear" is used in many ways both literal and figurative and does not always imply a physical presence; and in this instance the context will not allow it. This is clearly a revival of Zion by the Lord "from heaven" and this interpretation only is compatible with the massive testimony of the New Testament that Jesus will not return until the restitution of "all things."

No, this passage is clearly millennial with an expanded concept of Zion comprised of both Jew and Gentile which can only be the "house of God, the church of the living God" in the day of her glorious victory.

Such Jew/Gentile passages abound in Scripture (see also Isa. 11:6-10; 42:1-12; 52:7-10; 60:3-5; Joel 2:28-32; Amos 9:11, 12; John 10:16; Acts 9:15).

We see then that both the Old and New Testaments 1) put the Jews in the church along with the Gentiles, 2) that the New Testament presents the church as the final form of the house of God, 3) that the gates of hell will not prevail against it, 4) that through the church will be fulfilled the "eternal purpose of God in Christ," 5) that the last earthly institution addressed in the Bible is the church (Rev. 22:16), and 6) that there is to be "glory in the church by Christ Jesus throughout all ages, world without end" (Eph. 3:21).

From these things it is an easy conclusion — in view of the direct teaching in the Scripture that Jesus will never reside on this sin-cursed earth again — that converted Israel will serve through the church with the Gentiles. And this institution will reach the zenith of its power during the millennium.

Now all these things present a great theological problem for the premillennial position. It is according to the eternal purpose of God that His church be the agency to make known the manifold wisdom of God contained primarily in the Gospel of Christ to the powers and principalities. This biblical truth has been distorted and perverted by the doctrine that the church is a mere intercalation — a sort of *afterthought* — in the purpose of God. Premillennial theology makes the very apex of the development of the House of God, the earthly agency for the spread of His truth, a stop-gap measure, an afterthought, and a failure.

The late radio evangelist, Oliver Green, once said the "... visible local church has failed as no other group has ever failed." I marvel at how a theological proposition can so crassly contradict the Word of God (Matt. 16:18, 19; Eph. 3:10, 11) and thousands of good men never notice it. When Christ established His church, as Dr. B. H. Carroll has said, He did not intend for it to begin big at the head like a tadpole and then finally whimper out at the tail.

The theory is incredible that Christ tried and failed to establish an earthly kingdom here during His first advent, necessitating a second expedient to establish a stop-gap church which would fail and have to be raptured out. Then He would come again and reestablish an Old Testament-style Jewish theocracy with Himself as an earthly king.[7] What an anticlimax! Every line of the book of Hebrews cries against this theory.

The Jews are going to be converted, but they are going to work according to the "eternal purpose of God" in the church, just as they did in the first century. The conversion of the Jews in the first century did not rob them of their Jewishness; yea, it extended it. God never intended just a tribal *House*, but a world-wide institution. After God had accomplished His genetic purpose for Israel, He then included the Gentile in His *House*, the church, on an equal footing with the Jew. This makes their Jewishness even more vivid. The Abrahamic and Palestinian covenants were in no way affected by the establishment of the church. The promises will not be taken away from the Jews simply because they are now to work in the format of the "house of God, which is the church of the living God, the pillar and ground of the truth" (1 Tim. 3:15). But it is the power of the Spirit of God extended through the Gospel that will bring the righteousness that is to cover the earth as the waters cover the sea during the millennium,

---

[7] For a devastating treatment of this whole issue, see Philip Mauro, *The Gospel of the Kingdom* (Swengel, Pa.: Reiner Publications, 1974).

and the church will be His instrument in accomplishing this great purpose.

World conditions will then be inverted. Whereas *now* only maybe five or ten percent of the earth at the most is Christian, *then* it will be the other way around. With ninety percent of the world population saved — being disciplined members of unified, scriptural churches — the whole earth will bloom as a rose. Wealth and all of the conditions that come with righteousness will accrue to all people, simply because of the power of God through the Gospel. With no armies to maintain, no war destruction, practically no crimes or prisons, only a token police force, low taxes, honest business, full pay for a full day's work, there will be no need for welfare; and poverty will be practically banished. The poor among us will be primarily the handicapped, and they will not be a burden on such a society.

The Millennium and the Unity of the Faith

In the prayer of the Lord Jesus Christ, the night before He was crucified, He made a far-reaching request of God that so far has been realized in only a limited way. He asked: "That they all may be one; as thou, Father, art in me, and I in thee, that they also may be one in us: that the world may believe that thou hast sent me" (John 17:21). Now the world has never really seen that unity, and it does not see it today in a magnitude great enough to make an impression. But that prayer will be fully answered when the Gospel is presented in full power through a visibly unified church — in the true unity of God's people. This prayer involved a unity that would be *visible* to the *world*. Then the world will believe that God has sent Christ.

But now, today, what the world sees is disunity. It sees division. It sees strife. It sees all the different denominations; it sees ecumenicalism, liberalism, fundamentalism. The world sees Catholics, Anglicans, Lutherans, Presbyterians, Methodists, etc., and a breach of the Scripture on every hand within every one of these movements. The present situation can *never* be seen as a credible representation of Jesus

Christ. But God will bring true biblical unity around the Word of God in answer to Christ's prayer. There must be one kind of church; only this is unity that the world itself is able to observe. The unity for which Christ prayed is one the world must be able to see. This obscurity and division is the reason the so-called invisible church cannot be the institution for this work. It is the most disunified entity ever conceived. Only unified local, visible churches can demonstrate true biblical unity before the world. That will have a tremendous impact on the world. The Gospel will be able to have its power and the church of the living God will thus be used to bring the manifold wisdom of God to the powers and principalities in high places "according to the eternal purpose which [God has] purposed in Christ Jesus."

Now God wants us to know the things in His outline for the future so that we can set our faces toward correcting these great problems and breaches that are among His people. God does not intend to permit all these diverse denominations that will not obey His Scriptures to stand forever. These institutions are represented in Scripture as the great whore (Rev. 17; 18), and she is to be blotted out — i.e., all of the counterfeit churches that do not correspond to that which is written in the Bible. But God calls to His people who carelessly and indifferently remain in these counterfeit churches:

> Come out of her, my people, that ye be not partakers of her sins, and that ye receive not of her plagues (Rev. 18:4).

There was a time a century ago when the different denominations debated issues like baptism — whether it was by immersion or by sprinkling, whether of infants or of believers only. They debated whether the church was hierarchical in form or congregational and autonomous. They debated whether a regenerate soul was eternally secure in God's grace or whether he might lose his salvation and be lost.

But these issues are now passé. Because these issues, which are rather simple on the face of Scripture, were not settled, the debate degenerated to the liberal-conservative debate. Is the Bible the Word of God or not? Was Christ virgin born? Did He literally rise from the dead?

Now these issues are growing old. Today the "venerable" councils are preoccupied with yet baser issues of debate than ever before: Should avowed and practicing homosexuals be ordained to pastor the flock of God? This degradation process was inevitable for those who resisted the simple truths of God's Word on the easy issues of the early debates. Stubborn resistance to the simpler truths of Scripture gave way in later generations to an outright rejection of Scripture itself. Then that rejection finally gave way to "vile affections" — to the baser elements in human nature — until the institutions claiming to be the churches of Christ are filled with immorality and corruption. It is developing just as God has said:

> For this cause God gave them up unto vile affections: for even their women did change the natural use into that which is against nature: And likewise also the men, leaving the natural use of the woman, burned in their lust one toward another; men with men working that which is unseemly, and receiving in themselves that recompense of their error which was meet (Rom. 1:26, 27).

Now God is going to destroy this corrupt system (Rev. 17:16-18). And He calls His people to "come out of her."

But in this chaotic situation, God's people who care for truth and righteousness will be seeking unity around the Word of God. We should even now be studying together, hearing one another, learning from one another, because unity is a commandment of God (1 Cor. 1:10). We should establish a strong, unified voice to stand when Gog of Magog mounts his attack, and Israel sees her need of Christ and the church she once rejected.

So then, we need to settle down and begin to search and to obey the Scripture. This splintered image of Christianity is an inexcusable reproach to Christ. The church is going to be here for awhile, and there *is* time to do these things. We have been sidetracked for over a century with premillennial doctrine which undermines the purpose of God through the church. Now God expects us to get back on the track and study the Scriptures and become unified in the faith that the world may see that God has sent Christ into the world. Then we will see that the church, according to the prayer of Christ, will have its intended power in the world. But under present conditions, the world cannot see Christ. We therefore need to "gird up the loins of our minds" and make some preparations for doing the will of God in view of these things that are coming upon the earth shortly.

In addition to plucking brands from the burning, we need also to disciple them for the long haul. Why should this generation not be used of God to begin to take seriously the things God has foretold in His Scripture? God will bring down the high places of the earth. These perversions of the church of the living God that have been perpetuated ever since the days of Constantine and a little before, both in the Roman Catholic and in the Protestant areas of Christendom, are not going to continue to stand. The world will finally get a chance to see the Gospel as it is. People will get a chance to see the Lord Jesus Christ represented once again as He should be represented. They will get to see what the church was intended to be. They will see the unity of the faith prevailing on earth. They will feel the power of the Gospel by the Holy Spirit. The followers of Satan will come to know the manifold wisdom of God, and the world will be converted.

There will literally be "peace on earth and good will to men" for a thousand years before Satan is released a little season as the time of the consummation draws near. Then the Lord will return after all these events, and God shall have wrought a great victory through the Gospel. The power of Christ through the Gospel of Christ, through the agency of the church of God, will gain the victory. And the prayer of Jesus Christ for unity will be answered.

Those who say this is impossible apart from the personal presence of Christ, as if He were any more powerful on earth than He is in heaven, should read Ephesians 1:18-23. If this passage does not describe sufficient power exercised from God's right hand on behalf of His church (v. 22), then Satan has won the victory already.

Achieving the Power of Biblical Church Unity

I want to discuss now a vital question that has been perverted, neglected, and in some cases scorned by Baptist churches and many Protestants as well for over a century: that is the question of the unity of the faith. At once I must hasten to say that I am totally opposed to the ecumenical movement. But we have so successfully avoided ecumenicalism, that we have also avoided unity.

Although there will be a true unity of the faith during the millennium, we must not wait for the millennium to seek it. It is a sin to make no deliberate effort to accomplish what God has commanded. God has commanded that we deliberately work at becoming truly unified around the Word of God (Eph. 4:3; 1 Cor. 1:10; John 17:21, 23; 13:34, 35). We have both the command and the example. We must deliberately meet and lay our differences openly on the table to settle them in a sincere and charitable search of Scripture truth. Two churches did this in Acts 15. That meeting stands as a textbook example of scriptural procedure, and it is sin to be negligent about unity when we have both the commandment and so clear an example to follow.

While the ecumenicalists are feverishly working to see how many of the doctrines of Scripture they can *exclude* and *disobey* so they will have *nothing to disagree* over, we who desire to obey God's Word (not just merely "believe" it) should be working to see how many of the doctrines of Scripture we can *include* and *obey* so that we have *everything to agree* over.

We must get rid of that sinful, cop-out notion that "doctrine divides" and "time is running out." This produces the hysterical notion that all we have time to do is to quickly have a few "unified" interdenominational evangelistic campaigns, high-pressure as many souls down the aisle as possible to say a repeat-after-me prayer, count them, divide them among the cooperating churches no matter what they teach, and often make them seven-fold more the sons of hell than before. If this is not the intent of many of today's fundamental and evangelical efforts, and I am sure it is not, it nevertheless is very close to an accurate expression of what often actually happens.

We should wedge in some serious time to establish a unified, biblical, doctrinal foundation of truth and then proceed to evangelize, disciple converts, and build churches according to the principles of this truth.

To become unified around biblical truth, we must be willing to let down our protective guards and begin to weigh our venerable traditions in the light of Scripture. Every church that loves the Word of God should be eager to have its doctrines and practices searched in a charitable spirit by others. But many Protestant as well as Baptist pastors are afraid to let another brother search their doctrines. Yet we are going to have to be willing to be searched before we can become a unified voice in a no-nonsense movement where we can genuinely "love one another" (John 13:34) and come to agree with one another (1 Cor. 1:10). It is impossible to move from a position of divided chaos to a position of unity without someone, if not everyone, repenting of something. When this happens, it will be a solemn time. Sacred cows will be flayed and quartered, shibboleths will be shattered, and clichés will crumble under the sheer weight of Scripture.

Now I want to call all of those who love the Word of God to consider a great but simple principle: *It is possible to be unified.* The Scriptures teach a *doctrine* of how to be unified, but we have neither learned it nor believed it. Most Christians are rather cynical toward division, discord, or lack of unity, holding that we must forever differ in our understanding of Scripture truth. Very few Christians take the biblical teaching seriously that we both could and should be unified.

Now the great sin of Christendom today is not that differences arise, but that we are willing to settle down with them permanently and accept discord as the Christian norm to the great jeopardy of the credibility of our message to the world and of the world's ability to receive it. This has gone on so long that practically all Christians living today have adopted the philosophy that the historic divisions of Christendom are inevitable. Most of the seminaries reinforce that notion by pointing their students to scholarship for answers rather than to ingrain in the students the faith that they can get the answers from Scripture. A seminary student in a large fundamentalist university in the southeast told me: "You can't learn doctrine from Scripture." That university had made "shipwreck" of that young man's faith in the Scripture — all the while claiming to believe the Bible! The professors teach a strange contradictory doctrine of "unity in diversity." So the student concludes, "What's the use trying to resolve our differences? We can't know the accurate interpretation of Scripture anyway."

Nevertheless, Jesus prayed that we might be one in such a way that the unbelieving world could visibly observe this unity and hence believe that Christ was sent from God; ". . . that they also may be one in us: *that the world may believe* that thou hast sent me" (John 17:21).

The Bible has commanded real unity — not compromise with discord. But we must distinguish between compromise, toleration, and unity. *Compromise* adapts itself to discord. *Toleration* admits of discord and forebears it in love while attempting to achieve unity. Toleration is a noble trait, but it is not the same as unity. *Unity* is the absence of discord, which we must achieve with truth. "Sanctify them through thy truth: thy word is truth" (John 17:17).

Compromise is out of the question for Christians, and to become satisfied with mere toleration is not a Christian option.

Paul wrote to the Corinthians: "Now I beseech you, brethren, by the name of our Lord Jesus Christ, *that ye all speak the same thing*, and that there *be no divisions among you;* but that ye be perfectly joined together *in the same mind and in the same judgment*" (1 Cor. 1:10).

This is both a commandment and a working definition of Christian unity. Anything short of this is not Christian unity. But is this possible to achieve? It must at least be practically approachable or else God is merely taunting us. It would be very wrong to look upon this commandment as a mere theological abstraction with no possibility of practical application. But unity is in one sense like perfection; we will never attain absolute perfection, but shall we therefore abandon the pursuit of it?

We may indeed approach perfection so closely as to be "blameless" (see Luke 1:6; Phil. 2:15; 1 Tim. 3:2, 10). Blamelessness is a state close enough to perfection that the world with its poor spiritual perception can find no real fault in us worthy of blame. With the proper attitude, the people of God can also arrive at a blameless state of unity — to "speak the same thing" and have the "same mind." To quibble, as some do, about the impossibility of reaching either perfection or absolute unity is but a ploy to avoid the grave responsibility of trying.

But to achieve this, we must first break free from the bondage of the man-centered conditioning of the times that says unity is impossible because God's people cannot interpret the Scriptures alike. Yet there are great principles to guide us; therefore, let us consider then how this may be accomplished.

The time has come to take a *positive look* at what *can* be done. We must not forever malinger in the shadows of what we are told cannot be done.

One of the mightiest principles ever expressed by Jesus Christ forms the foundation of the claim that we *can* obey the Apostle's command to be of the "same mind" and guarantees that it is possible to interpret the Bible alike.

But before I examine this great doctrine of Scripture, let me say I do not approach it as one who has climbed to the pinnacle of its glorious possibilities. I have seen it afar off and have been enthralled by what I see. I have tested it enough to know it is true and valid and that it works. I have climbed a short distance at the base of the mountain, and the vista, even from these lower altitudes, is marvelous. But mountain-climbing is a team effort, and this is only a call for help — for companions to climb together: " . . . get thee up into the high mountain; O Jerusalem, that bringest good tidings, lift up thy voice with strength; lift it up, be not afraid; say . . . behold your God" (Isa. 40:9).

How then may we reach unity? Jesus said: "If any man *will do* [is willing to do] his will, he *shall know* of the doctrine, whether it be of God, or whether I speak of myself" (John 7:17). In this is a principle and a promise which implies 1) if two people *want* to *do* the will of God, 2) if they are willing to change if necessary and *do* whatever the Word says, 3) if they go to the Word of God to find out what it says that they might *do* it, then 4) they will *learn* and *know* what it teaches. 5) If they each have truly *learned* and *know*, then they are truly *agreed*.

The principle turns then upon what I will call the *Great Willingness* to do God's will, which, we are promised, would enable us to *know* the doctrine. To *know* is to be accurate. If one looks at the words and lines of Scripture with this *Great Willingness* to obey in his heart, there will be no motive to resist its teachings. Then as he studies each Scripture truth with this willingness, only then is he truly taught by the Holy Spirit. If one wants to *know* and God wants him to *know*, who then is able to prevent understanding?

Therefore, if two brothers should come to the Scripture with the willingness to obey, they will both come to *know* the teachings. If they both truly *know*, they know alike. They will be of the "same mind"; they will "speak the same thing." Hence, it is possible to interpret the Scriptures alike — a marvelous privilege of which we desperately need to take advantage.

But the Scripture not only promises that we can *know* of the teachings, it also promises that we can be fully *assured* that we do know. We can know and know that we know. This is a great kindness from God.

My first reaction as I saw this thought in Scripture was a fear that it would produce arrogancy. But can a sincere recognition of one truth produce the breach of another? I think not. Many even suppose it is arrogant for a Christian to claim full assurance of salvation, but God will assure us of *any* truth as we meet His conditions.

Then consider Jesus. He knew *all* things and knew that He knew, but there was not an ounce of arrogancy in Him because of it. The more we truly know the will and teachings of God, the more it drives arrogancy from us and brings humility as we begin to really understand, little by little, His majestic purpose. How we are dwarfed before Him. As we move out into the ocean of His truth, how it awes us by its vastness and depth. The more we truly know as we study with the willingness to obey, the more we realize how little we do know. And if a person thinks he knows much, "he knoweth nothing yet as he ought to know" (1 Cor. 8:2).

Paul desired that the Colossians might have a "full assurance of understanding" (Col. 2:2). This full assurance of understanding — to understand accurately and to be assured that we do understand — is essential for the most effectual service and a holy boldness just as the assurance of salvation is essential to be an effective witness. One cannot be motivated to proclaim boldly that of which he is not positively certain — which doubtless is the main problem in pulpits and classrooms today.

Furthermore, such assurance of understanding is essential for comfort. It would be a distressing thing for one desiring to do God's will to be forever seeking but never able to have any assurance of finding it. But Paul has taught us that assurance is given for comfort: "That their hearts might be *comforted*, being *knit together in love*, and unto all riches of the *full assurance of understanding* . . . " (Col. 2:2). It should be carefully noted that this comfort of which Paul speaks involves two great principles: 1) the unity of the faith, i.e., "being knit together in love," and 2) the "riches of full assurance of understanding."

These two principles are closely related. Let me illustrate: A certain brother was troubled about a specific doctrinal matter. He went to the Scriptures determined to do whatever he found the will of God to be on the matter. He studied carefully and God gave him to know the matter according to His promise (John 7:17). But then this brother found himself standing essentially alone in this knowledge. His fellow believers, unwilling to go against tradition, scorned him for that knowledge.

The brother then felt a discomfort. "Did I understand this doctrine correctly?" he wondered. Being willing to change if wrong, he studied the matter again and reached the same conclusion even more positively. He *knew* but still was not comforted, for there was no one with whom he could be "knit together in love" on this matter.

Then the brother heard of some other fellow believers who had begun to study the matter. They had independently reached the same conclusion; they also *knew*. He went to them; he candidly allowed his conclusions to be searched by them. Then they all were "knit together in love" on the matter, and he was both "comforted" and "assured" that he had understood correctly. Then he boldly and gladly proclaimed it.

There are then three witnesses that work together for full assurance: 1) the witness of the Bible — the objective Word, 2) the witness of the Holy Spirit to the biblical truth, and 3) the witness of other brethren who also have the willingness to obey. All these combine to bring true understanding, full assurance of understanding, and the comfort of the unity of the faith.

Even Paul himself reached the full assurance of his doctrines this way: 1) he pored over the Old Testament Scriptures in Arabia for three years (Gal. 1:17, 18); 2) he was taught by the Holy Spirit (Gal. 1:15, 16); and 3) he later submitted his doctrines to be searched by other brethren —lest he "had run in vain" (Gal. 2:2).

This is the way God intends for His people to come to His Word, and to each other. We must get rid of the obnoxious argument: "Well, you have *your* interpretation, and I have *mine*." That attitude says, "I am not willing to do His will unless it agrees with *my* interpretation, so don't bother me with *yours*."

This attitude is remarkable for its shallowness and immaturity.

We are not likely to find God's interpretation if we are unwilling to allow ourselves to be searched by others who show signs of being willing to obey. Those who are willing to do His will have nothing to lose by being searched; but those who are not willing to obey will fear and may tenaciously resist even the mildest dialogue.

But we read in Proverbs, "He that is first in his own cause seemeth just, but his neighbor cometh and searcheth him" (18:17). It is profitable for us to be searched. If we long to do God's will an erring neighbor cannot destroy our understanding, but our righteous neighbor may be God's instrument for further correction.

We do not need, nor should we often engage in, dialogue with unbelievers. But unless we care enough for the brethren to search and be searched by their dialogue, we will never know the true comfort of being knit together in love; and the full assurance of understanding and probably understanding itself will elude us. An open and non-defensive spirit is essential to the unity of the faith.

But why is it necessary to be willing to obey a given truth before one can understand or learn it? To answer that question, it will be necessary to consider the negative side of this whole issue. Just as the Scripture states the positive side of the issue — if one is *willing* to do His will he shall know — it also states the negative case.

The Scripture definitely identifies the reason for our failure to correctly understand its teachings — and hence our lack of unity. I will call this reason the *Great Reluctance* in contrast to the *Great Willingness.*

Jesus introduced this principle and its consequences to His disciples in answer to their inquiry of why He spoke in parables (Matt. 13:10). His answer contained both a promise and a warning: ". . . it is given unto you," He said, "to *know* the mysteries of the kingdom of heaven" (a fact based upon the principle of the *Great Willingness*); but He continued, "to them (because of the *Great Reluctance*) it is not given" (v. 11). Jesus then further explained that to those who *have* will be given more, but from those who *have not* will be taken even that which they have (v. 12). They would hear the words but would not understand (v. 13). "Their ears are dull of hearing, and their eyes they have closed . . . " (v. 15).

Here then is exemplified the *Great Reluctance* in its ultimate form — in unbelief and rebellion toward the whole of God's redemptive truth in Christ.

However, the principle of a reluctance to hear is applicable to individual truths even in the life of a believer. Jesus taught that even some who are "in the kingdom of heaven" will resist certain of His commandments and will even "teach men" to break them (Matt. 5:19). Hence even the believer is not immune to the effects of the *Great Reluctance* when it comes to certain specific truths which he does not like or which go against his biases or traditional beliefs in some way. This is a sobering truth which should move us all to solemn self-examination. These Jesus called "least in the kingdom of heaven."

This is the class which the writer of Hebrews calls ". . . dull of hearing" (Heb. 5:11). In this way those who "have not" — the dull of hearing — lose even the understanding they once may have had.

Now if we analyze this phenomenon of reluctance to obey a given truth or commandment in the life of a Christian, we will readily see that it is impossible to learn a given truth or doctrine while resisting it.

No one, especially not a Christian, will stand before a commandment or truth of God, admit it to be a commandment or truth of God, and then openly defy it. If he is reluctant to obey, then the only recourse is to rationalize.

Ask a Presbyterian if baptism is by immersion, and he will typically say, "No." Turn with him to Romans 6:4 and read ". . . we are buried with him by baptism . . ." and he will proceed to explain why that passage cannot mean that baptism is a burial — that it really means something other than what it says. He literally persuades himself that this simple statement somehow means to sprinkle. To obey the direct statement would involve such radical implications in terms of traditions, associates, churches, family ties, etc., that his psyche will not permit him to *learn* the true doctrine of baptism.

Ask a five-point Calvinist if the atonement of Jesus was not for believers only but also for the sins of the whole world, and he will typically say, "No" — or something that means "no." Turn with him then to 1 John 2:2 and read, ". . . not for *ours only*, but also for the sins of the *whole world*," and he will proceed to explain why that simple, direct statement cannot mean that Christ died for everyone. The implications are too great in terms of associates, traditions, losing face, church affiliation, prestige, etc., that his psyche will not allow him to *learn* the true doctrine of the atonement.

Why does this occur? A person does not know the doctrine because when he reads it or is taught it, there is a reluctance to face the often traumatic consequences of obedience to it. Hence he rationalizes: "that passage of Scripture really means something other than what it seems to say." An erroneous interpretation is invented to avoid the correct one, and he then sincerely believes the erroneous one. Such persons have deceived themselves — not permitting themselves to truly understand, and it becomes a serious blind spot.

A person may continue in this state of self-deceit (see Jer. 17:9) for many years or a lifetime; the rationalization may be so thorough that he literally *forgets* (see James 1:23, 24) that there was ever an issue when once, long ago, there was a brief moment of truth which was rationalized away only to be rediscovered at the "judgment seat of Christ" (Rom. 14:10-12; 1 Cor. 3:11-15).

The root of the problem of Christian discord is therefore exposed. The Scriptures are subconsciously misinterpreted because we are reluctant to obey the true interpretation. Since we all are vulnerable to this problem, it would behoove us to be on our knees before God and deliberately resolve to begin a life-long process of examination, adjustment, and conformity to every detail of Scripture regardless of the cost in position, prestige, association, or finances.

This may not be the most welcome news to some, but if we really want to cut the tap-root of the problem of discord, we may now do it. There is nothing mysterious about it; we can examine ourselves before God, purge out the *Great Reluctance*, humble ourselves in willingness to obey the will of God, interpret the Scriptures accurately, submit ourselves "one to another" (Eph. 5:21) to search and be searched, and persist until we are "knit together in love."

Now it will do us no good to have considered the scriptural doctrine on how to "know the doctrine" if we are reluctant to obey even this doctrine. But we can *learn* it and implement it if we will.

Even in this matter the Scriptures set before us the

practical example of how to achieve a unity of the faith when discord has arisen. There arose among the early churches a very divisive issue concerning circumcision (Acts 15:1f). It caused great dissension and serious concern among the brethren. They were not "knit together in love," and this caused great discomfort.

They were unwilling to accept a state of division and discord as irreversible and inevitable, so the churches of Antioch and Jerusalem met together to face the issue candidly. After carefully weighing the evidence, and searching the Scriptures, being willing to obey the truth rather than tradition, they reached agreement (Acts 15:25).

They sent word of this agreement to other churches, and when the news of their agreement was carried back to Antioch, ". . . they rejoiced for the consolation" (v. 31). Thus the validity of Paul's teaching in Colossians 2:2 was exemplified in their consolation. They were "*comforted*, being *knit together* in love, and unto all riches of the *full assurance of understanding* . . ." This principle was actualized in their experience; it can be in ours also.

All the doctrines of Scripture are immensely practical. Religious experience must be guided by the doctrines of Scripture. No doctrine of Scripture is intended to be a mere theological abstraction but rather truth that grips the soul, guides the emotions, and directs the experiences of our personal interface with Christ through the Holy Spirit.

But the question remains, are we ready to search ourselves for the *Great Willingness* and to be searched in love by each other? I know this may seem like a radical proposal in these days. But what is to prevent us from seeking a candid and charitable examination of each of our differences, point by point, under the searchlight of Scripture?

All of us, doubtless, would have to be prepared, rather should always stand prepared, to change as we would converge toward the center of Scripture truth. Some long-standing traditions would be shattered, but any "losses" would be repaid a hundred fold as shouts of salvation would rend the deadness of these times in the revival that would inevitably follow.

But before this can happen, someone must care that the name of Christ is reproached by this discord and raise his voice with others who care.

To actively pursue unity and reach one accord is a challenge which none but the most mature Christians could or would accept; we must come to each other with stark honesty, no cynicism, but rather absolute sincerity. There must be unselfishness, humility, infinite patience, " . . . brotherly love; in honour preferring one another" (Rom. 12:10). There must be the willingness to sacrifice prestige, position, crowds, time, and effort to reach unity in truth, as did those of Antioch and Jerusalem.

We must get rid of the unscriptural notion that Christian people cannot interpret the Bible essentially alike. We are not helpless victims of discord as if the Bible were an insoluble riddle. We have been made free to understand by the Spirit of God.

But there must be a rallying point for unity — something to be unified around. This cannot be a slogan, a creed, a tradition, a program, a mission board or movement, a denomination, a man, a school. It must be *objective* in nature; subjectivism is an unreliable guide. The rallying point or criterion for unity must be worthy of the allegiance of all. It must be of universal authority, cosmic in stature and significance, timeless in its principles, impeccable in righteousness, and immutable in truth. Only one objective standard on earth satisfies these requirements and is worthy to hold up as a standard to all Christians. That standard is the Word of the living God as revealed in the Bible which derives its timeless authority from the Holy Trinity: God the Father, the Person and Lordship of Jesus Christ the Son, and the Holy Spirit who breathed the inerrant message of this Word. "Sanctify them," Christ prayed, "through thy truth. Thy word is truth" (John 17:17).

This has been a rather brief study of a very important matter. It is a difficult matter, I admit. But how it would glorify the Lord's name and what great profit would accrue to the people of God and to the world if we could become settled from the Scripture not only on future things but all other matters as well. We could then settle down to the long-range task that the Lord has left us here to accomplish. We could then get down to the business of occupying until He comes.

There is a long road ahead. Is anyone interested?

Now to summarize: the things I have discussed in this section surely indicate that there is yet to be fulfilled a conversion of the Jews. There will be, in answer to the prayer of Christ, a true unity of the faith — if not before, then in the millennium. There is yet to be fulfilled a millennial period when national Israel will live in the covenant borders of her homeland, and both Jew and Gentile will be united in the church for the greatest earthly harvest of souls in the history of the world. Then toward the end of the millennium there will be a "great falling away" (see 2 Thess. 2:3)[8] which will introduce a final but short period of tribulation. Then will come the end.

But until the very time of the end, the Gospel is still the power of God unto salvation. Yet under the circumstances that now prevail in Christendom, that Gospel cannot be very powerfully felt. However, the Holy Spirit through the power of unified churches in obedience to the Word of God can cause this world to tremble to its very foundations; and the Lord is going to have such a victory before He returns to destroy the earth. I urge my brethren everywhere to give an humble and an honest reconsideration to the doctrine of Scripture pertaining to the unity of the faith. It is possible; it is essential; it is right. We must confront the issues that would draw us together around the Word of God in such a way that the *world can see* it. Then "the world may believe," as Jesus said, "that thou hast sent me" (John 17:21).

---

[8] Some feel that we are now in the time of the "great falling away" spoken of by Paul. However, one cannot "fall away" from a state he has never reached. There has never been a time since the end of the third century that the majority of Christendom has not been nearly apostate concerning the major truths of Scripture, let alone revived. That was a falling away. But it could not be what Paul had in mind, for on the heels of Paul's "great falling away" the "man of sin" is to be revealed (2 Thess. 2:3). This great apostasy of which Paul speaks will be the apostasy that terminates the millennium with the release of Satan.

Characteristics of the Millennium

Without going into great detail in the interpretation of the Scripture references pertaining to the millennium, I want to list them for your study and to make a few general observations concerning the nature of the millennium. Some of the main passages that relate to either the conversion of Israel and/or the millennium are Deuteronomy 30:1-10; Isaiah 2:1-5; 11:6-16; 60:1-18; 65:18-25; Revelation 20:1-6. This is not an exhaustive list, but these are some of the main passages. On these passages I make the following observations:

1. **Deuteronomy 30:1-10.** This is a clear expression of the final regathering of Israel from a world-wide dispersion. It involves their national sovereignty over the land of the Abrahamic covenant, their conversion and spiritual blessing, their wealth and temporal blessing.

2. **Isaiah 2:1-5.** This speaks of the universal faithfulness of the people of all nations to the house of the Lord. It is called here a "mountain" denoting the generic or kingdom-wide aspect of the church, and it is said to be established in the top of the "mountains" (plural) denoting the local aspect of the churches throughout the nations. Jerusalem and Zion are to be understood here in the church format of the "house of God," just as Peter interpreted "Zion" in Isaiah 28:16 (cf. 1 Pet. 2:5, 6). However, the millennial church at Jerusalem, as in the first century, will doubtless always be a center of influence — a symbol of the faithfulness and power of God among all churches. As long as the world stands, especially after the Jews are converted, Jerusalem as an ancient symbol of the "house of God" will be venerated, and rightly so, for its historic and nostalgic association with the name of God and as a center of power and influence among the millennial churches. It would be wholly appropriate, I think, for Israel to rebuild the temple as a symbol of their national heritage, but it can never be biblically used for ritual worship and animal sacrifice again. The true "house of God" on earth will be the church. Therefore, in a double sense, it is literally true that

"out of Zion shall go forth the law, and the word of the Lord from Jerusalem" (Isa. 2:3).

3. **Isaiah 11:6-16.** Starting with the nativity of Christ (v. 1) and looking forward to the millennium (v. 6f), the remarkable thing about this passage is the peaceful union of natural enemies. I cannot settle the debate as to whether this is to be interpreted as the natural relationship of the animal kingdom, or figuratively as the peaceful relationship of warring factions of religious or political strife. I like to think the animal kingdom will again enjoy the relationship implied in pre-flood times (cf. Gen. 1:30, 9:2-5). But this very fact (if it proves to be a fact) is such an apt illustration of the union of the broken human relationships that I feel certain it refers to peace in the religious and social realm and may well have this double meaning.

The listing of the clean animal at peace with the unclean animal answers to the Jew (the clean) and the Gentile (the unclean); in just this way Peter was shown (Acts 10:10-15) that they would come together in the church. The effect is so striking that it strongly suggests a symbolic meaning of the Jew and Gentile union in the church. But the animal relationship, I believe, may also be actual.

Here, too, is perhaps the most significant description of the millennium in the Bible. It is characterized by universal righteousness (v. 9). For the first time in history, angels, devils, and all mankind may see what a difference righteousness makes in human society. This is one of the reasons, I believe, why God will bring the millennium through the Gospel and His church, so that He may vindicate and prove before every intelligent being at the judgment that true, voluntary righteousness brings untold blessing. Then when the great accuser, Satan, says the conditions on earth were rotten, it can be demonstrated to everyone's satisfaction that the reason was primarily because of his own instigation of sin. This will effectively cut the ground from under Satan as he accuses the brethren.

4. **Isaiah 60:1-18; 65:18-25.** These passages foretell the general millennial blessings. Observe, however, one note of

caution: sometimes prophetic passages rather suddenly change time-frames or subject matter; for example, Isaiah 60:19 suddenly changes from the description of millennial blessings to the New Jerusalem (cf. Rev. 21:23). Likewise, Isaiah 65:17 speaks of the new heaven and new earth (cf. Rev. 21:1; 2 Pet. 3:10, 13), but Isaiah 65:20 speaks of sin and death. Then verses 21 and following speak of the natural human lifestyle including reproduction. None of this goes on in the new heaven setting (see Matt. 22:29, 30). However, an unusually long life span is implied here. If the non-predatory nature of the pre-flood animals is restored, we might expect also the longevity of the antediluvian patriarchs to be restored. But this does not imply a lifting of the Edenic curse; sin and death still exist (v. 20). Sin and death will not be eliminated until the restoration of "all things" (Acts 3:21) in the new heaven and new earth. The last enemy to be destroyed is death (1 Cor. 15:25, 26).

Again we have mention of the clean and unclean beasts in peaceful relationship; therefore I conclude Isaiah 60:1-18 and 65:18-25 are millennial passages and speak of the "latter day glory."

5. **Revelation 20:1-6.** This is the only passage in the Bible that names the duration of this special time of blessing — a thousand years (I will treat this chapter in greater detail later when we make a detailed study of Revelation). But here we learn that Satan will be bound and that a certain class of martyrs will be resurrected to celebrate the millennial victories with Christ.

As Christ with the martyred saints enjoy the victorious reaping of the fruit of the earth from their vantage point in the heavens, so those who love His eternal purpose will enjoy here on earth the blessings of Zion's glad morning. Though times seem spiritually hard now and the heavens seem as brass; yet, soon now, we will be seeing the events unfold which will introduce an unprecedented period of victory for the Gospel. "Therefore, my beloved brethren, be ye stedfast, unmovable, always abounding in the work of the Lord, forasmuch as ye know that your labour is not in vain in the Lord" (1 Cor. 15:58).

Ramifications 6

So far I have relied mainly upon five rigorous propositional truths to establish the general framework of eschatology whether it is pre- or postmillennial. Furthermore, I am confident that these propositions will not be soon shaken, because they are rigorously drawn from the very fabric — the words, sentences, and inspired logic of Scripture. These propositions stand alone. Therefore in taking them at face value, there should be no great concern that the rest of the Scripture will not be compatible with the conclusions established by them.

However, I well remember how anxious I was, even after the logic of the Scripture had forced me from my former position, to learn if all the other areas of Scripture were easily and naturally compatible with my new conclusions. I wondered about all the ramifications of a framework of eschatology that was so simple and directly defined on the surface of Scripture. If it were true, I thought, why was it held as such a minority position? Then I remembered that the general majority has seldom been right on spiritual matters, especially on complex matters that can easily be exploited as sensational. Yet, I thought, there surely must be many other Scriptures that necessitate a different view. So over the period of a year I spent from three to five hundred hours searching every other passage of Scripture that had a bearing on the subject to determine if all of them were easily compatible with the framework of eschatology that I had seen.

Now I want to share a brief summary of the ramifications and implications of a few of the major prophetic passages of Scripture that may trouble someone. Obviously, in treating these important passages in a work of this size, I cannot be exhaustive. But brevity is to your advantage. I will set forth the kernel of the thought in different issues and the related Scripture references dealing with it, then leave you to search the matter. Remembering then the injunction of the Lord to "Prove all things; hold fast that which is good" (1 Thess. 5:21), we embark on an investigation of a few of the ramifications.

The Question of Imminency

One of the most widespread impressions held by many Christians of all ages is that Christ may return at any moment. This idea is sometimes called the doctrine of imminency. Most Christian scholars who have studied Scripture prophecy, to the extent that they have reached strong conclusions on a position of eschatology, do not hold the doctrine of imminency unless their broader doctrine of eschatology embraces it. Most people, however, do not read analytically but impressionistically, and this probably explains why many people never realize that God wants us to know that certain prophecies must be fulfilled before Christ returns.

To illustrate the carelessness with which many people read the Scripture, even pastors and teachers, I want to call attention to the first few verses of the Lord's discourse on future things (Matt. 24; Luke 21). I have heard a multitude of sermons from my youth, mostly by premillennial preachers, on the signs of the second coming of Christ wherein great emphasis was put upon earthquakes, pestilences, wars and rumors of wars, as positive signs that Christ was coming any minute now. Voluminous statistics have been poured forth, ranging from the destruction of Pompei to the eruption of Mount Saint Helens or falling debris from satellites, as evidence that the second coming of Christ is imminent. Yet, an accurate reading of the passages from which these "signs" were taken will show that the very opposite effect was intended by the Lord.

When the apostles had asked Christ about His second coming and the end of the world (Matt. 24:3), His most immediate concern was to warn them not to be deceived by the doomsayers, sensationalists, and false prophets (Matt. 24:4; Luke 21:8). Then He mentioned wars, etc., and instead of saying these are signs of the end, He said ". . . for all these things must come to pass, *but the end is not yet*" (Matt. 24:6; cf. Luke 21:9). That is to say, these are things that must happen, but that is *not* a sign of the end. It is a sign that the end is *not* imminent. It is a sign that things are proceeding normally and that the end is *not* soon — not "by and by" or not "immediately" (Luke 21:9, NKJV).

I had misread these Scriptures many times, and I will never forget my astonishment when I noticed that Christ was expressly warning us not to be deceived by those who teach imminency and who think these are signs of His soon coming. But rather, He was setting forth a doctrine that many things must be fulfilled *before* He would return. He said, "Take heed that ye be not deceived: for many shall come in my name, saying, I am Christ; and *the time draweth near: go ye not therefore after them*" (Luke 21:8). There are some today who say "I am Christ," but there are many today who say "the time draweth near" and yet all the prophesied events have not yet been fulfilled. Many Christians today regard it as a mark of spirituality to make frequent use of the term "the soon-coming of the Lord." *We are not to go after them*!

The very first thing that is said to be a sign of the end is that "this gospel of the Kingdom shall be preached in all the world for a witness unto all nations; and then shall the end come" (Matt. 24:14). That event has not occurred as yet and probably will be literally fulfilled only in the millennium. You see then that by not reading the Scriptures carefully and by listening to preachers who do not read the Scriptures carefully, it is easy to get an impression just opposite from what is actually taught.

Now there are at least two views of eschatology in which imminency is held. These views are premillennial pretribulation rapture and amillennial. The views in which it is not held are: premillennial post-tribulation rapture, and postmillennial. Since this question may be settled by an independent investigation of Scripture, it is not appropriate merely to accept or reject imminency on the basis of your view of eschatology. The question to be answered is this: has the Bible taught that beginning any time after the moment Christ was taken up in the cloud (Acts 1:9) all things were fulfilled for His return? Or has the Bible taught from the beginning that certain things must be fulfilled before He returns?

We must distinguish between the *doctrine* of imminency beginning from the ascension of Christ and the logical proposition that at some point in time, after all prophecies are fulfilled, that His return will then be imminent. The latter will obviously be true, since we are expressly told that His coming is "immediately after the tribulation" (Matt. 24:29). Therefore, those in the tribulation time should expect Him almost any moment, for the instant the tribulation starts may be difficult to recognize and there is no exact information in prophecy as to its duration.

But that is not the *doctrine* of imminency. That doctrine says that after Jesus ascended out of the sight of the apostles, they immediately began to look for His return. Jesus told them on the same occasion that they would be His witnesses "... both in Jerusalem, and in all Judea, and in Samaria, and unto the uttermost part of the earth" (Acts 1:8) and that they were to "teach all nations, baptizing them . . . ", etc. (Matt. 28:19). Now that takes a little time. But never mind, Pentecost says, " . . . the very men who received such announcements themselves believed that what *would be the natural course of history* [emphasis mine] could be interrupted by the translation of the believers out of the sphere in which history unfolds and held to the imminent return."[1]

---

[1] Pentecost, *Things to Come*, p. 168.

Now this raises a serious question. Does God in Scripture teach His saints to believe that even His own prophecies and purposes are to be truncated and to believe that which He Himself knows to be false? He has plainly taught us: "... When ye shall *see all these things, know* that it is near ... " (Matt. 24:33), but not before. "But ye, brethren, are not in darkness, that that day should overtake you as a thief" (1 Thess. 5:4). God has clearly revealed a timetable but not the very day.

But *did* the apostles believe, as Pentecost says, that the coming of the Lord was imminent? I want now to examine those passages of Scripture that are thought by some to teach imminency. I am going to list the Scriptures cited by Pentecost[2] as teaching imminency for your study convenience. But let me suggest that in order for a passage to teach the imminent return of Christ, it must say something about timing relative to other prophesied events. If any event is prophesied to occur in the normal course of developing history, Christ's coming cannot be considered imminent until that event occurs, unless we are *told* plainly that He would come *before* that event. And since the Bible clearly states that *all* prophecy must be fulfilled before Christ returns (Acts 3:21), we need not look for Scriptures stating or implying the contrary.

Nevertheless, let us look at Pentecost's list to see if this conclusion is valid:

1. *John 14:2, 3.* These verses confirm the *fact* of Christ's coming, but nothing concerning *timing* or imminency.

2. *Acts 1:11.* (Same as comment number 1).

3. *1 Corinthians 15:51, 52.* There is a comment here relative to other prophesied events, but this comment, far from teaching the doctrine of imminency, utterly destroys it. The event treated here is the rapture, and it is put at "the last trump." However, the last trump sounds *after* the tribulation (compare Matt. 24:29, 31; also see Rev. 11:12-18, especially v. 15). When Jesus comes at His revelation (Matt. 24:31) there is

---

[2] *Ibid*, pp. 168, 203.

a trumpet sound, and since we have seen that event terminates the universe, it is the *last* trump. This shows again that the rapture and the revelation are the same event and both occur after the tribulation. Therefore this reference shows the rapture as *not* imminent.

4. *1 Corinthians 1:7.* While this passage, as it reads in English, might more reasonably be thought to imply imminency since the Corinthian church is "waiting" for this coming, yet it would only *allow* the interpretation of imminency if it were otherwise established; it could not establish imminency, especially in the face of Scriptures which preclude it. In fact there have been other prophecies fulfilled since then, e.g., the destruction of Jerusalem, but the Corinthians are still "waiting" albeit in their graves. But then a closer look at the word "coming" proves too much, for the Greek word is *apokalupsis*, meaning the *revelation* (the showing or manifestation) of Christ which everyone agrees, both pre- and postmillennial, must occur after the tribulation. Hence, again, imminency is proved impossible by this passage also. This passage is also in conflict with the whole idea of the rapture of the church in a "secret" coming of Christ seven years prior to the visible return or *revelation* of Christ. The *church* is "waiting for the *revelation* of our Lord . . . ."

5. *Philippians 3:20.* This passage standing alone would *allow* the interpretation of imminency if it were otherwise established, but since we are told that the Corinthian church was waiting for the *revelation* of Christ which occurs after the tribulation, we know that the Philippian church does likewise. There is nothing in the passage to controvert that reasonable interpretation. It does not teach imminency, for although the Philippian church did "look" for Christ from heaven, it says nothing of *when* He was to arrive or when they looked for Him to arrive.

6. *Colossians 3:4.* (See comment number 1).

7. *1 Thessalonians 1:10.* (See comment number 5).

8. *1 Thessalonians 4:16, 17.* Notice the phrase "trump of God." Everyone admits this to be the same occasion as

1 Corinthians 15:51, 52 at the "last trump"; hence this event follows the tribulation and cannot be imminent (see comment number 3). Apart from this significant fact, nothing is mentioned about timing or order here.

9. *1 Thessalonians 5:5-9.* (See comment number 1). Also notice verse 4 says that day should not overtake the brethren "as a thief." That means they know the approximate time frame because they "watch" the prophetic events unfold (see Matt. 24:32, 33), and if there are prophetic events to come there is no imminency.[3] Pentecost says the church should watch for Christ, not the prophetic events. What must we do, ignore the prophecies and go outside every hour or two and look up in the sky to see if He is on the way?

10. *1 Timothy 6:14, 15.* This is simply an injunction for Timothy and all who follow him to keep that commandment perpetually until Christ comes. Then "in his times" pointing to a future event, He will show His power. If God by verse 14 intended for Timothy to believe Christ might come before he died, He would have misled Timothy; for God knew very well that Christ would not so come.

That unsavory implication in the imminency doctrine is one of its worst features. It makes God a party to encouraging His saints to believe something that He knows is not so. It makes God the author of a sort of "tongue in cheek" threat that He *might* come at any time to keep us in line.

The true servants do not need that "threat." "Who then is a faithful and wise servant, whom his Lord hath made ruler over his household, to give them meat in due season? Blessed is that servant, whom his lord when he cometh shall find so doing" (Matt. 24:45, 46). The faithful will be serving *whenever* He comes, even if he knows it to be a distant event. If he is faithful only because the Master might come soon, he is not faithful at all. The picture is as a man travelling into a "far

---

[3] As to "wrath" (v. 9), this refers to God's wrath upon the wicked (cf. v. 3). It is contrasted with "salvation" and cannot have reference to the tribulation. The real wrath of God is reserved for the terminal event at the revelation of Christ (cf. Rev. 6:16; 14:10, 11, 19, 20); hence it has no relevancy to the doctrine of imminency.

country" (Matt. 25:14), and his servants know it is a *far* country; it is no quick trip. The righteous serve him knowing it will be a "long time" (25:19). They make long-term investments of their talents; then "after a *long time* the lord of those servants cometh." The righteous are faithful though there is no "threat." The wicked would be wicked if there were a threat (see Matt. 25:14f).

All that God has said is to be faithful until Christ returns; it says nothing about how long. You do not know the day or hour, but if you "watch" prophetic events you will know the general season. The wicked will not watch, and though he is gone a "long time," they will be caught unawares. There is no doctrine of imminency in the Scriptures.

11. *James 5:7, 8.* The injunction is to patience, because the Lord "waiteth" for the "latter rain." The "latter rain" will fall during the millennium. There can be little doubt that the "latter rain" is a reference to the great millennial harvest. This being so the passage not only proves that the Lord's coming is not imminent for that prophecy is not yet fulfilled, but it also proves that the coming of the Lord will be after the millennium. That, in fact, is exactly what He is waiting for, as Peter said: " . . . account that the long-suffering of our Lord is salvation . . . " (2 Pet. 3:15).

No the latter rain has not yet fallen, but God has "long patience" for it. Therefore, we are also to be "patient." Because it is so long in coming, James adds the comforting reminder that it is drawing nearer — He will come. The word translated "draweth nigh" is in the perfect tense and would literally mean "has drawn near." Now, if this means "near" as men understand near and two thousand years later it still has not occurred, we have a problem with the credibility of Scripture. Doubtless this is an example of the prophetic tense which speaks of events in the distant future as already fulfilled, e.g., "ye *are come* unto Mount Sion . . . " (Heb. 12:22), or "unto us a child *is born* . . . " (Isa. 9:6). To interpret the passage in James to mean actual *nearness* as men normally think of *near* not only casts a shadow on the promise of God, but it is completely out of harmony with the tenor of the whole context.

This entire passage implies a long wait — watching, working, waiting — until God gets His final harvest. The reference to "drawing near" is doubtless given to confirm the certainty of Christ's return, in view of the long wait, lest we be discouraged. No imminency can be found here. The Gospel is to be preached into all the world (the latter rain); *then* the end will come (see Matt. 24:14).

12. *Titus 2:13.* (See comment number 5.)

13. *Revelation 3:3.* I have pointed out above that only the wicked would be caught as a thief (1 Thess. 5:4). The wicked, impenitent sinners are in view here, yet nothing is said about timing or order.

14. *Revelation 3:10, 11.* The argument that verse 10 teaches a rapture before the tribulation is far too vague to have any significant bearing on imminency. In view of the evidence that there is no pretribulation rapture (see pp. 57-59), this is only a reference to God's providential mercies during the hour of trial. The word *quickly* (v. 11) can mean *soon*, but it also means *suddenly*. If God meant *soon* as men understand it, we already, as in James, have a problem with the credibility of Scripture. Therefore it cannot mean *soon* as we normally think of it — two thousand years is not "soon" to us. It may be "soon" to God, but if that is the way it is to be understood, it has no bearing on imminency. But we should probably understand it in the sense of *suddenly*. Imminency would be allowed here if otherwise established, but it is not taught in this passage.

15. *Revelation 22:20.* (See comment number 14).

16. *1 Peter 3:3, 4* (sic). Pentecost actually gives this reference (p. 203), but probably he intended 2 Peter 3:3, 4. If so, Peter's concern is not with imminency but with certainty. The events Peter associates with Christ's coming, the destruction of the heavens and earth, *must* follow the millennium and the tribulation. This passage is devastating to the theory of imminency.

Now these doubtless are the most convincing passages in Scripture to establish imminency. Pentecost would surely have found more convincing passages if they had been there. But it is plain to see that these do not support the doctrine of imminency; they destroy it.

I have already discussed the teachings of Jesus that bear on the question of imminency. These are found mostly in His Olivet discourse (Matt. 24:4-14, 32, 33; Mark 13:5-10; Luke 21:8-24, 29-36; see also parables Matt. 24:36-51; 25:1-30). He positively teaches that there are many things to come before He returns.

Now I want to examine the question: Did the apostles expect Christ to return in their lifetimes?

Peter. We read that Peter knew he would die instead of being raptured. Jesus positively predicted Peter's death (John 21:18, 19). Peter understood it and accepted it completely and lived with that expectation (2 Pet. 1:13-15). In view of this expressed knowledge by Peter of his death, "... even as our Lord Jesus Christ hath shewed me" (v. 14), I cannot trust a theory that tries to make Peter believe in imminency. Such a theory seriously compromises the credibility of our Lord's words and of Peter's own confidence in them. There is a better way to handle the Scripture.

John. While there is not a direct prediction of John's death, yet John himself was not party to the rumor going around that he would live until the Lord came. John implies that he actually expected death (John 21:23), but after receiving the prophecies of Revelation, surely he knew for certain the Lord's coming was not imminent.

Paul. Again by Paul's own words he was not expecting the Lord to come at any moment and definitely not within his own lifetime (Acts 20:22-24; Phil. 1:20-26; 2 Tim. 4:6-8). Furthermore, he did not want those to whom he wrote letters to believe in imminency. The Thessalonians had mistaken his meaning in his first letter, just as many do who have not read carefully, but he wrote a second letter to correct their mistaken interpretation. In his second letter he carefully explains:

> Now we beseech you, brethren, by the coming of our Lord Jesus Christ, and by our gathering together unto him, That ye *be not soon* shaken in mind, or be troubled, neither by spirit, nor by word, *nor by letter as from us*, as that the day of Christ is at hand. Let no man deceive you [remember our Lord's similar warnings to be not deceived — Matt. 24:4; Luke 21:8] by any means: *for that day shall not come, except* there come a falling away first, and that man of sin be revealed, the son of perdition (2 Thess. 2:1-3).

Paul here is earnestly persuading them not to take the things said in his first letter (which we have already discussed) as teaching imminency.

Now if neither Paul, Peter nor John believed the doctrine of imminency, we need not look further. Even if some of the early disciples did believe it, it does not make it so unless the inspired Scriptures teach it. But as we have found, far from teaching imminency, they rather reject it.

The doctrine of imminency as an organized doctrinal system relating to a pretribulation rapture was unheard of until the early 19th century. Emmanuel Lacunza, a Jesuit priest, wrote a book called *The Coming of Messiah in Glory and Majesty* (1812) in which the concept of a pretribulation rapture was born.[4] From this beginning Edward Irving, J. N. Darby, and C. I. Scofield, each in turn contributed to the development and spread of this unscriptural doctrine among the people of fundamentalism until it permeated the movement down to the very grass roots. We need now to throw off this false doctrine. Many have done as Jesus and Paul said they should not do. They have allowed themselves to be deceived.

Interpretation of Daniel's Seventy Weeks — Dan. 9:24-27

One could do no better for the interpretation of this passage than to refer to Dr. B. H. Carroll's *Interpretation of the English Bible.*[5] I strongly urge this study upon those who

---

[4] Bray, *Origin.* See also MacPherson, *Cover-Up.*

[5] B. H. Carroll, *Daniel and the Inter-Biblical Period* (Nashville, Broadman Press, 1947), pp. 92-126.

desire to study this prophecy thoroughly. However, I will make a brief study outline for the aid of those who may not have access to Carroll's works or who would prefer to examine these brief suggestions for themselves in the Scripture, but again I strongly urge personal study regardless of whose interpretation you read.

I will merely list here the salient features of the prophecy and make some observations which, I believe, will show that the seventy weeks comprise one coherent, continuous, undivided time span which includes the times of the first advent of our Lord, and that the theory which projects the seventieth week into the future as the tribulation period is untenable.

The prophecy may be outlined as follows:

I. Verse 24 gives the subject of the prophecy: (a) "thy people" Israel, and (b) the "Holy City" Jerusalem. Both these entities are in view here.

II. Verse 24 also enumerates all the factors which must be fulfilled during the seventy-week period. That is, these seventy weeks are allotted for the accomplishing of six significant things, and they all must occur within the limits of these seventy weeks. These six things are:

A. To finish the transgression. This has reference to the full outworking of the sins of the Jewish people, particularly in Jerusalem, to the fulness or climax of the apostasy of the Jews beginning before the Babylonian captivity and culminating in the crucifixion of their Messiah. God once said to Abraham, "the iniquity of the Amorites is not yet full" (Gen. 15:16); yet when the time came that their iniquity was complete and ready to judge, God sent Israel in to take the land. Likewise the sin of the Jews was to reach its apex during the seventy weeks. Hence Jesus in the final week of this period said:

> *Fill ye up then the measure of your fathers.* Ye serpents, ye generation of vipers . . . *O Jerusalem, Jerusalem,* thou that killest the prophets, and stonest them which are sent unto thee . . . Behold, *your house is left unto you desolate* (see Matt. 23:32-38).

B. To make an end of sins. The idea is to accomplish a sealed, finished or closed transaction. In only one sense can it be said that sin was finished or closed during the seventy weeks, and that is by the death of Christ.

> . . . but now once in the end of the world hath he appeared to *put away* sin . . . Behold the Lamb of God, which *taketh away* the sin of the world . . . he was manifested to *take away* our sins (see Heb. 9:26; John 1:29; 1 John 3:5).

The Jews will continue to sin, like all others, as long as the world stands. If one interprets that as an end to sinful behavior, that will not happen until the final destruction of this world. There is sin during the millennium and serious sin after the millennium (Rev. 20:7-10).

C. To make reconciliation for iniquity. This is a similar thought using different words. It means "to cover" (cf. Lev. 6:30; 8:15; 16:19, 20; Ezk. 45:15, 17, 20). Only Christ through His death can make reconciliation for sins (2 Cor. 5:19). Some premillennialists say the "end" and "reconciliation" for sin are accomplished by the Jews in the tribulation by their suffering. But they wholly confuse the nature, purpose, and timing of the tribulation, not to speak of the doctrinal error in what is required for reconciliation to God. Men cannot make reconciliation for sin by their personal suffering.

D. To bring in everlasting righteousness. Once again everlasting righteousness is accomplished only through Christ: "For by one offering he hath *perfected forever* them that are sanctified" (Heb. 10:14). " . . . to declare *his righteousness* for the remission of sins that are past" (Rom. 3:25).

E. To seal up the vision and prophecy. The idea is to give the seal of confirmation to the Messianic vision and prophecy so far as the work of His first advent is concerned.

> . . . Jesus Christ was a minister of the circumcision for the truth of God, to *confirm the promises* made unto the fathers (Rom. 15:8; cf. Isa. 42:6; Mal. 3:1).

Jesus has finalized, confirmed, and validated the promises of the prophets by means of (a) miracles (Acts 2:22); (b) His death and testament in blood (Luke 22:20); (c) His resurrection (Acts 1:3); (d) by the Holy Spirit (Acts 1:4; 2:1-4), (e) through His church (Acts 4:29-33). In all these ways Jesus confirmed the covenant to the Jews in the seventieth week.

F. To anoint the most Holy (see Acts 2:30-36; 4:27; 10:38; Heb. 1:8, 9, 13; 8:1, 2).

Now the accomplishing of these six things is the purpose for determining the seventy weeks on the Jews and Jerusalem.

III. Verse 25 gives us the event from which the beginning of the seventy weeks is to be calculated, which I will discuss later.

IV. Verse 26 conveys two significant facts:

A. The death of the Messiah will be after the sixty-two weeks, i.e., after sixty-nine weeks, since there are seven weeks preceding the sixty-two weeks. Therefore, the death of Christ is in the seventieth week. It must be within the seventy-week period, as required by verse 24, otherwise the very kernel of the prophecy is destroyed.[6]

B. There is to come a people who will destroy the "city and the sanctuary" by a siege filled with desolations. It is not difficult to interpret this event since both the city and the temple were destroyed by Roman armies in 70 A.D. This destruction, however, is not to be counted within the seventy weeks because verse 24 does not include it.

V. Verse 27 likewise conveys two significant truths:

A. The entire final week of the seventy-week period will be dedicated to confirming the covenant or the Messianic

---

[6] The premillennial interpretation of this prophecy suffers from this problem. It terminates the sixty-ninth week with Christ's triumphal entry and then arbitrarily divides the last, or seventieth week from the sequence and relegates it to a time yet future during the great tribulation. This division, to say the least, is a very artificial approach to a prophetic period which has a definite length and no suggestion in the prophecy of a gap. If I were to accept the gap interpretation with all the necessary ramifications, the special "prophetic year," etc., and would relegate it to the great tribulation, it would be no less compatible in a postmillennial framework than in a premillennial one. But in either view, when the tribulation is properly understood, the gap is an arbitrary and needless complication. The best sense is the simplest, most natural sense.

promises to the people upon which this period is determined, namely the Jews. The "he" of verse 27 refers to Christ, the subject of the prophecy, not to antichrist.[7] Christ came to Israel, not to the Gentiles, and first confirmed His Messiahship (Matt. 15:24). Paul expresses this truth concisely:

> Now I say that Jesus Christ was a minister of the circumcision for the truth of God, to *confirm the promises* made unto the fathers (Rom. 15:8).

In many passages this central biblical truth is expressed: see Isaiah 42:6; Malachi 3:1; Luke 1:72; Acts 3:25, 26; Galatians 3:15-17; Hebrews 7:22; 8:6, 10-13; 9:15-24; 12:24. Christ confirmed Himself to Israel by miraculous works until His ascension. Then through the miraculous works of the Holy Spirit, He continued to confirm the covenant to Israel only until the Jews finally turned on the church once and for all about the time of the death of Stephen. After that the church was scattered and turned to the Gentiles (see Acts 8:4; 10:44-48; 11:15-20). This takes us to the end of the seventieth week.

B. The second thing we learn from Daniel 9:27 is that there is a cessation of the acceptability to God of the Jewish sacrificial system. Again this is accomplished by Christ and not by antichrist. In the midst of the last week, just prior to the death of Christ, He denounced the Jews for their rejection of Messiah, then told them they had filled up their full measure of wickedness (Matt. 23:32-36), wept over Jerusalem (v. 37; Luke 19:41), and said "Behold, your house is left unto you desolate" (v. 38). After the veil of the temple was rent (Matt. 27:50, 51), God never accepted another sacrifice from that desolate house, and He never will. Sacrifice and oblation ceased, and "for the overspreading of abominations he shall

---

[7] It is specifically said that the covenant is confirmed for "one week." The premillennial theory is that antichrist makes a false confirmation (which is no confirmation at all) and breaks it in the midst of the week. When Daniel 9:27 is compared with Daniel 11:30-32, all is contrast. There is no confirmation of the covenant there, but only indignation against it. Only Christ confirms, validates, the great covenant of the promise of the Messiah (Rom. 15:8).

make it desolate . . ." (Dan. 9:27). That house will be desolate until the consummation of it — or its destruction, which destruction was later poured upon those left desolate — both Jerusalem and the Jews in 70 A. D.

The Jews said let "His blood be on us, and on our children" (Matt. 27:25), and so it has been. Prior to His death Christ had established another house which He called "my church," and when the Jews repent they will be in this new house — no more "sacrifice and oblation" (see Heb. 10:4-9).

Now I will treat the matter of the beginning and the termination of the seventy-week period. I think it is unnecessary to belabor the point that the seventy weeks are "weeks" of years. The text literally reads *seventy sevens* are determined. The time-scale of the prophecy, including the rebuilding of Jerusalem after the Babylonian captivity, makes it clear that the *seventy sevens* are seventy groups of seven years each or 490 years.

We are told that the beginning of this period of 490 years is with the "going forth of the commandment to *restore* and to *build* Jerusalem" after the Babylonian captivity (Dan. 9:25). The determination of this event would seem easy enough except that the commandment went forth on several occasions. Now it is our task to discover which of these occasions is the beginning of the seventy-week period. There are four possibilities:

1. The first decree was given by Cyrus (Ezra 1:1, 2) in 536 B.C. This was a commission to build the temple only — not to "restore" (in the sense of establishing the Jews again in Jerusalem as a civil entity) or "build" the city itself. Then, too, no chronological scheme can reach the time of Christ from this date.

2. A second decree was issued by Darius Hystaspes (Ezra 4:5, 24; 6:1, 6-12) in 519 B.C. This only permitted the continuation of the temple in accordance with Cyrus' former decree.

3. Then a third and broader decree was issued by Artaxerxes I Longimanus (Ezra 7:1, 6, 7, 10-13, 18, 25, 27, 28). This decree is dated 457 B.C., and it contains much broader provisions: 1)

It restored civil polity. Ezra appointed judges and exercised the penalties of law over the people. 2) It restored all the people who were willing to return. 3) It gave permission to start to rebuild the entire city in accordance with Ezra's desire (see 7:10, 13, 17, 25), not merely the temple.

4. A fourth narrow commission was later given by the same king, Artaxerxes I (445 or 446 B.C.) to Nehemiah to rebuild the walls (Neh. 1-2). This was a short, but difficult, work and was finished in less than two months. Ezra and many Jews had already been living in the city a number of years under a rudimentary civil government. Neither the work of Nehemiah nor the time frame of this commission can satisfy the terms of Daniel's prophecy.

Now of the four possibilities, only the third broad decree under Artaxerxes I can satisfy the terms of the prophecy to *restore* and *rebuild* Jerusalem and also satisfy the chronology in a simple, direct way without resorting to the mental gymnastics of creating special units such as the "prophetic year" of 360 days each. Of course if a person is free to create his own units, he can make any system of numbers support his position. But God set lights in the heavens (Gen. 1:14) "for signs, and for seasons, and for days, and years." The whole human race, including the Jews, has counted the years by the sun. Although they had a lunar calendar system, yet they intercalated a certain period of time periodically to make their years keep pace with the sun. Hence, we must deal with normal solar years or we do not have years at all.

We must now examine the chronological aspect of the prophecy. We are told that from the decree to restore and build Jerusalem unto the Messiah would be seven weeks and sixty-two weeks. This is sixty-nine weeks, or 483 years. It is a simple matter then to calculate from the first decree of Artaxerxes I (Ezra 7)

$$483 - 457 = 26 \text{ A.D.}$$

as the end of the sixty-nine weeks. If we calculate from his second decree (Neh. 1-2)

$$483 - 446 = 37 \text{ A.D.}$$

we would have to adjust these figures considerably[8] to bring the end of the sixty-ninth week into the lifespan of the Messiah who died 30 A.D. Roger Rusk, a physicist for many years at the University of Tennessee, made computer calculations of the passover dates and has rather settled the date of the death of Christ as Thursday (not "Good Friday"), April 6, 30 A.D.[9]

Now using the normal solar year, and the first decree of Artaxerxes I, the end of the sixty-ninth week brings us up to 26 A.D. What then is the significance of this occasion as it serves to bring us "unto the Messiah the Prince" (Dan. 9:25)? To answer this we must first consider two things. The first is that the "Christian era" (the B.C., A.D. system of reckoning time) was invented by one Dionysius, a monk, who lived about A.D. 496-540. The problem is that he made a mistake in the date of the birth of Christ by approximately four years. Christ was born prior to the death of Herod the Great. Herod died near April 1, 750 A.U.C. (*Anno Urbis Conditae*, from the foundation of the city — of Rome). The Christian era (1 A.D.) was fixed to begin on January 1, 754 A.U.C. Hence Christ was actually born about 4 B.C.

Now Luke tells us (3:22, 23) that when Christ was baptized by John, identified to Israel as Messiah by the voice of God Himself, He was about thirty years old. We therefore calculate:

30 years - 4 B.C. = 26 A.D.

This brings us, at the end of Daniel's sixty-nine weeks, to the shores of Jordan just as Jesus presented Himself as Messiah and began His official Messianic ministry.

Now in the final week of Daniel's prophecy, the Messiah was to confirm the covenant to Israel, which we have

---

[8] Premillennialists make this adjustment by use of the special prophetic year of 360 days. For example: [360 (days in prophetic year)/365 (days in solar year)] x 483 (prophetic years) = 476 solar years. Then 476 - 446 = 30 A.D., which just barely catches the end of Messiah's ministry if at all.

[9] Rusk's findings are detailed in "The Day He Died," *Christianity Today*, XVIII (March 29, 1974), 4-6.

formerly discussed. In the midst of this last, the 70th, week (in A.D. 30), He caused "sacrifice and oblation to cease," and left the temple "desolate." He was "cut off" but rose again and continued to confirm the covenant by His resurrection, by sending the Holy Spirit, and by miraculous works through the church. The last three and a half years from His death would take us to about the time of Stephen's martyrdom and the conversion of Cornelius and the beginning of the ministry of the Gospel to the Gentiles. That is the end of the seventieth week of Daniel. Shortly after that Paul said:

> It was necessary that the word of God should first have been spoken to you [Jews]: but seeing ye put it from you, and judge yourselves unworthy of everlasting life, lo, we turn to the Gentiles (Acts 13:46).

This is a simple and uncomplicated interpretation of Daniel's great prophecy of the Messiah. It satisfies all the terms of the prophecy in a very biblical, natural, and satisfying way. It must be accurate.

An Interpretation of Matthew 19:27, 28 and Luke 22:28, 29

> Then answered Peter and said unto him, Behold, we have forsaken all, and followed thee; what shall we have therefore? And Jesus said unto them, Verily I say unto you, That ye which have followed me, in the regeneration when the Son of man shall sit in the throne of his glory, ye also shall sit upon twelve thrones, judging the twelve tribes of Israel (Matthew 19:27, 28).
>
> Ye are they which have continued with me in my temptations. And I appoint unto you a kingdom, as my Father hath appointed unto me (Luke 22:28, 29).

The reward according to Matthew is twelve thrones and rulership over Israel, and according to Luke it is a kingdom. Doubtless these refer to the same reward.

1. In Matthew the conditional phrase is *the regeneration* and in Luke it is *my temptations.* These phrases seem to be two descriptive aspects of something in which the twelve have followed Christ.

2. If Matthew meant the *new birth*, then the "following" would apply to more than the twelve. If he meant the new heaven and new earth, then it would have no relevancy to Luke's "temptations." If he meant the millennium, he may have reference to the apostles raised in the first resurrection sitting on thrones with Christ in heaven as in Revelation 20:4.

3. Both terms, "my temptation" and "the regeneration," respectively, are compatible with the *suffering* and *resurrection* of Christ — the firstfruits. Likewise then the apostles *suffered* and will be *resurrected* in the "first" resurrection, and sit on thrones with Him (Rev. 20:1f; see the discussion of the "first resurrection," Chapter 2).

4. As to determining the eschatological framework, these passages are neutral. The premillennial view would have the apostles on earth, and the postmillennial view would have them in heaven or possibly in the new heaven and new earth.

5. The most probable meaning is that the twelve would follow Christ both in *suffering* as martyrs ("my temptation") and then in the *first resurrection* ("the regeneration"), and reign with Him from heaven in the millennium. This interpretation accounts for the different emphasis in Luke and Matthew.

An Interpretation of Zechariah 12-14

These three chapters (Zech. 12-14) appear to be a series of random prophecies given without regard to chronology.

12:2-9. This passage sets forth the military struggle of Israel with the nations just prior to the millennium when God is establishing them again for the final time in their homeland. It parallels Ezekiel 39.

12:10-14. This passage describes the conversion of Israel which occurs within or immediately after this struggle and regathering. The words translated "look upon" are elsewhere translated "regard" (Isa. 5:12; Lam. 4:16; Amos 5:22) or "consider" (Psalm 13:3; Isa. 18:4; Lam. 1:11; 2:20; 5:1) and do not necessarily imply, let alone prove, the personal presence of Christ. The Jews at that time will *consider*, turn their attention to, their Messiah; they will *regard* Him as their

Savior and will be saved. The thought of mourning "apart" (12:12-14) implies individual, personal repentance as the essential Scriptural response to the Gospel in salvation. There is no such thing as national conversion except by individuals.

Another proof that Jesus is not physically present when the Jews are converted is the theology of salvation itself. Salvation is through faith not by sight. In contrast with His first advent when there was nothing about the visual appearance of Jesus to distinguish Him from other men, His second advent will be unmistakably, catastrophically, awesomely, visually convincing. When Jesus rends the heavens and descends with a shout, every eye shall *see* Him. This is *sight* not faith.

Premillennialism inherently contains a serious affront to the doctrine of salvation by grace through faith by entertaining a doctrine wherein sinners on earth continue in rebellion and unbelief until forced by the *sight* of Jesus in "power and great glory" to "believe." When they see the sun darkened and the moon not giving light, the stars falling, and they "see the Son of Man coming in the clouds of heaven with power and great glory," then there can be no other response but surrender. In that day they will all say with one accord, "Oh! I see! Now I think I will repent after all." But anyone who understands the biblical doctrine of salvation knows that bowing the knee after Jesus is "revealed from heaven with his mighty angels, in flaming fire taking vengeance on them that know not God" (2 Thess. 1:7, 8) is not saving repentance and faith. Faith is the evidence of things *not* seen, not of things *seen*.

It is elementary truth in Christian doctrine that when Jesus comes, the day of salvation is over (see Matt. 24:51; 25:12, 30, 41; 2 Thess. 1:7-10; 2:11, 12). If it were possible to be saved by sight, hell would be totally empty.

13:1f. This chapter abruptly reverses chronology from the yet future conversion of the Jews to prophecies of the first advent of Christ. This passage shows the wounding of Christ (13:6, 7) as if He were a false prophet in the house of those who should be His friends. The occasion is the crucifixion of Christ (cf. Matt. 26:31; Mark 14:27). Then it looks forward a few years (13:8, 9) to the final dispersion of Israel, after the death of Christ; then on to their subsequent regathering and conversion. For commentary on the "third part," see Ezekiel 5:11, 12.

14.1f. As we look at this chapter, I want to acknowledge that if the premillennial view was not so thoroughly irreconcilable with the rest of the Scriptures, this one chapter would at least be reasonably compatible if premillennialism could be otherwise established. This chapter, along with the sequential order of Revelation 19 and 20 (which we will discuss later), are the only relevant passages in Scripture that are reasonably compatible with the premillennial view. But, even so, it cannot be said that either of these passages *teach* premillennialism.

God, for His own purpose, has established the sequence of material in this chapter. And until we see that purpose, the sequence complicates the interpretation no matter what your view of eschatology. As we look at this chapter, at first glance it is a little puzzling as to why the Lord put it in this order. But as we begin to examine the content, the purpose becomes clear. Let us see if we can discover God's message in this passage.

Verses 1-7 unmistakably discuss the phenomenon of the "day of the Lord." As we have already seen from our former Cluster Study on the "day of the Lord" (review p. 25), this phrase denotes an on-going concept, or phenomenon of God's major judgmental intervention events in the history and future of the world. The smaller local or even global judgment events, sometimes called the day of the Lord, are all prototypes and warnings of the final "great and notable" day. This phenomenon has had periods of manifestation in the past and continues to develop in the future toward that ultimate and final expression of judgment in the "*great and notable* day of the Lord" (Acts 2:20; see 2 Pet. 3:10).

What we have in Zechariah 14 is the generalized expression of God's intervention in retributive judgment and of blessings as a phenomenon rather than language confined to any specific event. The reason the chapter has what appear to be abrupt changes in subject matter — from judgment (vs. 1-7), to blessing (vs. 8-11), back to judgment (vs. 12-15), and again to blessing (16-21) — is because the Lord's purpose here is to reveal concepts and phenomena — not specific events.

The vehicle for such phenomenal revelation is what we can call Telescopic Prophetic Vision, and that is what we have in Zechariah 14 which explains the rather mixed order and generalized language of the chapter.

Let's look more closely, then, at the Lord's use of Telescopic Prophetic Vision to see how it works. A rather simple example of it is found in Ezekiel 28:12-19. The Lord takes up a lamentation on the king of Tyre, but the language telescopes out to a greater evil and a greater judgment than the king of Tyre. The language can only be fully true of Satan himself. This concept may be illustrated by the following diagram:

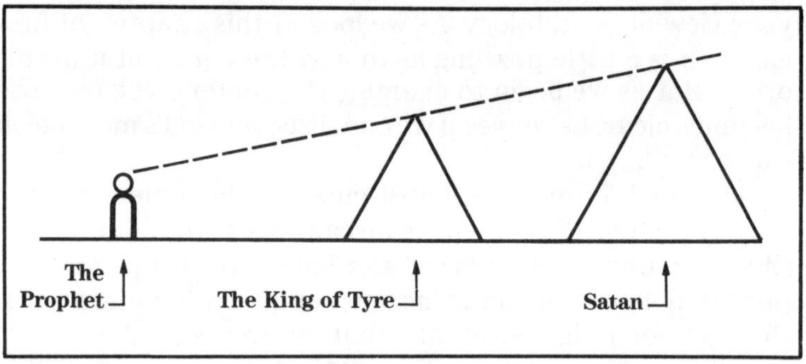

The prophetic field of vision contains two objects of similar characteristics. As the prophet describes what he sees, the king of Tyre in the foreground blends in with the more distant background and is identical in essence to the larger image of Satan himself in the background. This is a simple example of Telescopic Prophetic Vision.

Another example is in Isaiah 65:17-25. Blended in this view are two times of great blessing, a lesser and a greater. The lesser is the millennium, a powerful, long, but temporary revival on this earth (cf. Rev. 20:1-9). The greater is the new heaven and new earth when all things are restored to their pristine purity and the curse of sin and death is eternally lifted (cf. Rev. 21:4; 22:3).

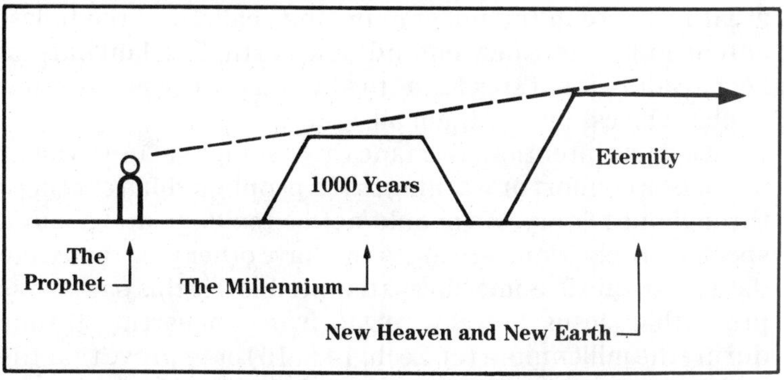

Again the prophet sees the greater object in the background and the lesser but similar object in the foreground and the passage discusses features of both.

Zechariah 14 is a more complex example of Telescopic Prophetic Vision because it carries two themes. The first theme is the concept of the "day of the Lord" and the second concept is of millennial and/or eternal blessing. These could be illustrated as follows:

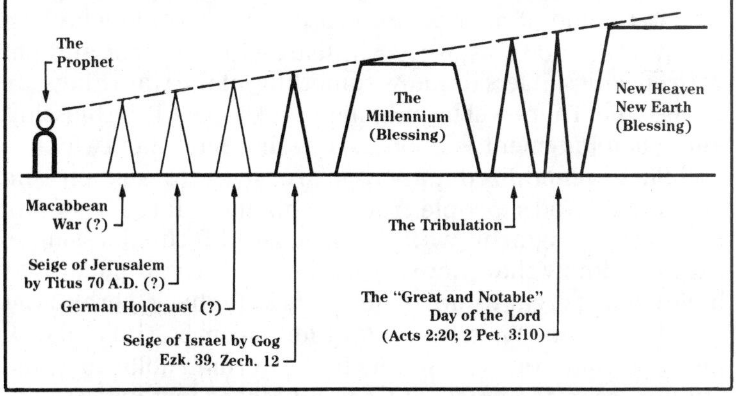

The first theme of judgment may relate to any of a number of events while probably looking more particularly to the "*great and notable* day of the Lord," the final event. The second theme is that of the blessing of the Lord as realized in great measure in the millennium and realized to the fullest extent in the new heaven and new earth. The language of Zechariah 14 is not specific as to any of these occasions, but it depicts the essence of them all.

God has intentionally made this passage vague so that it might be a comfort or warning to His people at different times throughout history. We should not be too dogmatic about a specific proposition here unless we have other more concrete data to sustain it. Some have attempted to use this passage as proof that Jesus literally reigns from an earthly throne during the millennium (cf. Zech. 14:9, 16) or to prove that the millennial worship will be a restoration of the Old Testament economy including animal sacrifice (cf. v. 21). But neither of these are sustained when this passage is interpreted in the light of the rest of the Scripture instead of vice versa.

The Lord will indeed be "king over all the earth," but He is that even now. "The Lord hath prepared his throne in the heavens; and his kingdom ruleth over all" (Psalm 103:19). The Lord can and does rule over the earth without being located on the earth (cf. 1 Sam. 12:12). However the consciousness of His Kingship will be enhanced during the millennium because of the obedience of His subjects.

The value of such a prophecy to the people who first received it, and to us, is that it deals with essences and not with specifics. It lets us know something of the way things are going to be. There will be judgment and there will be blessing; and when judgment is upon us, blessing is not far away.

Such generalized passages are given to sustain and encourage God's people, those who have faced times of retributive judgment, with the promise of future blessing so they may know that there is yet a future. This prophecy may have been of great value to the saints as far back, perhaps, as the Maccabean revolt, the siege of Jerusalem by Titus, 70 A.D., perhaps even to some believers in the German holocaust, and still future in the battle of Gog and Magog just prior to the millennium, and finally in the great tribulation and the approach of the "*great and notable* day of the Lord."

Now to examine the text a little closer, probably factors pertaining to the siege of Israel prior to the millennium are in view, and almost certainly factors pertaining to the final battle of Armageddon are in view (vs. 2, 3); this probably parallels Revelation 16:14, 16; 20:7-9. Then the second advent of Christ is partially described (vs. 4, 5) and parallels the catastrophic events connected with it in the New Testament (Matt. 24:29f; Rev. 6:12f). As the stars converge on earth (vs. 6, 7) from every direction, there will be a period of time just before the end, when the eerie blue-shifted light from the converging stars will give light all around the earth at once. See footnote number 4, Chapter 2.

14:8-11. At this point the prophecy again abruptly changes to the theme of blessing. The passage probably refers to millennial times. These verses may also refer to the character of the new heaven and new earth, in somewhat symbolic language.

14:12-15. At this point the chronology and subject matter reverses again and we see again certain features of the day of the Lord. It sounds very much like the effects of a "fervent" heat wave (see 2 Pet. 3) preceding a nuclear holocaust from the falling stars. If that is not the message, then it could refer to the battles just before the millennium (Ezk. 39; Zech. 12) where very likely atomic weapons would be involved.

14:16-21. Then once again the prophet returns to a discussion of millennial conditions through the end of the chapter. This prophecy is randomly organized to convey essences, for God's own good reasons, but this abrupt chronology change is not unusual in prophetic writings. Rarely or never does a lengthy organized, chronological treatise appear. We must obtain the total picture "here a little and there a little" (Isa. 28:13).

A Brief Interpretation of Revelation

7

There was once a man whom, they say, had taught the entire book of Revelation one thousand times, and he got it wrong every time. This is an example of an extreme case of tunnel vision. I had read the book of Revelation numerous times as a premillennialist trying to feel comfortable with a serial interpretation of the material from chapter four to chapter twenty. I accepted the theory that it was describing the events of the tribulation, all of which were yet future. There were, I thought, seven serial seals, then seven serial trumpets, and then seven serial vials — one after the other — and the last thing before the millennium was chapter nineteen when Christ would come on a white horse. But every time I read these chapters, I came repeatedly to a finale — to an end of things — long before I reached chapter nineteen, and it gave me an uneasy feeling.

First, I found the end in chapter six (vs. 12-17), and I had to rationalize. Then another end appeared in chapter eleven (vs. 15-18), again in chapter fourteen (vs. 14-18), and in chapter sixteen (vs. 15-21), and chapter nineteen (vs. 11-21), and finally in chapter twenty (vs. 7-10), and I had to rationalize each time. Now this troubled me. How could this age have so many ends? How could there be any final events before chapter nineteen? But the only way to avoid acknowledging these passages as describing the events of the end time — the destruction of the world, the second coming of Christ, the judgment, etc., was to "spiritualize" them like Dr. Ironside. He saw Revelation 6:12-17 as political and social turmoil — not actual stars falling or every island and mountain being removed or the heavens departing (see Chapter 2).

But that did not satisfy. I reasoned that if I already had my mind made up about the material from chapter four through nineteen — that these chapters set forth the tribulation events in serial form — then why bother with the words? No need to read words and sentences unless they themselves were to form and shape my thinking. And if I was unwilling to let my mind be changed by the words, what good was it to go through the book a thousand times?

I decided upon a daring course of action. I decided to go through the book of Revelation and let each section or coherent prophetic unit give forth its individual message. Then I would see if the individual messages formed a larger picture, were serial or parallel and repetitive, or were complementary one to another or to other passages of Scripture.

When I had finished, I did see a larger picture. Many passages were repetitive and therefore reinforced one another. Many were complementary and each expanded the picture of the other, adding clarity and completeness. And above all they each confirmed the other passages of Scripture that speak directly to prophetic issues throughout the Bible.

Now I want to go through the book of Revelation and write a brief synopsis of what I will call prophetic units (which do not necessarily correspond with chapters). Then I will show how the prophetic units form a coherent picture of prophecy complementary to the more rigorous prophetic passages of Scripture already discussed.

Unit 1 (1:1-20)

The first coherent unit is essentially coincident with

chapter 1. As would be expected, this unit is primarily introductory material, and contains information essential to any proper understanding of the visions and prophecies to follow:

1. We learn from this passage that Christ is the Revelator — that He sent an angel and signified the things to be revealed to John (1:1). The revelation was "signified" primarily by visions: "What thou *seest*, write in a book . . . " (1:11). This is an important interpretive principle which I will discuss more fully later.

2. In this passage also we learn that the book is addressed to the churches (1:4, 11; 22:16), not to Israel. It is a message to the churches that contains information vital to the churches about events relating to the churches; the book opens and closes with this thought (1:4, 11-13, 20; 2:1-3:22; 22:16). The message broadly is to prepare the churches for the trying times to come, to enlighten them concerning events to come starting from the time of John, to assure them of victory as the overruling and conquering power of Christ at the right hand of God is exercised on their behalf (compare Eph. 1:19-23; 3:10, 11, 20, 21).

3. This passage tells us the general nature of the contents of the book: " . . . things which must shortly come to pass . . . " (1:1). But the book is not limited to events future from the time of John but contains also information about things "which are" or were contemporary with John: "Write the things which thou hast seen, and the things which are, and the things which shall be hereafter" (1:19). Also in chapter four we are told that John would be shown "things which must be hereafter" (4:1), and again in chapter twenty-two we are reminded that these prophecies were to show "the things which must shortly be done" (22:6).

The events future from John's day, particularly those events which will transpire during the career of the churches and affect their success, are primarily in view here. However, we must not make the mistake of interpreting this generalization about the events of Revelation as if it were an iron-clad rule which would exclude another understanding of some of the passages of the book. For example, if we take that approach we could not handle the obvious reference to the birth of Christ (12:5) since it was already past when the revelation was given.

Furthermore, the events of history repeat themselves, in kind, in future events. Hence, most of the providential events of prophecy are, in essence, one with the events of the past. They differ mainly in time, location, and perhaps degree of intensity, but not really in kind. Therefore, we should not lock ourselves out from the valuable insights of past historical events, from the foundation of the world, as we interpret the events of Revelation.

Someone has said, "The past is the key to the future," and the understanding of Revelation will depend in some measure on understanding the past. This principle is inherent in the statement of Jesus, "As it was in the days of Noe, so shall it be . . . " (Luke 17:26). "As it was . . . so shall it be." This is a statement true of all things where the same characters are creating the events. The interaction of mankind, Satan, and God, none of whom change fundamentally, will cause history to repeat itself. The only change will be a change in degree or intensity — not in kind.

Not only should we, therefore, understand the outline of past history, but also of past prophecy, i.e., prophecy of the past that has found fulfillment. Then as the prophecies of Revelation emerge, though given generally to the churches to enlighten them of things to come starting from the days of John, the nature of these future events may be better understood by extrapolating backwards in some instances. For example, to understand the nature of the "beast" (chapters 13 and 17) clearly depends upon this backward extrapolation to the worldwide historical empires (see Dan. 2, 7, 8). This method gives the church living in the final days a clear picture of the nature of the phenomena by which it is confronted.

Some have so doggedly insisted on the interpretation of every line of Revelation as an event peculiar to the future that they lose the grandeur of the panorama of God's providential works as His eternal purpose sweeps from ancient history to the distant future with unbroken continuity.

Unit 2 (2:1-3:22)

This next unit in Revelation includes chapters two and three and is comprised of specific messages to the seven churches of Asia to whom the whole book is addressed (1:11). These messages treat specific problems within each church, whereas the remainder of the book treats the broader issues that are relevant to all churches alike (22:6, 16).

The number seven in Scripture is used quite consistently to depict completeness or totality and should be so understood here. Hence the seven churches of Asia are representative of all churches everywhere in all time. There is no sound reason to make these to represent seven progressive historical periods of the church age. All attempts to do this are transparently artificial. There are churches having these kinds of problems in every generation. There are always churches moving toward apostasy; there are always churches standing true and always will be until Jesus comes.

These two chapters reveal, as B. H. Carroll has discussed in his interpretation of Revelation, the human and earthly agents involved in the eternal purpose of God; but weak as they are, Christ walks among His churches (1:13) guiding, strengthening, encouraging, rebuking. The picture looks like this:

Church	**Commendation**	**Rebuke**
Ephesus	Yes	Yes
Smyrna	Yes	No
Pergamos	Yes	Yes
Thyatira	Yes	Yes
Sardis	No	Yes
Philadelphia	Yes	No
Laodicea	No	Yes

Two of the seven churches are almost apostate; they receive no commendation. Three of the seven are both commended and rebuked. Two of the seven are wholly pleasing to the Lord and receive no rebuke. Every church should take hope because of the standing of Smyrna and Philadelphia. *It is possible to please the Lord.*

I cannot accept the carnal notion that a church because it has imperfect people in it must inevitably become a "cess pool." A perfect church is a church which points lost sinners to Christ through the Gospel, baptizes them, then begins to teach them and nurture them with all their imperfections until they grow more and more toward the fullness of the stature of Christ (Eph. 4:11-16). The individual members will sin, but a church may act scripturally as an institution toward those who sin within it. If it thus fulfills the purpose for which Christ ordained it, might it not be called perfect? We should take hope and not let down the standards. It is possible for a church to please Christ and need no rebuke, and that is an encouraging thought.

Now this unit gives us a picture of the human and earthly side of God's purpose. True, it is not all it should be. But with the aid of the divine and heavenly side of the picture which begins in chapter four, there will be success. As we shall see, God will execute His providential and redemptive purposes until the victory is won for Himself and for His people.

Unit 3 (4:1-5:14)

With chapter four we are to be initiated into the unseen realities of the divine side of the picture. The churches, God's human and earthly agencies, though weak and discouraging, are nevertheless God's chosen vessels to be the custodians of the Kingdom of God on earth (Matt. 16:19; 18:18). But the heavenly, the divine side is glorious, powerful, and altogether encouraging. Through His power the weak not only can stand but can be victorious.

First, John sees a throne of deity (4:2, 3). About the throne are twenty-four elders (4:4) representative of the earthly agencies of God's house:[1] twelve for the tribes of

---

[1] For an examination of the nature of God's "House" on earth — the earthly representation of His name — see: William C. Hawkins and Willard

Israel, and twelve for the apostles. There is powerful activity from the throne: "lightnings and thunderings and voices" (notice this recurring phrase as we go through the book). Seven lamps, representing the universal, omnipotent and omnipresent Spirit of God (seven spirits), burn before the throne and extend into all the world executing the providential purpose of God everywhere (4:5; 5:6; compare Ezk. 1:12, 20, 21). There are four living creatures, mighty spirit beings, who are constantly attendant unto the One upon the throne (4:6-11; compare Ezk. 1:5-28).

This is the scene in heaven — a glorious scene — in contrast to the scene on earth. Powerful and mighty works are to be exercised in pursuit of God's purposes and in behalf of His weaker earthly vessels.

Now John's vision focuses more closely on the throne (5:1). There is a scroll with seven seals, and a Lamb in the midst of the throne (5:6) who will open the scroll (5:7). The elders and living creatures exult with a new song:

> Worthy art thou to take the book, and to open the seals thereof: for thou wast slain, and didst purchase unto God with thy blood men of every tribe, and tongue, and people, and nation, and madest them to be unto our God a kingdom and priests; and they reign upon the earth (5:9, 10 ASV).

The angelic hosts join in (5:11) and exalt the name of the Lamb for what He is about to do (5:12, 13) — open the book of God's redemptive purpose. The heavenly setting of chapters four and five introduce us to what we might call in today's terms the "combat information center" or "command headquarters" where the battle strategy against the powers and principalities is being formulated. Powerful angelic agencies are dispatched in support of the earthly forces, the churches, whose prayers rise up before the throne (Rev. 5:8; 8:4; compare Acts 12:5-17; Eph. 1:21, 22; 6:10-20; Phil. 4:19; Col. 4:12, etc.). All these heavenly and earthly agencies are orchestrated according to the great redemptive purpose of God written from the foundation of the world in the book to

---

A. Ramsey, *The House of God* (Simpsonville, South Carolina, Hallmark Baptist Church, 1980).

be opened by the Lion of the tribe of Judah, the son of David, even the Lamb in the midst of the throne.

Now this heavenly scene did not originate the instant John was called up to heaven (4:1). Although the book of Revelation is oriented toward revealing things that will relate to the future plight of the church and the course of God's providential works in her behalf from the time of John, yet that same kind of work has been going on in behalf of God's earthly agencies since the foundation of the world. The same "command headquarters" has operated from ancient times and will continue until the consummation (see 1 Kings 22:19-34; 2 Kings 6:14-17; Isa. 10:5-16; Dan. 10:10-21; Psalms 45:3-6; 68:29-35; 89:18-29; 110:1-7). These are but a few examples of the power of God working His redemptive purpose through His providential works on earth. And now in the next prophetic unit of Revelation, Christ is about to open the seven-sealed book and show us the complete providential picture (all seven seals) as He executes His redemptive purpose through the Gospel by means of His churches (Eph. 1:19-23; 3:10, 11).

Unit 4 (6:1-17; 8:1)

Now as we enter into the interpretation of this passage, we must rely heavily upon the deductive method of interpretation. The failure to make primary use of the deductive method in this passage would reduce any person's interpretation to a series of arbitrary speculations about the meaning of symbolic language. The failure to bring the broad background of truth from the rest of Scripture to apply to the unique language of Revelation leaves us open to the imaginative theories of sensationalists with no bench mark to judge the soundness of their speculations. Therefore, we must look at the broader purpose of God as directly taught in the plain-language passages of Scripture and let these clear purposes set the boundaries for our interpretations. Nothing in Revelation can be out of character with the God of Genesis, Psalms, Matthew, or Romans.

We have already seen what wide emphasis the New

Testament Scriptures put upon the passage from Psalms: "Sit thou at my right hand, until I make thine enemies thy footstool . . . " (110:1). We have seen this emphasis to highlight the program and purpose of God from the time of the ascension of Christ until He comes again at the destruction of the earth. It has been rigorously established from Scripture (see above, pp. 32 - 40) that Christ's current program is to reign at the right hand of God while He continuously makes His enemies His footstool:

> But this man, after he had offered one sacrifice for sins for ever, sat down on the right hand of God; *From henceforth expecting till his enemies be made his footstool* (Heb. 10:12, 13).

That is His program from the ascension to the second coming which covers the period of time from John's receiving the Revelation until the Great White Throne Judgment (Rev. 20). Therefore when the voice told John "I will shew thee things which must be hereafter" (Rev. 4:1), the "hereafter" has to be the time from near the beginning of His Session (Acts 2:32-35) until the time when death itself, His "last enemy," is fully conquered (1 Cor. 15:25, 26). The last enemy is fully conquered only when this present universe has "passed away" at His coming, and a new heaven and new earth is created. Therefore the interpretation of the events of Revelation *must* be made in the light of all the purposes of God during the Session of Christ. Revelation, therefore, describes, in general, *the events that were and are to transpire as Jesus executes His providential purposes and wins His victories from the right hand of God:*

> The Lord said unto my Lord, Sit thou at my right hand, until I make thine enemies thy footstool. The Lord shall send the rod of thy strength out of Zion: rule thou in the midst of thine enemies . . . . The Lord at thy right hand shall strike through kings in the day of his wrath. He shall judge among the heathen, he shall fill the places with the dead bodies; he shall wound the heads over many countries. He shall drink of the brook in the way: therefore shall he lift up the head (Psalm 110:1, 2, 5-7).

He executes His rulership from the heavens:

> The Lord hath prepared his throne in the heavens; and his kingdom ruleth over all (Psalm 103:19).

He rules in behalf of His earthly agency, the church, as He executes His purpose to conquer His enemies either by salvation or by judgment:

> . . . when he raised him from the dead, and set him at his own right hand in the heavenly places, Far above all principality, and power, and might, and dominion, and every name that is named, not only in this world, but also in that which is to come: And hath put all things under his feet, and gave him to be the head over all things *to the church*, which is his body, the fulness of him that filleth all in all (Eph. 1:20-23).

And it is His "eternal purpose" to bring His manifold wisdom (the Gospel of Grace) before the powers and principalities by the means of the church:

> To the intent that now unto the principalities and powers in heavenly places might be known by the church the manifold wisdom of God, According to the eternal purpose which he purposed in Christ Jesus our Lord" (Eph. 3:10, 11).

Now the period of time in which all these things are to be accomplished, in the greatest measure, is that period of time covered by the prophecies and visions of Revelation from the time of John's visions (Rev. 1:1) until the general judgment (Rev. 20:11); including the victorious work of the church during the millennium and the short reign of terror of the "man of sin" during the tribulation.

We may teach through the book of Revelation a thousand times, but we will get it wrong every time unless we interpret it in the light of the program outlined above executed from God's right hand. This program is outlined in Peter's sermon (Acts 2) wherein he teaches that the course of this age is bracketed by Pentecost and the "great and notable day of the Lord" (Acts 2:16-20). This program is what the book of Revelation is all about. Furthermore it is this program, with its broader implications of God's providential purposes which He began in the past and continues from the time John received the Revelation, that comprises the seven-sealed scroll which only Christ can open.

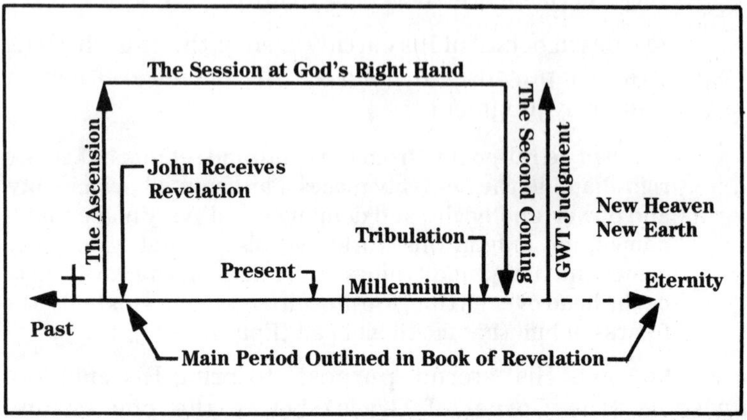

Our interpretation must be guided by and in harmony with these plain-language teachings of Scripture; otherwise it will be sheer speculation. Now with this plan as a guide, we are prepared to look at this book as Christ opens its seals and lays the contents bare for all to see:

The Vision. "And I saw . . . ." (6:1): This phrase is the primary key to the beginning of the prophetic units in Revelation. The information is imparted in visions, hence John generally begins these units with "I saw."

The First Seal (6:1, 2). One of the four "beasts" or living creatures (cf. 4:6-8; Ezk. 1:5-25; 10:9-22) shows John a horseman seated upon a white horse.[2] This rider has a weapon and a crown. He goes forth "conquering, and to conquer;" his purpose is to conquer, and he does conquer. He is victorious. A study of the symbology of the white horse in other passages and his conquering rider must represent the

---

[2] For a study of the symbology of the colored and white horses see: Zech. 1:8-11; 6:1-8; Rev. 19:11, 14. The study of these passages makes it clear that these horses represent providential agencies at God's disposal, whether good or bad, by which He executes His sovereign will in pursuit of His conquering purpose.

pure and righteous agencies of God's purpose (Zech. 1:8; 6:3; Rev. 19:14) of which the chief and royal agent is Christ Himself (Rev. 19:11). Hence Christ sets out to make His enemies His footstool, to conquer them, and He does conquer them both in time, providentially and redemptively, and at His coming, judgmentally and eternally (Rev. 19:11f). That is a reasonable interpretation of the first seal and is compatible with the broad purpose of Christ, reasoning deductively, and is compatible with the victorious white horse symbology, reasoning inductively.

There is a theory among premillennialists that this white horse represents antichrist! This theory is compatible with nothing in Scripture; it is sheer speculation.

The Second Seal (6:3, 4). The second living creature calls to John. It is significant that each of the four living creatures is, as it were, "in charge" of his own peculiar aspect of these providential horsemen and their works. This second living creature shows John a red horse, the color of blood. This horse represents evil agencies which instigate wars which are and have always been used of God in His providential purposes[3] (consider Psalm 76:10).

The Third Seal (6:5, 6). The third living creature showed John a black horse and the phenomena associated with this horse speaks of poverty, famine, and scarcity. By far the majority of the peoples of the world has languished in poverty wherever the pall of sin has blanketed any people. Yet in all these things God causes the wrath of men to praise Him, and all things are working together, ultimately, for good to those who love the Lord and are called in accordance with His purpose (Rom. 8:28). In all these things He is working toward victory. Though God has no pleasure in human suffering, yet the fruits of sin are turned by God into victory for the righteous and His righteous purpose (e.g., see 1 Kings

---

[3] To see examples of how this works out in real life, study 1 Kings 22:1-37; Isa. 10:5-16. Consider then, in the same light, the fall of Babylon, the Medes and Persians, Greece, Rome, the Crusades, Napoleon, the Third Reich, etc.

17; consider the poverty of Africa and India in the latter half of the 20th century).

The Fourth Seal (6:7, 8). The last living creature shows John a pale horse. The name of the rider was death, and Hades followed him. The description is of violent forms of death — not of good men dying in a ripe old age in the bosom of loved ones. A fourth part of the earth is affected. We should not think of any of these as events peculiar to some special time. Probably on an average twenty-five percent of all the people of the earth have died a violent or unnatural death. It would not be accurate to think of this as a momentary event in time when one person out of four suddenly was killed. That would not be one-fourth of the "earth" since people are continually being born year after year.

All these four seals represent long-range operations of God's providence in pursuit of His goal to put all enemies under His feet while gaining souls through the Gospel. Christ is head over all these things in behalf of the work of His church (Eph. 1:20-23).

The Fifth Seal (6:9-11). Here is highlighted an aspect of the battle for righteousness that is almost forgotten in Western Christendom — the Christian martyr. The earthly agents who are co-laborers with God in this battle for truth, have seen millions of casualties since our Lord went to the cross before us. Not only were there martyrs in the early centuries under pagan Rome, but hundreds of thousands have died in the Dark Ages at the instigation of the Catholic Church. The noblest and most biblical Christians — the covenant people of God, the true churches of Jesus Christ called heretics by most Catholic and Protestant historians — were peculiarly the objects of persecution from the fourth century through the eighteenth century. In the ninth century the Paulician churches suffered death by the thousands for their faith. Gibbon writes:

> . . . the prize [for persecution] must doubtless be adjudged to the sanguinary devotion of Theodora, who restored the images to the Oriental [Catholic] church. Her inquisitors explored the cities and mountains of the lesser Asia, and the

> flatterers of the empress have affirmed that, in a short reign, one hundred thousand Paulicians were extirpated by the sword, the gibbet, or the flames.[4]

The churches that retained the New Testament principles, after the apostasy of the Roman Catholic Church, were scattered throughout Europe and have been variously identified as Waldenses, Vaudois, Paulicians, Albigenses, etc. From 1180-1200 in the provinces of the Albigois it is estimated that 200,000 Albigenses were put to death.[5] The best estimates of the number of martyrs of these Christians from the fourth through sixteenth centuries approach fifty million.

These then, with all the martyrs from "righteous Abel to Zacharias the son of Barachias" (Matt. 23:35), are the souls under the altar (6:9-11). These, God's choicest servants, are to be joined by others before they are finally and completely avenged by the Lord's return.

I find no identity with the interpretation that limits these martyrs to those only who were martyred during the tribulation; not only is it arbitrary, but it implies that God does not take special account of all those in every age who have paid with their blood. God is telling us that in the great battle against the powers and principalities there are casualties, but the victory is certain. And there will be more casualties yet. The unscriptural theory of a pretribulation rapture will leave the people of God ill-prepared to stand in the days of persecution which may occur again both prior to and after the millennium.

The Sixth Seal (6:12-17). Now we have clearly a climax of the seven-sealed book. This passage has been previously discussed at some length in Chapter 2. I have recognized the

---

[4] Edward Gibbon, *The Decline and Fall of the Roman Empire*, The Great Books, Vol. XLI (Chicago: Encyclopaedia Britannica, Inc., 1952), p. 331.

[5] W. R. Downing, *The New Testament Church* (Sunnyvale, Ca.: Lakewood Baptist Church, 1982), p. 217. For an excellent summary of the doctrines, migrations, and sufferings of these biblical Christians (still called heretics by Catholic, Protestant and interdenominational Christians today), see pp. 192-234 of Downing's book.

symbolic nature of the horsemen of the first four seals. But I have interpreted the events themselves as literal in kind. The fifth seal also is literal since martyrdom is literal. The sixth seal is certainly literal. This passage is unquestionably a parallel passage to Matthew 24:29f, and that whole section in Matthew is direct, plain-language, prophetic narration by Jesus Himself. I therefore am compelled to interpret Revelation 6:12-17 in the same way. Both passages are undoubtedly discussing the same occasion.

The book of redemption, written by the Trinity in the counsels of eternity opened and prosecuted by Jesus Christ, is near completion with His second coming. At this point the work of providence through the various agencies, pictured under the symbology of the horsemen, is brought to completion as the last of the enemies of Christ are put under His feet when the stars fall, the saints are rescued and the earth is destroyed (Rev. 6:13).

The Seventh Seal (8:1). We are not told specifically what the event under the seventh seal is. However, it should not be impossible to discover the meaning. There is a short but profound silence in heaven. Ordinarily around the throne of God there is a resounding jubilation (see Rev. 5:9-14). When a sinner is converted there is rejoicing in heaven (Luke 15:7, 10). Such a silence therefore would suggest an opposite emotion. What then happens, reasoning deductively, as a finale to the purpose of God which might cause such a reaction? The finale of God's book of redemptive purpose, symbolized by the seventh seal, is closed by the most solemn assembly ever to be gathered in the annals of eternity — the judgment before the Great White Throne. There the wicked will be separated forever and cast into the lake of fire (see Rev. 20:11f; Matt. 25:31-46).

God has no pleasure in the death of the wicked (Ezk. 33:11), and neither will His saints or the righteous angels. The voices of praise will be silenced in a temporary expression of awesome sorrow at the pronouncement of the immutable sentence. For the very first time the actual realization of God's awful holiness will dawn on every spirit. Every voice will be muted in a profound sense of awe at the execution of ultimate justice. God will say " . . . depart from me ye cursed . . . ," and the book of the redemptive purpose of God will slam shut, never to open again.

"But the Lord of hosts shall be exalted in judgment, and God that is holy shall be sanctified in righteousness" (Isa. 5:16). So the paean of praise will spontaneously rise again to be silent no more.

This seven-sealed book is the most comprehensive of the visions John received. It begins with the purpose of God to conquer sin from eternity past. It outlines His use of all agencies, good and evil, to purge the universe of sin and to put the whole possibility of sin to rest. Peace will reign when God reconciles the elect and commits the rebellious to the prison-house of the universe:

> And, having made peace through the blood of his cross, by him to reconcile all things unto himself; by him, I say, whether they be things in earth, or things in heaven (Col. 1:20).

Now God's activities in time have been to this end. His activities are both through righteous agents, conquering through the Gospel message, and through all other agencies — men, angels, devils, nature — in His providential works causing the wrath of both men and angels to praise Him. Finally He will come again, judge the world, and the book will be closed. That is the all-comprehensive significance of the seven-sealed book.

To better envision the time relationship of the seals, see the illustration on page 191.

Unit 5 (7:1-17)

This prophetic unit also starts with the familiar "I saw." That phrase sets the vision apart from the first six seals with the explanation: "and after these things I saw . . . ." We must be careful not to make the serious mistake of taking this sequential suggestion of "after these things" as meaning that the events depicted in the vision occurred sequentially after the events depicted by the first six seals, but this means only that John *saw* the vision of chapter seven *after* he saw the vision of the first six seals.

John is merely a recorder of visions (1:11), not an interpreter. If we make the substance of the vision to be John's *meaning* of "after these things," he then becomes an interpreter of the meaning of the visions, but worse than that the Word of God is made to be a self-contradiction. God has left the interpretation to those who read the book.

It is quite evident from the standing of chapter seven between the sixth and seventh seal, that this passage is parenthetical. That is, there is a pause, for God's own reasons, to explain some important facts before proceeding to the seventh seal.

Now these facts are, as before, set forth in somewhat symbolic language. A vision of four angels, on the four "corners" of earth holding four winds, is symbolic; hence it is our task as interpreters to determine what this means.

The number four is significant here. It corresponds to the four living creatures which are so integrally connected with the execution of God's providence on earth (Ezk. 1; 10; Rev. 4; 6). The four living creatures cover the four points of the compass. They move everywhere like lightning without turning around (study carefully Ezk. 1 and 10), because one is always facing forward. Here, then, we reason that the four winds and the four angels depict the universal coverage and control of the affairs of God's providential acts to the four points of the globe.

The vision is to show us that the "winds" (doubtless representing spirit forces) are held, or delayed, from the execution of their roles until some important work is finished. The work is to seal the "servants of God," and after this is done the implication is that the winds will be allowed to blow and produce a harmful effect on the earth, sea, and trees (7:1-3).

Now we must consider what this harmful effect might be. We reason thus: If we are correct in the interpretation of the first four seals as representing the whole providential purpose of God acting in the earth, then the effects of these four winds must be related to this same phenomenon. There is therefore a special seal applied to these special servants of God in view of the coming events.

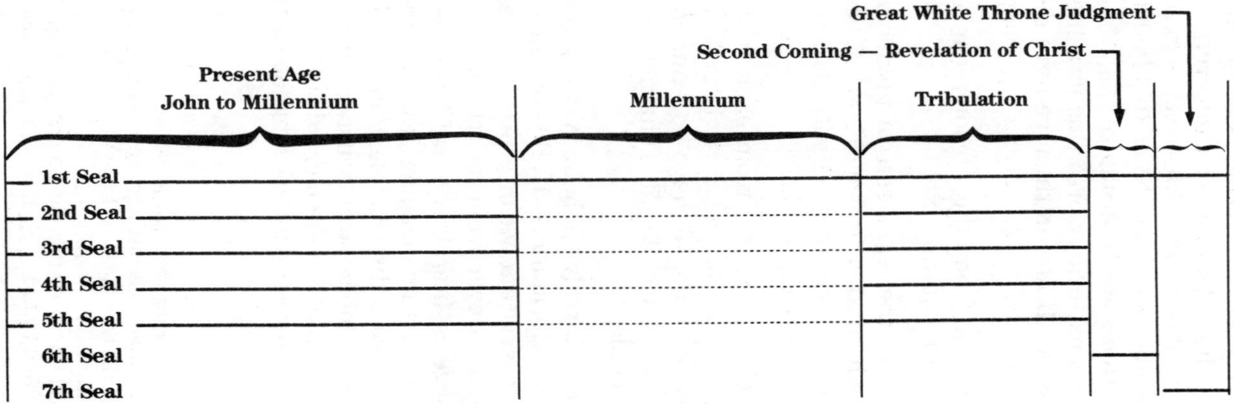

1. This chart depicts the duration and chronological order of the seven seals, representing the conquering and redemptive purpose of Christ at the right hand of God "expecting till his enemies be made his footstool" (Heb. 10:12, 13).
2. The first four seals (Rev. 6:1-8) represent the long-range, providential phenomena used of God to achieve his conquering purpose by means of both good and evil agencies (compare Zech. 1:7-11; 6:1-8). These four as well as the fifth seal are continuous, on-going phenomena that have continued in kind from near the foundation of the world, although John's vision anticipated future events.
3. The sixth and seventh seals, the second coming of Christ and the judgment respectively, are unique, singular events finalizing God's conquering and redemptive purpose.

The Seven Seals

Who then are these servants? They are called the "children of Israel" (7:4). They are said to be from every tribe of Israel and an equal number from each tribe — exactly 12,000 (7:4-8). The total number then comes to 144,000, a perfect square of twelve times one thousand.

Now does God expect us to interpret this in a literal sense or in a symbolic sense? If literal, then we have these problems:

1. We must suddenly switch from the obvious symbolic context of the four winds[6] to a literal text.

2. A literal interpretation of the equal sets of numbers of favored people from each of the twelve tribes of Israel forming a perfect square number conflicts with all known statistical phenomena.

3. The literal sealing of exactly 12,000 from each tribe of Israel with a literal mark in the forehead trivializes God's dealing with His choicest servants. We have no example of such a thing in the past, and it is wholly out of character with God to visibly mark His people.

4. This action is set in a book largely symbolic in character in which God is conveying information. If His message is contained in a symbolic passage and we interpret it literally, we will shut ourselves out forever from its true meaning. Conversely, if His message is literal and we interpret it symbolically, again we have lost its meaning. It is extremely important, that the difference is discernable. Hence, in this instance, God has made the numbers so obviously contrary to literal statistical experience that we are alerted sufficiently to His intended purpose that here is symbolic language with a special meaning.

---

[6] There are those who might literalize the four angels actually holding on to the north wind, the south wind, the east and west winds, but God knows that a sincere seeker for His true meaning knows better than that. Whenever all factors call for a literal interpretation, it should always be the first consideration, and a literal interpretation should always be applied except when it would trivialize God's Word or conflict with known reality.

Therefore I conclude that this is a revelation of truth in symbolic language. What that truth is can be better understood when we come to chapter fourteen. God leaves us here without an explanation until then. It serves at this point to show that God singles out special servants for special consideration in view of the providential "winds" about to blow. I leave the matter here, and will return to it later when more data are before us.

Now to consider the second half of this unit (7:9-17), the main elements of the passage are these:

1. A vast multitude; not a discrete number as before (7:9).

2. They are before the heavenly throne described in chapters four and five with the Lamb, the four living creatures, and the elders (7:9).

3. They are from all nations and are engaged in a great victory celebration (7:9, 12).

4. There is the inquiry concerning the origin of this throng and the answer that they came out of the great tribulation (7:13, 14).

5. The last three verses give the continuing service and state of this throng. They are serving before the throne. They are eternally blessed. They dwell with God and every tear is wiped away (7:15-17).

This passage does not have the symbolic characteristics of the first half of the chapter. A literal interpretation here does not conflict with any known principles nor does it trivialize the Word of God. We remember from other plain-language passages that the rapture of the saints and the end of this present universe comes immediately after the tribulation (Matt. 24:29-31). These saints are identified as those coming out of the tribulation and are in heaven with the Lord. Therefore, these must be the saints raptured at the second coming of Christ entering into and enjoying the bliss of heaven.

The timing (as seen by verses 15-17) is parallel to that of Revelation chapter twenty-one. The language is very much the same. This passage just follows the great white throne judgment in chronology (cf. Rev. 20:11; 21:1f). The awful silence of chapter eight (v. 1) is past at this time, and every tear is wiped away (cf. 7:17; 21:4). Chapter eight (v. 1) then flashes back to the final seal after the parenthetical vision of chapter seven.

The great multitude of 7:9f differs from the 144,000 of 7:4-8 in that the former is in heaven. The 144,000 in chapter seven are sealed for life on earth and marked by God for special consideration during the providential events of the seals. But we will see this group again — in heaven.

Now having considered the interpretation of Unit 5, and before introducing Unit 6, we must again discuss the matter of literal versus symbolic interpretation as it pertains to Unit 6. A fully literal interpretation would be quite compatible with the main eschatological postmillennial framework previously established by rigorous, plain-language passages (see Chapter 2), for the proof of this framework turns on other grounds. A wholly literal interpretation of the seals, trumpets, or vials, would fit nicely in the framework I have set forth. The first four trumpets could be set in the intensified period of tribulation at the beginning of the millennium and interpreted as strictly literal and be perfectly compatible with a postmillennial view. None of these four trumpets speak of universal catastrophic destruction as does the sixth seal. The effect of each, if literal, would have a serious effect on the earth; however, they are all partial in their effect (one third part) and life could survive until these effects pass. Egypt survived some similar effects during the time of the Mosaic plagues.

However, there are reasons to believe that God may have intended for us to understand these passages differently, and my object is to discover, if possible, exactly what God wants us to know by these words and sentences — not to prove a tradition. These words were written to *reveal*, not to *conceal*. Hence we can understand the general meaning now. And those who live through these events can identify the specific meaning, even the details, as the events transpire.

Serious logical dilemmas arise with the typical premillennial interpretation that these trumpet passages are all *literal and chronological* or *serially* related to the seals and the vials. A logical dilemma never arises when the Scriptures are properly interpreted, but it would be worthwhile to consider the types of inconsistencies that arise when we apply both a *literal and a serial* interpretation to the seals, trumpets, and vials.

1. In chapter six the sun has become black, the moon as blood, and the stars have fallen to earth, the heavens therefore have departed, and every island and mountain moved out of its place as a part of the process of the destruction of earth. Then in chapter eight we find trees (8:7), seas with living animals and seagoing vessels (8:8, 9), a star falling from heaven (which has already departed), rivers and springs (8:10, which could not exist if 6:12f had already occurred), the sun and moon were shining for two-thirds of a day (8:12), there were armies, millions of people still alive on earth (9:16, 20), etc.

2. Then when we come to the vials (16:1-21) again we find seas, living people, a scorching sun (16:8), great armies being gathered (16:14, 16), every island and mountain again fleeing away (16:20).

So the literal-chronological interpretation is contradictory and not logically feasible. Now, we can have it one of three ways:

1. Symbolic and chronological (serial);

2. Literal and not chronological: i.e., the heavens actually departing and the stars falling (6:12f) after the trumpets and vials have already occurred; even though it occurs first in the text.

3. Some passages literal and some symbolic; and some events serially chronological and some parallel.

But we cannot have it strictly literal with a strictly chronological progression, i.e., seals, then trumpets, then vials. It is remarkable that the one way it cannot be is the way most premillennial interpreters make it — remarkable!

Now how do we decide? The first thing I want to do is look at what we have observed in the prophetic units so far. Unit one was introductory, setting the ground rules; and it contained both plain-language passages and symbolic passages, e.g., candlesticks (churches), stars (angels) are examples of symbolic language. In the same text we find both types of language; and God knows that generally, we can sense the difference. In unit two the seven churches are in view. Again, there is some plain language ("I know thy works, and thy labour, and thy patience . . . " 2:2) and some symbolic language (" . . . I will come unto thee quickly, and remove *thy candlestick* . . . " 2:5). Plain language is predominant in this unit. Unit three has both symbology and plain language.

In unit four (the seals) there are symbolic characters — four horsemen — accomplishing real, essentially historical, kinds of things: war, poverty, violent death. These are the kinds of things history is made up of, both before and since John's vision, and the future will see more of the same. Under the fifth seal the death of the martyrs is quite literal, and we know from Hebrews 12, Matthew 24 (and the other Gospels) that the sixth seal is literal — the actual destruction of the heavens and earth at the Lord's return. Based on what we have seen so far, we find the texts contain a mixture. The seven churches of Asia represent seven parallel or synchronous views of the problems of the churches all occurring at the same time. All these conditions existed at once, and there is nothing in the text to suggest a serial or chronological interpretation. We are not to think the events relating to Ephesus (2:1-7) occurred, and then after these were finished the events relating to Smyrna (2:8-11) occurred, etc., in serial fashion. We have here seven parallel views of churches, each view giving us some additional information until we have a full understanding of the nature of church problems and what to do about them.

The four horsemen of chapter six and the events relating to them must also be parallel in nature. War, poverty, death, etc., all occur together and are essentially continuous. But the horsemen give us synchronous (not serial) views of different aspects of God's providence, each view giving additional information until we understand the nature of providence by which Christ is gaining the victory ("all things work[ing] together for good" Rom. 8:28) through both good and evil agencies. The fifth seal is also parallel to the first four, since martyrdom has been proceeding intermittently since the time of John's vision, as well as before, and will continue into the future.

When we come to the sixth and seventh seals, the events themselves are not continuous in nature but are unique events of short duration in time. The stars can only fall once. The heavens can only depart once. Christ shakes the heavens and the earth "once more" (Heb. 12:26, 27). So we cannot lock in on any single scheme; the material does not prove to be all serial or all parallel; neither is it all symbolic or all literal.

What rules then can we establish for the interpretation of this book, particularly of the trumpets and the vials and of their relation to the seals and to each other? Such decisions cannot be made arbitrarily. We are forced then to these conclusions:

1. We must recognize a mixture, in all these texts, of both symbolic and literal language as well as parallel and serial events.

2. We must therefore decide how to interpret the material text by text. We cannot approach this material with a single neat preconceived plan that fits all passages. What each passage says must provide its own clues for interpretation.

3. In the discernment of what is symbolic and what each specific symbol means, we must be guided by the following principles:

A. Every conclusion must be in character with all we know of the nature of God and the rest of Scripture truth.

B. It must never contradict another known fact whether theological, historical, or scientific.

C. It must make coherent sense with the immediate context in which it is found and with the broad context and plan of Scripture.

D. We must allow other passages using similar symbology to interpret for us whenever such passages are available.

4. In discernment of what is serially chronological and what is parallel, we must be guided by the following principles:

A. Events of the kind that experience and history prove to be of a continuous nature must be interpreted as parallel views, e.g., war (6:4) and violent death (6:8).

B. Events that are unique and occur once at a point in time must be fitted into a reasonable chronological order with other events, e.g., heavens departing (6:14).

C. Events of the kind that are dependent upon prior events must be considered chronological to the prior event, e.g., Satan's being cast into the bottomless pit (20:2, 3) must precede Satan or beast ascending out of bottomless pit (9:1-11; 11:7; 17:8; 20:7).

D. Repetitive material describing the same event, though in different language, must be considered parallel views of the same event, e.g., destruction of earth (Matt. 24:29-31; 2 Pet. 3:10, 12; Rev. 16:20; and 20:9,11) which can only occur once but is described repeatedly in many places.

E. Chapter division and order in the text must not be used to establish chronological order in prophetic passages if such order conflicts with any of the above principles.

With these conclusions, we are now ready to interpret the material of Unit 6 and are better prepared to interpret the rest of the book of Revelation.

Unit 6 (8:2-11:19)

At this point another major vision is introduced with the familiar words "and I saw . . . " (8:2), and the subject matter of this vision continues to unfold to the end of chapter eleven. However, chapter ten is parenthetical in nature and might be, like chapter seven, considered separately. Yet it is closely related to chapter eleven, and these chapters will be easier to understand when considered together.

In the beginning of this unit we note that the sounding of

the trumpets is preceded by a description of certain activities around the heavenly throne similar to those just preceding the opening of the seals. The smoke or odors of incense, which are said to be the prayers of the saints, ascend up before the throne of God (cf. 5:8; 8:3, 4).

We have seen that the Scriptures teach clearly that Christ is head over "all things," providentially, on behalf of the church (Eph. 1:21-23). Elijah prayed that it not rain, and it rained not. He prayed for rain and it rained (James 5:17, 18). The church prayed and Peter was released from prison (Acts 12). Now, in this unit (8:2f), God pulls back the curtains of heaven to let us see the heavenly reception of the prayers of His people. The seals (see 5:8) and trumpets (8:2f) are the providential events continually executed by God in pursuit of His conquering and victorious purpose in response to the prayers of the saints who prosecute the affairs of His kingdom on earth:

> Verily I say unto you, Whatsoever ye shall bind *on earth* shall be bound *in heaven*: and whatsoever ye shall loose on earth shall be loosed in heaven. Again I say unto you, That if two of you shall agree *on earth* as touching anything that they shall ask, it shall be done for them of my Father which is *in heaven* (Matt. 18:18, 19; cf. 16:19).

Now as soon as the prayers of the saints rise up before the throne of God *in heaven* (Rev. 8:4), things begin to happen *on earth* (8:5); and the trumpets begin to sound (8:6). Then four phenomena take place on earth as the first four angels sound their trumpets. These phenomena involve 1) the earth and vegetable life, 2) the sea and sea life, 3) fresh-water fountains and streams, and 4) the celestial bodies, sun, moon, and stars. In each case only a partial effect is made — a "third part."

If we consider these literally and chronologically with the seals, we have a logical dilemma with chapter six as previously noted. Furthermore, it seems generally out of character with God to proceed directly in this manner: e.g., hail and blood falling down, a great mountain falling into the sea, a single star falling on all rivers, etc., especially since the close of the canon of Scripture and the discontinuation of signs and wonders originally performed in the confirmation of Scripture[7]. Yet this is not impossible. It could be that God will choose to use these actual means in some way, in response to prayer (8:4), to bring the victories to His people in the conflagration prior to the millennium, just as He used plagues to bring the deliverance of His people from Egypt in Moses' day in response to prayer (Ex. 3:9). But a dogmatic literalism employed to avoid the difficulties of interpreting these messages from God, may work to obscure the very message God wants us to see. In the absence of strong corroboration from plain-language passages, we should always proceed cautiously.

I would not rule out, either, the possibility that these first four trumpet events could represent certain effects of man-made phenomena connected with modern warfare. For example, "hail and fire mingled with blood" (8:7) is a fair description of atomic or other destructive means of warfare with the resultant bloodshed and the destruction of plant life, "trees and grass." Then a gigantic fireball "*as it were* a great mountain" — not actually a mountain — fell into the sea (8:8, 9) with the destruction of a part of the marine life and the sea-going vessels. This could be atomic phenomena or some futuristic aspect of battle from space orbit. The blood could refer to a coloration of the water or to massive bloodshed.

The "star" (8:10, 11) which fell from heaven, causing the fresh-water sources to be bitter or polluted to the extent that many people died because of them, is hardly to be understood as a real star comparable to our sun. The clue is that the effect described here, the embittering of one-third the fresh water supply, is much too mild. The catastrophe of Revelation 6:13, 14 and Matthew 24:29, where not "a star" but "the stars" converge upon earth, results, we are told, in total destruction

---

[7] For a thorough discussion of this principle see Willard A. Ramsey, *Modern Charismata vs. the Revelation of God* (Hallmark Baptist Church, 1988.)

of the heavens and earth; these obviously are real stars. But in Revelation 8:10-11, we must understand some fiery object "burning *as it were* a lamp" polluting a significant part of the fresh-water sources. To say more than this would be speculation. In the absence of other supporting Scripture passages to give rigor to our interpretation, as we have in the case of Revelation 6:12f (where over a dozen major passages throughout both the Old and New Testaments corroborate the interpretation of the total destruction of the universe), it is better to avoid sensational speculation.

Proceeding with the theory that these first four trumpets may describe literal phenomena resulting from modern warfare, the effect in the sun, moon, and stars (8:12) could represent a diminishing of the light from these celestial bodies because of the tremendous atmospheric pollution resulting from the other phenomena previously described — perhaps a "nuclear winter."

Now I freely admit that there is no rigor attached to these suggested interpretations, but those who live in these times, if these things are literal, will definitely recognize them. Hence we "watch and wait." And yet, as in some other prophecies, these trumpets could have a double meaning and a double fulfillment. A literal event can have a symbolic meaning (cf. Luke 17:26-30). In any case, however, the interpretation, whether literal or figurative, is compatible with a postmillennial framework of eschatology and is irrelevant to my primary thesis.

Now having said all this, I have the feeling, based on the general tenor of Scripture and the character of God, that He does indeed have another message for us wrapped up symbolically in these first four trumpets. To discover this message I call to witness other symbolic passages of Scripture. Of course it is inappropriate to be dogmatic when dealing with any symbolic passage, but no less so than to declare, arbitrarily and dogmatically, a passage to be literal where no scriptural rigor attaches to it or when many senseless problems arise with such a position. In most other books of the Bible the literal interpretation of a passage is easily identified by the language of its context, but in

Revelation we do not always have literal supporting passages from other books of the Bible as we do, for example, in chapter six (cf. 6:12f; Matt. 24:29f).

We compare then the first and second trumpets (8:7-9) with Revelation 7:1-3. There is about to be an effect on the earth (with trees and grass) and on the sea (7:1-3) during the opening of the seals, and just so the first and second trumpets affect the earth and seas respectively. From passages like Isaiah 60:5; Daniel 7:2; Revelation 13:1; 17:15, it is clear enough that the "sea" ordinarily figures the unbelieving Gentile multitudes comprising the world *political* environment. Contrast this with the apostate *religious* figure, the "false prophet," of Revelation 13:11 rising out of a religious environment figured as the "earth." Using this approach then, comparing Scripture with Scripture, it is not inappropriate to search for other possible messages from these visions.

The First Trumpet (8:7). The "earth" then, which is the subject of a judgment of hail, fire, and blood under the first trumpet, may reasonably represent the world *religious* environment — "churches" or religious bodies, including Islam and/or Israel. If this concept is true, that the "earth" represents the visible aggregate of institutional religion, it follows that some of them (one-third part) are "burned up" (destroyed or hindered in some way) under God's providential power. God presently exercises restraint — two-thirds are not burned; "Surely the wrath of man shall praise thee: the remainder of wrath shalt thou restrain" (Psalm 76:10; cf. 2 Thess. 2:6, 7). All this is in response to the prayers of the true saints for relief from oppression and the perversion of truth by these apostate institutions at different times in history. Consider, for example, the ravages of the black plague, or the destructiveness of the Crusades on Islamic nations and Catholic-dominated Europe in the Dark Ages. And there is coming prior to the millennium, a more complete destruction of apostate religion (see Unit 12: 17:15-18:24).

The Second Trumpet (8:8, 9). Under the second trumpet the "sea," representing the secular world and political environment (see Isa. 60:5; Dan. 7:2; Rev. 17:15), is partially judged, or restrained (8:8, 9). This is in consequence of the shock waves of a gigantic burning "mountain" falling into the "sea." A "mountain" sometimes refers to a kingdom (cf. Rev. 17:9, 10; Dan. 2:34, 35, 44, 45), and the shock waves of the fall of the Roman Empire to this day reverberate throughout the Western world. But the tyrannical power of world political kingdoms has been restrained (one-third part) no doubt in response to the prayers of thousands of God's faithful saints and martyrs.

The Third Trumpet (8:10, 11). Then the third trumpet sounds and a "star" falls, looking like a burning lamp. We have already seen the use of the symbology of "stars" to represent angels (Rev. 1:20; 9:1, 11; 12:4, 9; 20:1). This "star" (8:10) then could be Satan in his role as an "angel of light" (2 Cor. 11:14) to pollute, poison, and embitter the "rivers of living waters," as Jesus symbolized His truth and salvation (John 7:38; 4:10, 14), that went out from the true church. Satan's intent was to pollute these waters completely, but he is restrained. The true Gospel, through apostate pastors and churches, is only partially (one-third part) polluted, as the restraining power of God in response to the prayers of His saints is exercised; the gates of hell do not prevail.

The Fourth Trumpet (8:12). The fourth trumpet is like the third. As we compare the description of what must be Israel as God's ordained institution about to give "birth" to a "man child" (12:5), we see a figurative reference to the sun, moon, and stars as part of her adornment (12:1). The ordained "house of God" has continued in the New Testament era as the church, and the adornment is doubtless the same. We find then that these sources of light — sun, moon, and stars — are partially obscured under the fourth trumpet (8:12) as some churches have become corrupt or apostate and have blotted out part (one-third part) of the glorious light, even as the fresh-water streams were polluted. But God has restrained Satan in response to the prayers of the saints so that the effect is not total.

Now this is not a rigorous but a reasonable interpretation of the first four trumpets, well supported by other Scripture truth, definitely true to the providential restraint on both the sinful apostate secular and the apostate religious worlds. God has not yet totally destroyed them; neither are they as bad as they would be if totally unrestrained (cf. Psalm 76:10; 2 Thess. 2:6, 7).

Also, these four effects are occurring simultaneously, not serially; therefore the first four trumpets, like the first five seals, are parallel views of different phenomena. This is a continuing revelation of the providential works of Christ as He sits at God's right hand "from henceforth expecting till his enemies be made his footstool" (Heb. 10:13). I feel more comfortable with this interpretation than with the literal alone, because it conforms to the deductive conclusions of Scripture. Yet, a literal interpretation may be all that God intended, but those who need to know the exact meaning will understand it at the appropriate time. One who says, "I don't know for sure," should not be blamed if wrong; but one who says, "I know for sure" and then proves to be wrong in the end, is to be blamed.

The Fifth Trumpet (9:1-12). Now beginning with the fifth trumpet (9:1), in accordance with a solemn warning (8:13), the character and timing of the events under the last three trumpets change sharply — especially in intensity. They are called "woes" (cf. 8:13; 9:12; 11:14). In verse one of chapter nine, we are given a very significant clue which enables us to establish a benchmark in time. This clue is the opening of the bottomless pit (cf. Rev. 20:1-3, 7-9) which marks the end of the millennium and the beginning of the "short space" or a "little season" (17:10; 20:3) of time between the millennium and the consummation of all things when Christ returns at the last trump, destroying the earth and judging all mankind (cf. 11:15-18; 20:7-15). With this benchmark, we can now proceed with a more rigorous interpretation than with the first four trumpets.

That "little season" of time is the tribulation. As previously established, the destruction of the heavens and earth comes "immediately after the tribulation" (Matt. 24:29); therefore, the millennium must occur prior to the tribulation. Now in the release of Satan from the bottomless pit under the fifth trumpet, or the first "woe," we have a clear and rigorous landmark establishing positively the termination of the millennium. Therefore, Revelation 9:1 is a parallel event with Revelation 20:7. Judging then from the nature of the events from the end of the millennium (9:1) to the end of the world at the last trumpet (11:15), this entire period would surely be called the great tribulation. Therefore, again, Revelation 9:1-11:18 is an expanded view of the same period covered by Revelation 20:7-15. I will discuss the length of this period later.

I now want to discuss the rigor of this interpretation. As noted above, the clue is the opening of the "bottomless pit" and what comes out. The Scriptures are abundantly clear that Satan and the other fallen angels are roaming the earth today: "... as a roaring lion, walketh about, seeking whom he may devour" (1 Pet. 5:8; cf. Matt. 17:15-18; Mark 5:9-12).

The text (Rev. 9:1, 2) says an angel unlocks the "bottomless pit" and there emerges a horde of "locusts"[8] (9:3) which can only be demonic beings. Their king is "the angel of the bottomless pit" named Abaddon or Apollyon (9:11). This can only be Satan himself. Now for Satan and his demons to emerge from the bottomless pit, they must first have been placed there and "locked" up by some great power.

We must now answer the question: When is Satan locked in the bottomless pit? We are told very clearly; at the beginning of the millennium (20:1-3) an angel binds Satan and casts him into the bottomless pit. We are told that after the thousand years "he must be loosed a little season" (20:3, 7). The fifth trumpet then is the loosing of Satan and his demons who were bound at the beginning of the millennium. (Remember we have seen that the book of Revelation *cannot* be interpreted in a strict serial chronology.)

Therefore, we have a very important guidepost to help us establish the order of events. The first four trumpets very obviously reveal the activity of Satan; he is under limitations

---

[8] These are not literal locusts, because these "locusts" have an intelligent king (9:11), they respond intelligently, though demonically, to leadership. Ordinary locusts do not do that.

and restraints (one-third part) but not locked up. That is his present and historic status — on earth, active, but partially restrained (Psalm 76:10; 2 Thess. 2:6, 7; Job 1:12; 2:6). Hence, the first four trumpets signify events in the providential operations of God that occur before the millennium. The last three trumpets, or the three "woes," signify events that occur after the millennium. This is graphically illustrated on page 217.

Now with this outline of the trumpets before us, knowing the three remaining trumpets or woes are tribulational, we can proceed with our interpretation of the events. The beings which ascend out of the bottomless pit could be literal embodiments of demonic spirits in some gruesome form as described (9:7-11). This interpretation is perfectly compatible with the broad postmillennial framework. However, it seems more in keeping with the nature of the context and the deductive understanding of Scripture, history, the Gospels, and the character of God, to interpret these as demonic activity through the agency of men who have abandoned themselves to every evil and wicked influence.

Toward the end of the millennium as the "man of sin" is about to be revealed, there will be a great "falling away" (2 Thess. 2:3) of men who will have turned away from the influence of the church. During the millennium, with the binding of Satan, the church will be a powerful, stabilizing influence. The true church during and immediately after the millennium will be the only visible institutional religious movement. Prior to the millennium, visible institutional religion was (or is) a conglomerate of apostate denominations and true churches, hence God's partial judgment (8:7f). At the end of the millennium, however, institutional religion is pure; hence the demonic activity, by the decree of God, is to not "hurt the grass of the *earth*, neither any green thing, neither any tree . . . ," as it did prior to the millennium, but the ungodly only (9:4). God during the great tribulation, then, protects His people generally (Rev. 3:10; 12:14-16). However, we will later see a special class of saints who voluntarily throw themselves into the battle and become martyrs for the faith as many before them have already done.

Having been recently released from his thousand years of imprisonment, Satan's first objective is now to regain control of the political and military systems of the world — to revive and give life again to the "beast" (13:3, 4; 17:8); he needs the "beast" again. He finds those who have "fallen away" from the influence of the church, or perhaps their offspring, ready to his hand. But he must first subject them. The methods of subjection of tyrannical forces are always cruel. Therefore cruel and torturous means, possibly involving drugs, though not intended to kill (9:5, 6), are used to bring the masses of the ungodly under his control and enlist them in what appears to be a massive military force of some type (9:7-10). He is then ready to lead them — Gog and his people (9:11; cf. 20:8); this is the end of the fifth trumpet or the first woe, and the approach of the next two woes is announced (9:12).

The Sixth Trumpet (9:13-21). The sixth trumpet introduces a voice from the horns of the golden altar (9:13) suggesting, again, a response to the prayers of the saints (see 8:3-5). Four angels are loosed which have been reserved by the foreknowledge and determinate counsel of God for a special time and purpose. The purpose: to instigate a calamitous battle in which the enemies of God are further subdued and a third part of men is slain (9:14, 15). A vast army is described and such cruel warfare as has never been known to mankind (9:17-21). This war is prosecuted by the army gathered by Satan and the demonic forces described under the fifth trumpet. At its head no doubt is the "man of sin," the final antichrist, and by these wars he conquers the now-apostate people of the world, regains his power as the revived "beast," and becomes the undisputed world leader.

I want to list for your study several parallel passages in the Scripture that deal with the same general time period and class of events during the tribulation just prior to the second coming of Christ at the seventh (last) trumpet. This list is not necessarily exhaustive: Ezekiel 38 (but not Ezk. 39, which precedes the millennium); Daniel 7:21-25; 11:36-12:1, 7-13; Matthew 24:15-22; Mark 13:14-20; Revelation 9:1-21; 11:7, 8; 12:12-17; 13:3-18; 16:1-16; 17:10-14; 20:7-9.

Chapter ten, as before mentioned, is parenthetical in

nature. There is a pause in the events leading up to the last trumpet, and when it has sounded the "mystery of God should be finished" (10:7). But the angel of chapter ten delivers a bitter-sweet message to John in the form of a "little book" (10:8-10). The events of chapter eleven no doubt comprise the message. It is sweet in that the great purpose of God is about to be finalized and the victory is about to be won as He makes the last of His enemies to be His footstool. It is bitter in that there is yet more suffering for *some* of His faithful saints. Those faithful saints in the vicinity of Jerusalem, where the "man of sin" has determined to set up his throne in the very house of God (2 Thess. 2:4), take a strong and resolute stand against him even unto death (Rev. 11:7).

Chapter eleven, after the parenthetical comments of chapter ten, resumes the events under the sixth trumpet or second woe. This trumpet discloses the final attempt of the "beast that ascendeth out of the bottomless pit" to silence the church of God (11:1-7). I am amazed at the arbitrary speculations about the "two witnesses" when we are all but told who or what they are. We are told:

> These are *the two olive trees*, and *the two candlesticks* standing before the God of the earth (11:4).

All we now must do is to look into the Scriptures and see what witnessing entities have gone under these names before. This same book of Revelation settles the meaning of the symbology of a candlestick or lampstand (cf. 1:12, 13, 20). ". . . The seven candlesticks . . . are the seven churches" (1:20). In Romans chapter eleven we have most clearly set forth the symbology of the wild olive tree (Gentiles) and the good or natural olive tree (Jews) which in Paul's context can only be the New Testament church comprised of the union of both Jew and Gentile (cf. Eph. 2:11-22).

I have previously shown that Israel will be converted prior to the millennium, and, nationally, she will remain Israel with her own peculiar national covenants but will not revert back to the Old Testament priesthood. The Jews will be, as were the early Jewish Christians, in the New Testament church. Paul argues they are the natural olive branches growing out of Christ, the root that bears both Jew and Gentile. The Jews are the natural branches; we Gentiles are grafted in:

> For if thou wert cut out of the olive tree which is wild by nature, and wert graffed contrary to nature into a good olive tree: how much more shall these, which be the natural branches, be graffed into their own olive tree? (Rom. 11:24).

There are many symbols in the book of Revelation concerning which we have little help from other Scripture passages, but the identity of the two witnesses does not suffer from this problem. Only a little faith in the principle of the self-interpretation of Scripture settles conclusively that the two witnesses are to be understood as Jew and Gentile, God's covenant people, unified in the church of the living God witnessing together before the "principalities and powers . . . the manifold wisdom of God, according to the eternal purpose which he purposed in Christ Jesus our Lord" (Eph. 3:10, 11). Moreover, this very symbology is prophetically foreshadowed in the Old Testament (Zech. 4:1-14). The candlestick and olive tree symbology is used in a beautiful picture of the Spirit and power of God through His covenant people, witnesses, expressly defined for us:

> . . . These are the two anointed ones, *that stand by the Lord* of the whole earth (Zech. 4:14).

Then in Revelation we are told:

> These are the two olive trees, and the two candlesticks *standing before the God of the earth* (11:4).

Compare also the seven candlesticks standing before Christ (Rev. 1:13). What could be a more positive identification?

The reason the obvious biblical interpretation of these two witnesses is rejected by premillennial interpreters is that in their scheme of doctrine, the church no longer exists as an earthly witnessing entity. They must therefore resort to arbitrary interpretations. Some say these two are Moses and Elijah; some say Enoch and Elijah, etc. There is nothing to connect these persons uniquely to olive trees and candlesticks.

Now the events of chapter eleven continue the visions under the sixth trumpet. From the time periods mentioned here, forty-two months or 1260 days, we are able to get some rough notion of the length of the tribulation period or the "little season" between the time of Satan's release from the bottomless pit and when Christ returns. We are told that the Gentile will tread the "holy city" underfoot for forty-two months.[9] But when do the forty-two months begin? That is not a question we can answer, nor can anyone ever answer it exactly except in retrospect. These saints are finally overcome and killed by the final form of the "beast" revived from the bottomless pit (11:7; cf. 17:8). The 1260 days terminate with the death of the two witnesses who are resurrected approximately three days later (11:11-15).[10] But it may be hard for Christians who live in those days to discern the exact time when, in God's mind, the forces of Satan gain ascendency over the holy city. However, those who live in those days, while not knowing the day nor the hour of Christ's coming, may certainly know the season is near (see Matt. 24:32, 33; 1 Thess. 5:4), and this will be an immense encouragement to stand fast with the witness as prophets of truth through that period. Only in those last days will the second coming be imminent as all things are fulfilled.

---

[9] We should be careful not to confuse this time with the Gentile domination of Jerusalem from the fall of Jerusalem in 70 A.D. (see Luke 21:24) until the Jews return when the "times of the Gentiles be fulfilled." The Jews regain control of Jerusalem prior to the millennium. Perhaps even now in God's mind this is so, but there are still many Gentiles there and a Muslim shrine on or near the ancient temple site. But this will change and they will have full control throughout the millennium and until the "beast" retakes the city (Rev. 11:2).

[10] We should remember the saints who were martyred prior to the millennium shared with Christ in the special "first" resurrection as "firstfruits." It is not surprising then that these latest and probably the last martyrs share in a special resurrection even if only a short time before the general resurrection. If this group of martyrs too are considered by the Lord to be a part of the "firstfruits," it is significant that they, like our Lord, were resurrected after approximately three days. This would be a singular expression of honor for those who had given all for the name of Christ.

The length of the "little season" then is something more than forty-two months, for it will take some time for Satan to amass his forces after his release from the bottomless pit and then to gain control of Jerusalem. The commonly-believed "seven years" tribulation period is derived from an erroneous interpretation of Daniel's "seventieth week" (see Dan. 9:24f, see also the discussion of this passage in Chapter 6). If the tribulation is seven years long, it is a coincidence; there is no way to tell for sure. The Bible does not tell us. The places where times are mentioned are as follows; I give them for your study:

1. a time and times and the dividing of time (Dan. 7:25)
2. unto two thousand and three hundred days (Dan. 8:14)
3. the seventy weeks of Daniel (Dan. 9:24-27)
4. it shall be for a time, times and a half (Dan. 12:7)
5. a thousand two hundred and ninety days (Dan. 12:11)
6. the thousand three hundred and five and thirty days (Dan. 12:12)
7. ye shall have tribulation ten days (Rev. 2:10)
8. the "locusts" torment the wicked for five months (Rev. 9:5)
9. they tread under foot forty and two months (Rev. 11:2)
10. they shall prophesy a thousand two hundred and three-score days (Rev. 11:3)
11. a thousand two hundred and three-score days (Rev. 12:6)
12. a time, and times, and half a time (Rev. 12:14)
13. continue forty and two months (Rev. 13:5)

Seven of these referenced time periods are the same. An examination of the context in these seven cases strongly, and most of them quite rigorously, indicates they are dealing with the same occasion or time period.[11] This one time period is

---

[11] It should be noted, lest anyone should overlook this important point, that if we use an average month of 30 days, then 42 months, 1260 days, and a time, times and half a time (1 + 2 + .5 = 3.5 years) are all equal. It is likely then that these three values represent the same time period and are

characterized in several different ways, or by its different aspects, as follows:

1. **Daniel 7:25.** The saints are "given into his (the 4th beast) hands" for 3.5 years.
2. **Daniel 12:7.** This is more ambiguous, but 3.5 years is implied to be the time required to "scatter (or shatter, NKJV) the power of the holy people."
3. **Revelation 11:2.** The time the Gentiles tread the Holy City underfoot is 42 months.
4. **Revelation 11:3.** The two witnesses shall prophesy in sackcloth, i.e., under this condition of oppression for 1260 days.
5. **Revelation 12:6.** The woman is protected and fed in the wilderness for 1260 days.
6. **Revelation 12:14.** The woman is nourished and protected from the serpent for 3.5 years.
7. **Revelation 13:5.** Power was given unto him (the revived beast) for 42 months.

It is clear from all this that the revived beast from the bottomless pit (Rev. 11:7; 13:5) will make an attempt to exterminate the saints, the church. Some of the saints will take a stand in Jerusalem, and by calling on the power of God through prayer will "fight" against the beast by calling on the same providential powers the saints have always had on their behalf (remember the plagues of Egypt; Elijah — 1 Kings 17:1; 2 Kings 1:9f; Elisha — 2 Kings 6:13f; see Eph. 1:19-23). But during this time, just before the end, God will intensify His pressure on the forces of Satan in answer to these saints, the two witnesses, and will bring the same types of plagues, but more intensely (see 11:5, 6; cf. the vials 16:2-16).

However, in God's providence this dedicated troop of latter-day prophets standing by the truth at Jerusalem, like Stephen, Paul and thousands of lesser known martyrs in past

---

probably intended to be approximations. Otherwise 3.5 years and 42 months equals 1277.5 days.

history, will be permitted to gain the martyr's reward (11:7-10).

Now as we reach chapter twelve, we will find that not all of the churches existing throughout the world, as we might expect, will be concentrated at Jerusalem at that time. And though the persecution of the churches by the beast will be a world-wide phenomenon, God's providential care will provide them with a place in the "wilderness" for safety.[12]

Now to note the final events under the sixth trumpet as described in this marvelous and informative chapter eleven, the martyred people who took their stand in the very teeth of the "beast" were resurrected and caught up to God before the eyes of all the people in Jerusalem (11:11, 12;). Then, within the hour a tremendous earthquake rocked the city, leaving seven thousand dead and shaking the people's confidence in the "beast" not a little (11:13).

With this event the sixth trumpet, the second woe, closes and the third woe follows quickly. The time between the close of the sixth trumpet and the sounding of the last or seventh trumpet, if any, is a mysterious period. I strongly suspect there is some time-lapse (perhaps days) for two possible reasons:

1. In chapter 10 John tells us of hearing "seven thunders" utter some messages, but he was not permitted to record them (10:3, 4). Then immediately an angel proclaimed that there would be no more delay in time but that when the seventh trumpet sounded, the "mystery of God" would be finished (10:6, 7). Now this implies some event or events under the seven thunders which may occur just prior to the last trump.

---

[12] This situation is not unlike that in the early days of the church under pagan persecution, and then later in the Dark Ages under the Catholic persecution of the church. In those times the Novations, Donatists, and Paulicians fled from the populous cities of the world and lived for centuries in "the wilderness" — the Piedmont valleys of the Alps and in southern France and other secluded parts of Europe — to avoid some of the persecution. I suspect the wilderness sojourn of these saints near the last days is for a similar reason.

2. In Daniel chapter twelve, there are two mysterious time references set in the same time frame with the more familiar 3.5 years which, so far as I can tell, are not accounted for in Revelation unless they account for the thunders and/or the vials.

A. The first time reference is a period of 1290 days (Dan. 12:11) "from the time that the daily sacrifice shall be taken away" (which probably had been reinstituted by apostate Jews toward the end of, or after the millennium). This period likely begins when the "man of sin" moves into the temple and takes over the holy city (cf. 2 Thess. 2:3, 4; Rev. 11:2). But the end of this 1290-day period, thirty days after the two prophets have been slain, is the mysterious part. What happens then?

B. The second time reference is a period of 1335 days (Dan. 12:12) which implicitly starts at the same time as the 3.5 years (Dan. 12:7; Rev. 11:2, 3) and the 1290 days (Dan. 12:11) and ends 45 days after the 1290 days. One coming to the end of that time period is blessed. I assume therefore that at that time the "mystery of God" is near completion or the seventh trump is about to sound. We are told enough that the events beginning and ending the 1260-day period are rather certain, but the beginning and end of the 1290 and the 1335-day periods are more obscure. Yet those who live through the days of this period will doubtless be able to understand the significance of these time periods even though they will not know the day or hour they begin and end.

Then what can we say for sure? It is certain that when the second woe is past (Rev. 11:14) the third woe, the last trump comes quickly. Does this mean 75 days later (1335 -1260 = 75)? I cannot say.

The Seventh Trumpet (Rev. 11:15-19). I do not think it necessary to dwell at length on the detail of this passage. I will only point out the salient features since this occasion has been discussed before in conjunction with the second coming of Christ (see Chapter 2).

Remember, however, that at this time a great calamity unknown to the unbelieving world is pending. The stars of the heavens are supernaturally hurtling through space toward earth at approximately or slightly less than the speed of light at that point in time. (Some of the more distant ones even now as I write these lines, at least 1000 years prior, may be speeding toward earth.) Due to the natural physical limitations of the speed of communications phenomena and the immense distance of some of the stars, there would be no possible way to detect such an event. But as the day approaches, subtle changes in light phenomena (the sun and moon darken) along with an intensifying gravitational shockwave will be noticed, and earthquakes and other catastrophic events begin to increase in intensity and severity until the very sudden engulfing of the earth in the converging stellar-atomic holocaust.

However, it is the time when Christ conquers all the enemies and kingdoms of the world and "shall reign for ever and ever" (11:15). Furthermore, it is the time of the general judgment when the dead, small and great, saints and sinners, will be judged and given their final rewards (11:18). It is the time when Christ's "wrath is come" (11:18; cf. 6:17). It is the occasion when Christ leaves the right hand of God to finalize the work of conquering all enemies, the time of the "restitution of all things, which God hath spoken by the mouth of all his holy prophets since the world began" (Acts 3:21). This event is approximately parallel with all the following passages: Matthew 24:29-31; 25:31-46; Mark 13:24-27; Luke 21:26-27; Acts 1:11; 3:19-21; 1 Corinthians 15:24-26, 51-54; 1 Thessalonians 4:14-17; 5:2-4; 2 Thessalonians 1:7-10; 2:8; 2 Peter 3:10-13; Revelation 1:7; 6:12-17; 14:14-20; 16:15-21; 19:11-21; 20:9, 10; Ezekiel 38:18-23; Daniel 7:22; 12:1-3 and others. See page 217 for graphic illustration of trumpets.

Unit 7 (12:1-17)

Having finished with the trumpet series, which spans the providential works of God from the time of John to the end of the world and is approximately parallel with the series of seals, the vision of chapter twelve flashes back to a time even before the time of John to give a broader, more general, synchronous or parallel view of the conflict of God and His people against Satan. I will deal with only two issues in this passage: 1) the identity of the characters — the woman, the man child, and the dragon — and 2) the relative timing of the events.

Since there is a rigorous identity of the dragon as "the devil, and Satan" (12:9), we need not belabor this point. Though he is symbolized as having seven heads and ten horns, the same as the beast of chapters thirteen and seventeen, this merely depicts him in his role as the energizer of the beast (13:2) and in his persistent career of trying to establish a universal empire ruling the whole world which project he has been prosecuting at least ever since Nimrod. He has nearly succeeded a number of times, but he has consistently been restrained.

Now the identity of the woman is more easily understood once we identify the "man child" (12:5). The major clues for identity of the child are given as one who would "rule all nations with a rod of iron" and one who is "caught up unto God, and to his throne." On the surface it appears conclusive that the reference is to Jesus Christ (Psalm 2:9; Acts 1:9; 2:34), and I so believe it is. However, there is another entity which has been suggested by B. H. Carroll[13] which also fits these qualifications. He says the child is the martyrs of the church as a class. They rule with a rod of iron and sit in his throne (Rev. 2:26, 27; 3:21). Carroll makes the woman to be the church exclusively, arguing correctly that the church cannot give birth to its founder, Jesus Christ.

The problem Carroll sees is that the woman's career extends to a late period in history (12:12-17), as does the church, and finds difficulty in accounting for national Israel as the woman in this setting. On the other hand, the futuristic school of premillennial interpretation sees Israel only in this setting since, they say, the church has already been rap-

---

[13] B. H. Carroll, *Revelation.* An Interpretation of the English Bible (Grand Rapids: Baker Book House, 1973), p. 137.

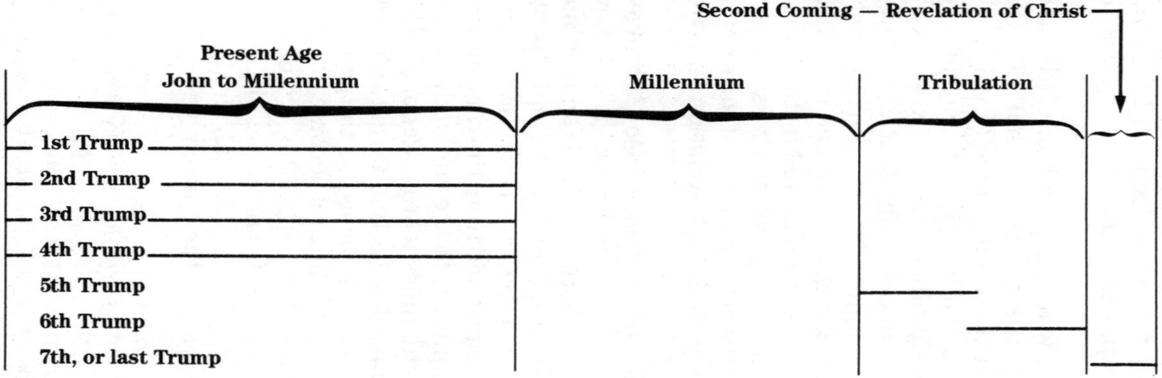

1. The providentially restrained (1/3 part) phenomena that occur under the first four trumpets (Rev. 8:2-12) occur prior to the millennium and perhaps continue, in kind, into the tribulation. I do not, however, rule out the possibility that these first four trumpets could represent catastrophic judgments or the devastation of modern warfare just prior to the millennium.
2. It is clear, however, that the fifth and sixth trumpets (Rev. 9:1-21) represent the detailed activities of Satan after the millennium through the revived beast. These two trumpets represent an enlarged view of the "short space" (Rev. 17:10) and "little season" (Rev. 20:3, 7-9) after Satan is released from the bottomless pit (Rev. 9:1, 11).
3. The seventh trumpet is unequivocally the terminal event, the second coming, the revelation, immediately prior to the judgment of all men (Rev. 11:15-18). This is the "trump of God" (1 Thess. 4:16), the "last trump" (1 Cor. 15:52), "a great sound of a trumpet" (Matt. 24:31).

The Seven Trumpets

tured.[14] We are back to the old problem previously discussed (Chapter 5) that some cannot allow national Israel to exist in a church relationship. I cannot feel comfortable with Carroll's position; and the futuristic position, as we have seen, is wholly untenable.

What then is the woman who gives birth to Christ and reaches into the future in the church format? In Old Testament times there was a covenant people (Ex. 19:5, 6) and an official earthly institution authorized, chosen, and sanctioned by God Himself as His official house (Ex. 40:33, 34; 1 Kings 8:10, 11). All the affairs of God's kingdom as it related to the earthly ministry and execution of God's purpose were the official jurisdiction of that agency of "the house of God." It was this covenant people, the official national institution of Israel that gave birth to the man child, Christ. (Mary exclusively cannot satisfy all the requirements of the woman in this passage. She is not the "woman" of Revelation 12 as the Catholics make her.)

Now the *format* of this *same* "house of God" changed after the Messiah was born. The new format is the New Testament church comprised of both Jews and Gentiles, but it has the same official sanction of God upon it, and it is the "house of God, which is the church of the living God . . . " (1 Tim. 3:15).[15] Its ministry has continued from the time of John on into the future and will continue to the end of the world.

At first in New Testament times it was predominantly Jewish. Now it is predominantly Gentile. But during and after the millennium it will again be largely Jewish as the people of national Israel submit to their Messiah and become pillars in the "house of God" in the church format. The "woman" of Revelation twelve represents the official "house of God" in any generation. She gave birth to the Messiah in the Old Testament format; she continues as the church.

---

[14] William E. Biederwolf, *The Second Coming Bible* (Grand Rapids: Baker Book House, 1972), p. 623.

[15] For a full treatment of this truth see: William C. Hawkins and Willard A. Ramsey, *The House of God* (Simpsonville, S. C.: Hallmark Baptist Church, 1980), pp. 12-34.

Now let's talk about timing. In verses one and two the woman is Old Testament Israel travailing under the oppression of Satan to give birth to the Messiah. In verses eleven through seventeen she is the Jew/Gentile church. Her work is about finished and God protects her in a place of safety while the dragon who "hath but a short time" is in the last throes of his wrath before his final destruction at the second coming of Christ.

It should be noted that the wilderness sojourn of the woman, which is God's provision for her safety in the tribulation (12:16), is the same length of time (1260 days or 3.5 years; cf. 12:6, 14) as the ministry of the two witnesses (1260 days; 11:3). It is also the same as the time of dominion of the revived beast (42 months) from the bottomless pit after his deadly wound was healed (cf. 11:2, 7; 13:3-5; 17:8). Also Satan has but a "short time" (12:12) which correlates with the "short space" (17:10) and the "little season" (20:3).

Therefore, it is rigorously established that the wilderness sojourn of the "woman," (then the Jew/Gentile church) follows the millennium. This event takes place during the tribulation period under the sixth trumpet. This gives us a picture of what is happening with the rest of the churches of the world while "the remnant of her seed" (12:17), the Jerusalem church (and perhaps others with her), are so valiantly defending the "faith once delivered to the saints" even unto death (11:3-8; cf. 12:17).

Moreover this passage gives us a broad overview of the career of Satan from the time of his efforts to destroy the Messiah (12:3, 4) until his last rebellion in heaven (12:7-10). The fact that John's initial vision of the woman and the dragon is said to have "appeared" in heaven must be interpreted, I believe, to mean that the visual heavens were the backdrop of John's vision. Israel was not in heaven; Christ was not born in heaven, and there is no wilderness in heaven. If that is not the case, then what we have here is a symbolic representation of a battle of spirit beings in heaven which was actualized on earth as Satan attempted to destroy the Christ-child two thousand years ago.

At verse six, however, the scene leaps forward by at least

three thousand years to the conclusion of this on-going battle, to the time of the tribulation after the millennium. God's prophesies often leap great periods of time. And now (12:7) there is another battle of spirit beings going on in heaven. It is Michael and his angelic host meeting Satan and his fallen angelic host, fresh from the bottomless pit, for a final showdown. This accords with Daniel's account of Michael during the tribulation, just a short time prior to the general resurrection (Dan. 12:1-3). I speculate, then, that when Satan was released from the bottomless pit after the millennium (9:2), he carried his rage straight to the courts of heaven (12:7). Then, being unable to be king of heaven and being cast out by Michael, he immediately brought his rage to earth and vented it against God's people in his last, short, desperate attempt to be king of the earth (12:10-13). He met the righteous resistance of the saints (12:11; 11:3-7) and the providential plagues of God in response to their prayers (9:1-11:18; 20:7-10) — resulting in final defeat at the last trump.

Unit 8 (13:1-18)

I have already defined the nature of the entity presented here under the image of the seven-headed beast (13:1-3) and have given a general outline of its career including his revival after the millennium (Chapter 4). I have not, however, dealt with the latter part of chapter thirteen from verse six to the end.

A very important aspect of the tribulation period and the revived "beast's" rise to power is here presented. Recalling that the "beast" with all its heads represents the great world-wide kingdoms, I want to review briefly my previous interpretation of the wounding and revival of the seventh head of the beast. It is "wounded to death" when Satan, the power behind all the world-wide political powers, is bound and cast into the bottomless pit. I know this because 1) he cannot energize the beast (13:2) at that time, and 2) as soon as he comes out of the bottomless pit, the beast is alive and well again (17:8f; 9:1f).

Now this gives us a benchmark in time to interpret the rest of chapter thirteen. Therefore, after the deadly wound is healed (13:3) the rest of the events of the chapter (13:3-18) occur after the millennium. This conclusion correlates well with the fact that the familiar 42 months of verse five fall during the tribulation as we have seen from chapter eleven. Furthermore, the same idea is introduced that the beast blasphemes every holy thing and makes war with the saints, overcomes them, and gains a world-wide following of the unbelieving world (13:6-8).

Another element is introduced in verse eleven that we have not directly encountered under the trumpets. That is a religious element in alliance with the beast, and this is probably the purpose of chapter 13 — to present this aspect of the work of Satan in the tribulation. Another "beast" comes up, not out of the "sea" as the first (13:1), but out of the "earth" (13:11). He doubtless will be an influential apostate church leader — rising out of the "earth." This new beast is elsewhere called a "false prophet" (19:20), and his function is to promote and religiously validate the political beast and his program to the people (13:12-17). As I have previously discussed, every successful political movement must have the blessings of religion or else it must be purely military and tyrannical. The revived beast, having such a short time to rise to world dominion, uses every means — military, political, economic, and religious tyranny. The thing is reminiscent of the Holy Roman Empire and differs only in degree, not in essence.[16] But by these means the beast's rise to power will be spectacular, and the world will "wonder after the beast."

I do not know what the mark of the beast is (13:16, 17), nor do I know what the number 666 means (13:18). I do not know anyone who does know. I know what the Bible says about salvation, and the saved will never receive that mark whether it be visible or invisible. Those who need to know will

---

[16] The ancient symbiosis of the state-church union returns after the millennium albeit in a different form, and the great harlot once again assumes her position on the back of the beast for their mutual benefit (cf. Rev. 17:1f).

be able to discern it. Millions of dollars have been fleeced from the fearful and the ignorant by those who live by speculating on the sensational — especially the mark of the beast. Since the "beast" has been around since long before the time of Christ, the mark has either been in existence since the origin of the beast or else it will be originated at some later time in history. If the mark is some invisible distinction, it may be presently worn by many of our unbelieving acquaintances (contrast 7:3; 9:4 and 13:16, 17; 20:4). I do not see a visible mark on any of God's people and feel it would be out of character with God to do that. Hence the mark of the beast may be invisible also. Yet I will never voluntarily receive a visible mark on my skin to identify me as a worshipper of the beast. If the mark is a visibly displayed distinction, it will doubtless be originated at a future time. Certainly it will be in existence in the tribulation (13:16, 17), but it would probably originate with Satan's next great effort for world supremacy just prior to the millennium (cf. Rev. 20:4). I have a feeling though, that the mark of the beast may be some invisible distinction, known to God but yet to be discerned by men.

Unit 9 (14:1-5)

Again we encounter the 144,000 which were first mentioned in the parenthetical chapter seven. At that time this perfect square number multiplied a thousand times — this special number of special people — were sealed or marked by God for some special reason. This was done before the providential winds of God began to blow (7:1-3). These people were marked, in the foreknowledge of God, while on earth — or perhaps before the foundation of the world.

Now in the passage before us, they have finished their earthly sojourn, have passed through death, and stand with the Lamb on Mount Zion (this is the heavenly Jerusalem, see Heb. 12:22, 23) — still marked for special treatment (14:1). Now in heaven "redeemed *from the earth*," they sing a special song that only they can learn (14:2, 3). Why this special mark? Not all the saved have it. Why the special distinction? The secret is their character, and the distinction is part of a special reward.

Their character is described as follows:

1. Not defiled with women, virgins. This does not imply celibacy, for the marriage bed is not defiled (Heb. 13:4), but moral and doctrinal purity — not fornicators morally or spiritually.

2. They followed the Lamb "whithersoever he goeth." Christ was obedient even to death. These true disciples were likewise. "If any man will come after me, let him deny himself, and take up his cross, and follow me. For whosoever will save his life shall lose it: and whosoever will lose his life for my sake shall find it" (Matt. 16:24, 25).

3. These were "redeemed from among men being *the first-fruits unto God and to the Lamb.*" These have been resurrected and glorified in heaven with God and with Christ. Christ also is called the *firstfruits* of the resurrection (1 Cor. 15:20, 23). He was the very first to be glorified from death, but there is a "first resurrection" (Rev. 20:4, 5) prior to the millennium comprised only of those who had given their lives for Christ. I have discussed these before (see Chapter 2). I believe this 144,000 is the same identical group of martyrs that were "under the altar" (6:9-11), "sealed" (7:3-8), and resurrected prior to the millennium; they "lived and reigned with Christ" during this glorious time when the cause for which they died is vindicated fully.

4. They are guileless and faultless "before the throne of God" (14:5; 20:4).

Then what of the martyrs after the millennium? They, too, share in a special resurrection prior to the general resurrection (Rev. 11:11, 12).

Now this interpretation is not rigorous, but it is reasonable. Yet I would not be dogmatic about relating this group to the group in 20:4. I feel, however, that we have quite rigorous evidence that chapter 14 shows the resurrected heavenly state of the same group sealed in chapter 7.

Unit 10 (14:6-20)

Concerning this passage, I will say only that it is another

parallel view of warnings to the wicked and encouragement to the saints (14:6-13), leading up to a rather symbolic picture of Christ's second coming to reap, "for the harvest of the earth is ripe" (14:14-20). It is another parallel view of the revelation of Christ.

Unit 11 (15:1-16:21)

This unit introduces another parallel set of seven events. They are called plagues (15:6). The events under the three "woes" were also called "plagues" (9:20), but this set of seven is further distinguished as the "last plagues" (15:1). In this set of plagues is "filled up the wrath of God," or "the wrath of God is complete" (15:1, NKJV), so they are set toward the end of the great tribulation, before the seventh trumpet. These plagues are executed by seven angels having seven vials, or bowls, "full of the wrath of God" (15:6, 7); and being the "last plagues" they would be poured out very near the end, just before the revelation of Christ.

Introductory to the pouring out of these plagues, we are allowed to glimpse a marvelous scene in heaven. There is a sea of glass. Standing on this sea of glass are those who had been victorious over the beast (15:2). They have harps and sing the song of Moses and the Lamb (15:3), just as Israel rejoiced in the wilderness after having been delivered from Pharaoh (Ex. 15:1-19).

Remember, the general resurrection has not yet occurred for these are the "last plagues" about to be poured out. Who then are these on the sea of glass delivered from the beast? Probably these are the resurrected martyrs, the 144,000 as well as the tribulational martyrs, from the Jerusalem church, and perhaps other churches, the "two witnesses" who stood faithful before the beast and gave their lives (11:2-7). But these "firstfruits" are resurrected (11:11, 12) and now rejoice in the anticipation of the final round of battle as the providential fires of God's judgment are intensified by the vials to a white heat, an unbearable pitch, on the beast, the false prophet, and those who follow them.[17]

---

[17] The premillennial view holds the tribulation period to be God's wrath

The scenario on earth is this: The witnesses of Jerusalem are resurrected and in heaven (11:11, 12). The rest of the churches are in the "wilderness" in relative safety (12:6, 14-16). After the resurrection of the saints at Jerusalem and the earthquake, some of the people began to see the truth and "gave glory to the God of heaven" (11:13). The zenith of the beast's popularity has past; his power is slipping. The forty-two months of power and glory are behind him. But Satan now drives the "man of sin" to a desperation-effort as these final plagues begin to fall, and their efforts will all end in Armageddon (16:13, 14, 16).

The scenes of chapter fifteen are preparatory, and now the orders are given:

> And I heard a great voice out of the temple saying to the seven angels, Go your ways, and pour out the vials of the wrath of God upon the earth (Rev. 16:1).

The vials, in John's vision, follow in rapid succession, i.e., John sees them in succession; they may, however, be executed synchronously or in parallel. They are short and intense. The effect is total and complete. It is important to notice that the objects of each of the first four respective vials are the same as that of the first four respective trumpets, but the trumpets were only partial in effect (one-third part). The effect of the vials is total. The vials are poured out on: 1) the earth, 2) the sea, 3) rivers and fountains. Notice the comment of the angel: "They [the rivers and fountains — polluted streams or religious institutions professing to give the water of life] have shed the blood of saints and prophets, and thou hast given them blood to drink; for they are worthy" (16:6). Literal rivers

---

on Israel. Nothing could be further from the truth. They bore their trouble scattered among the nations, in the death camps of Germany during World War 2, and in many other such times of suffering since being scattered in 70 A.D. But they are even now partially regathered, and prior to the millennium, will be converted. The past nearly two thousand years has been and still is the day of "Jacob's trouble" (Jer. 30:7-11). After their conversion God will not hide his face from them any more (Ezk. 39:29). In the tribulation God's wrath is poured upon the beast and his followers, not upon Israel.

and fountains do not shed the blood of saints. This institution of religion is "great Babylon" revived under the "false prophet" (13:11; 19:20) after the millennium now totally and wholly corrupt. The vials continue to be poured on 4) the sun, 5) the beast himself, or the "man of sin" (cf. 2 Thess. 2:3-9), and 6) the river Euphrates. The kings of the east get involved (see Dan. 11:44, 45).

At this point a strange thing happens. They are about defeated, but in desperation Satan, the beast, and the false prophet confer and agree upon a plan out of their "mouths" (16:13). They enlist the aid of every demonic power and spirit under the jurisdiction of Satan. They go to every king in the whole world and persuade them to contribute armies and equipment for the use of the beast in one gigantic stand against God and all that is righteous (16:14). A warning sounds, for Christ is about to come upon them as a thief (16:15; cf. 2 Pet. 3:10; 1 Thess. 5:2).

The army is gathered in a place not far from Jerusalem called Armageddon (16:16). Then simultaneously at least three prophecies are fulfilled: 1) the sixth seal is opened (6:12-17), 2) the seventh trumpet sounds (11:15-19), and 3) the seventh vial is poured out (16:17-21). This is the end:

> Immediately after the tribulation of those days shall the sun be darkened, and the moon shall not give her light, and the stars shall fall from heaven, and the powers of the heavens shall be shaken: And then shall appear the sign of the Son of man in heaven: and then shall all the tribes of the earth mourn, and they shall see the Son of man coming in the clouds of heaven with power and great glory. And he shall send his angels with a great sound of a trumpet, and they shall gather together his elect from the four winds, from one end of heaven to the other (Matt. 24:29-31).

The dead in Christ will rise (1 Cor. 15:52; 1 Thess. 4:16); the living saints, from their wilderness havens around the world (Rev. 12:6, 14-16) will be caught up (1 Thess. 4:17). The beast, "the man of sin," and the hordes following him will perish in the holocaust (2 Thess. 1:8, 9; 2:8-12; 2 Pet. 3:10; Rev. 6:12f; 11:15-19; 14:14-20; 16:21; 19:19-21; 20:9, 10) only to be

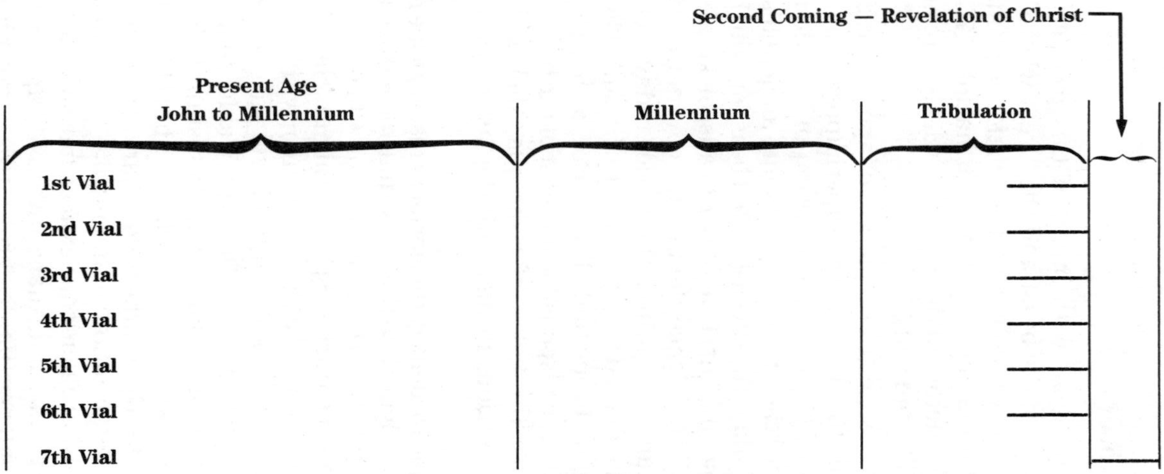

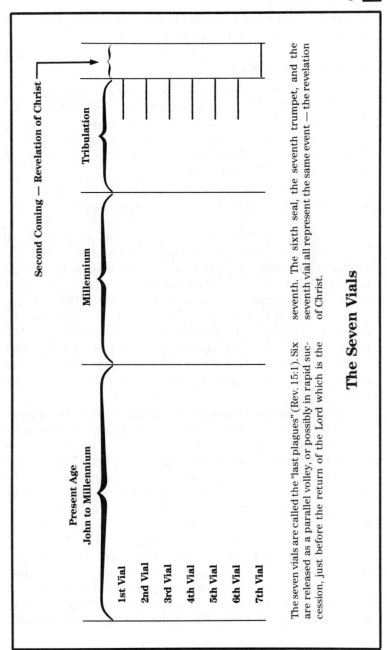

The seven vials are called the "last plagues" (Rev. 15:1). Six are released as a parallel volley, or possibly in rapid succession, just before the return of the Lord which is the seventh. The sixth seal, the seventh trumpet, and the seventh vial all represent the same event — the revelation of Christ.

The Seven Vials

resurrected for judgment and execution which occurs under the seventh seal (Rev. 8:1; 20:11-15).

Unit 12 (17:1-18:24)

I have already dealt with much of this passage in a previous discussion of the beast and the "great whore" (for this connection review Chapter 4). This section is primarily an account of the judgment of the great harlot (17:1). It recapitulates some details of the events which also are noted under the trumpets and vials.

17:1-6. This passage gives a picture of apostate religion which has, since history began, been superimposed upon the political systems of the world. This vision of "Babylon the Great," as apostate religion, reaches back into ancient history long before John's day. The seven-headed beast on which the harlot rides is also ancient. Five of the heads, or kings, had already fallen (17:10). Hence the picture covers the whole scope of history and the future. The harlot today includes (but should not be limited to) apostate "Christian" religions whether Catholic or Protestant. This harlot, as a universal phenomenon, has been responsible for most of the bloodshed of the saints since the blood of righteous Abel and will continue to be, in various forms, until the last martyr falls (17:6; 13:15).

It is very simple to identify the harlot in history. One need only look for the religious institutions that have instigated religious persecution on the followers of Christ. In the western world for centuries, starting about the fourth century, the apostate Catholic church in union with the state has been the consistent persecutor of the succession of Christians best described as the Donatist-Waldensian-Anabaptist-Baptist succession. During the Protestant Reformation, the "mother of harlots" (Rev. 17:5) gave birth to several daughters. True to their inherited characteristics; the daughters of the Reformation, in union with the state, also joined the persecution against the exact same succession of Christians, called at that time Anabaptists and Baptists. God, in His kind providence finally broke this state church relationship, and gave His people relief, in most of the western nations.

It is unequivocal, therefore, that in the western world, the *persecutor* has predominantly been the Catholic-Protestant succession, and the *persecutee* has predominantly been the Donatist-Waldensian-Anabaptist-Baptist succession (cf. Rev. 17:6).

This conclusion does not come from dark and mysterious lore. The concept of the "great whore" mounted upon the "beast" — church upon state — is a biblical and historical concept very clearly discernable to those who study history and the Bible. The language used, e.g., "mother of harlots," "great whore," "with whom the kings of the earth have committed fornication," "drunken with the blood of the saints," etc., is biblical language. We do not need more data than what is apparent by a casual study of the massive witness of history, to identify and distinguish the historical embodiment of this biblical symbology. The failure of learned Christian leaders today to acknowledge this identity borders on intellectual dishonesty, not to mention spiritual guile. Hence, God calls, "come out of her, my people" (Rev. 18:4).

17:7. This verse is an outline of the passage to follow in inverted order: the mystery of 1) the woman and 2) the beast carrying her. The beast is explained first (17:8-14) and the woman second (17:15-18:24).

17:8-14. For explanation of this passage, review the detailed discussion of the beast in Chapter 4.

17:15-18:24. The significant thing about this passage is that, like the beast, this religious "Babylon" (17:5) or "great whore" (17:1, 15) has an existence prior to the millennium (17:1-6) as well as after the millennium (13:11-15), but the institutional embodiment is not the same. Hence it is likely that 17:15-18:24 should be considered as the general career of apostate religion of every kind and interpreted as having a double, or perhaps we should say a split, fulfillment. The effect of this "Babylon" is predominantly felt in the long ages before the millennium, but it is revived for the short term after the millennium.

There will be the demise of the present apostate churches[18] prior to the millennium (17:16-18), but the final apostate system arising after the millennium under the false prophet (13:11-18) will be destroyed at the return of Christ (14:8; 16:19; 19:20). At the present time many of God's people — saved people — are mixed up in the harlot denominations. They ought to "come out of her" before they are forced out (18:4).

18:1-24. This passage is a general description of "Babylon the Great" and her character and fall. This passage, while possibly having a double fulfillment, seems to be more fully descriptive of the apostate religions prior to the millennium. Their demise will be rapid as the political and military build-up of the "would-be" or "hopeful" beast, prior to the millennium, reaches its climax and turns against the harlot through the ten horns (17:16-18). Chapter eighteen details her fall and the world reaction to it.

Unit 13 (19:1-10)

This is a picture of the reaction of the saints in heaven at the final defeat of the "great whore" (19:2). It is their exclamation of praise for the final victory over this ancient foe and persecutor of the true churches, and their anticipation of the "marriage supper of the Lamb" (19:7-10). I consider this "marriage supper" to be the same occasion described elsewhere as the great festal gathering, the "general assembly" (Heb. 12:22, 23).

---

[18] John's account of the destruction of "the whore" (Rev. 17:16) assigns this action to the "ten horns" under the influence of God (v. 17). The ten horns grow out of the sixth head of the beast (see chart, p. 93) and correspond to the toes of Daniel's statue (Dan. 2) and the fourth beast (Dan. 7:7, 8, 19-21). The ten horns, as we have formerly seen, are the European kingdoms of the disintegrated Roman empire. As the seventh-head leader begins his rise to power prior to the millennium (probably from among the ten horns), the European nations will be in league with him (Rev. 17:13). It will be to their advantage to get the "great whore" off their backs. Now institutional religion in the western world is predominantly Catholic and Protestant, especially in Europe. Therefore, we may look for the demise of these historic institutions as the conflict intensifies just prior to the millennium.

Unit 14 (19:11-21)

This is another view parallel to the sixth seal, the seventh or last trumpet, and the seventh vial. It is a somewhat symbolic picture (the white horses) of the second coming of Christ. The beast, as in the other parallel views of this time, is overcome and consigned to the lake of fire (cf. 2 Thess. 2:8).

Unit 15 (20:1-10)

This passage is unique in all the Scriptures in that it is the only place that gives any details about the length (1,000 years) and basic cause (the binding of Satan) of what we call the millennium (20:2). Read the passage carefully and see; there is not a hint that the "thrones" (20:4) or the "souls" of the martyred saints or their "reign with Christ" is on earth. Christ remains at the right hand of God until the time when His last enemy, which is death, is to finally become His footstool, and that event by no means occurs until after the millennium (see 20:7-9).

The salient features of this passage, to one who reads the Scriptures carefully, should be easy to discern. This is a distinctive vision, no continuity with chapter 19, as indicated by the familiar refrain, "And I saw . . . . " Then verses 1-3 provide the terminal bracket for the beginning of the millennium, and verse seven provides the terminal bracket for the end. Clearly, therefore, in the mind of God the primary and essential event to pave the way for that powerful and protracted world-wide revival is the binding of Satan. When Satan is bound, the millennium ensues — beginning with the conversion of the Jews, as we have seen, and the overspreading of the world with righteousness.

It is foolish to speculate about the "physical" whereabouts of the "bottomless pit" or whether it or the "chain" with which Satan is bound is literal. Since Satan is a spirit being, it is far more compatible with the broad theology of Scripture to understand this binding as a spiritual conflict in which God decommissions, overwhelms, confines, and imprisons Satan in order to allow His own sovereign purposes to come to fruition. Among those purposes is doubtless to demonstrate and document for the eternal record that Satan, and the propensity of men to follow him, is at the root of the deep persistent sin, and the grievous convulsions of human history.

Once Satan has been decommissioned and confined, the power of the Holy Spirit with the Gospel is more than an adequate cause for the millennial conditions. The premillennial claim that the conversion of the world is "impossible" without the physical presence of Christ is absolutely groundless. To the contrary, if there is any validity to the words of Jesus that "it is expedient that I go away," the agency of the Holy Spirit working through the church proclaiming the Gospel is a more expedient agency for winning the world than Jesus on earth localized to a body. Any ruling Jesus could do from earth could also be done from heaven. The binding of Satan will make a difference in the power of the Gospel that will astonish the greatest optimist among us.

Verse four describes a resurrection of a special group of martyrs. I have discussed this group and the "first resurrection" (vs. 5, 6) in Chapter 2. But verse four carelessly read and erroneously preached has become the basis of the widespread belief by laymen that "the Bible says Christ will reign on earth." Nowhere does the Bible teach that Christ will reign from a location on earth, least of all here. It is a grievous thing when well-meaning preachers mislead people by such loose and careless handling of Scripture.

By now we are familiar with the "little season" (v. 3), "short space" (17:10), or "short time" (12:12) that follows the loosing of Satan from the bottomless pit. Verses 20:7-10 are a brief summary of that period of time. This period corresponds to the great tribulation which is expanded and described in considerable detail in Revelation 9:1 through 11:19 and in other places as well. These passages establish clearly that the great tribulation follows the millennium and supports the discussion under the "First Rigorous Propositional Truth" that the tribulation is the last event in the history of this present earth (see discussion of Matthew 24:29f in Chapter 2).

While we are considering 20:7-10, we should take note of

a minority position among premillennialists that the millennium does not take place on this present cursed earth, but rather on the "new heaven and new earth" (21:1).

It is difficult to see why anyone who has read Revelation 20-22 carefully, or even casually, would hold this position. In the "new heaven and new earth," the following conditions prevail eternally:

God dwells with men (21:3). There is "*no more* death," no sorrow, crying, or pain (21:4). Righteousness dwells therein (2 Pet. 3:13). There will be "no more curse" (22:3).

Now if the millennium is in the "new heaven and new earth," then after a thousand years Satan is loosed to enter this perfectly holy place which God has restored to its pristine purity and to pollute it for a second time (20:7). He goes out on this perfect earth and deceives all nations (20:8a); he gathers them to battle against the "beloved city," now the new Jerusalem, and God, who resides in the new Jerusalem (21:22, 23), rains fire and brimstone from "heaven" to kill all the nations in the new earth! And only after this pollution of the new heaven and new earth is Satan cast into the lake of fire (20:10)!

In the name of common sense, how far will men wrest the Scriptures to protect a position? This view contradicts practically every line of Rev. 21, 22, not to speak of the entire theology of the Word of God.

Now I want to discuss the relationship of chapter 19 to chapter 20. Perhaps the strongest argument in the Bible for the premillennial position is the sequence of chapter 19, with the second coming of Christ, just preceding chapter 20 which introduces the millennium. That was the last ground I surrendered, along with Zachariah 14, when the rest of the Scriptures forced me from premillennialism. But after seeing so clearly that several parallel views of the terminal event or the second coming had already been presented in Revelation, some of them following the release of Satan from the bottomless pit, I finally gave up trying to force the rest of the Bible into harmony with these two misinterpreted passages. When I was able to accept chapter 19 as it obviously is, parallel to others preceding it in Revelation, as well as chapter 20 following it, then everything fell into place and became perfectly coherent.

I have already belabored the point that verses seven and eight in chapter twenty comprise a brief description of the tribulation (which is elaborately detailed under the "woes" and vials — 9:1f; 16:1f). Verses nine and ten are a brief description of the final advent or second coming of Christ as it relates to the destruction of Satan and the beast. It is parallel to 19:19, 20.

It is easy to demonstrate that the events of 19:19, 20 are parallel to those of 20:8-10:

1. The beast, under the leadership of Satan, has gathered a great army (19:19; 20:8).

2. This army-gathering, world-battling, and God-fighting activity of Satan and the beast follows his release from the bottomless pit (9:2; 11:7; 13:3-8; 16:14, 16; 17:8, 11-14; 19:19; 20:8; see also Ezk. 38:18, 22). Anyone who will take the time to compare these passages carefully will see that all of them follow the release of Satan from the bottomless pit after the millennium; all of them involve a gathering of armies against Jerusalem (cf. 11:2, 8 — the holy city, the great city, where Christ was crucified; 16:16 — Armageddon;[19] 20:9 — the beloved city).

3. The result in all these cases is the destruction of the beast, the false prophet, the devil and all who follow them. They are all cast into the "lake of fire" (19:20; 20:10, 14, 15).

Some have supposed that the statement: "and the devil . . . was cast into the lake of fire and brimstone where the beast and the false prophet *are* . . . " (20:10) is proof that the casting in of the beast and false prophet (19:20) was done a thousand years before. This passage (19:20) implies they

---

[19] If Armageddon refers to the ancient site of Megiddo, it is probably the location of the massive concentration of military forces from which the attacks against Jerusalem are launched. It may, however, be used only symbolically as the scene of the final battle (Jerusalem), for Megiddo is a famous battleground.

were "taken" right on the battlefield and "cast alive" into the lake of fire without dying in the holocaust of fire from heaven (20:9), whereas Satan was doubtless cast in later. It is therefore likely that the beast and false prophet were already in the lake of fire before Satan; but that this casting in occurred a thousand years before cannot be the case.

Furthermore, the Greek word *ὅπου* (translated "where") does not necessarily mean that the beast and false prophet were already in the lake of fire but only means the "place where" Satan, the beast, and the false prophet were cast is the same place. It should be noticed that the word "are" (20:10) is in italics. This was not in the original text and was supplied by the translator. It is significant that this is the only place in the New Testament where a verb does not follow soon after *ὅπου*. The absence of the verb, if we believe in verbal plenary inspiration, is deliberate. It could be added as possibly: *are*, *were cast*, or *are being cast*, or even *to be cast*. It is an interpretation by the translator. I think the evidence is that the true intent of the Holy Spirit in the absence of the verb was to project the idea that the devil, the beast, and the false prophet were all cast together in the same place. Perhaps the best translation would be that the devil "was cast into the lake of fire and brimstone *with* the beast and the false prophet," without any reference to time or sequence of casting. It is a peculiar use of *ὅπου* without a verb following, and it must be for the purpose above suggested.

One thing is certain, the verb *are* added by the translators is certainly not sufficient to prove that the beast, etc., was cast into the lake of fire a thousand years before Satan. More likely they were cast in before Satan, and the *are* is probably right. But if so, all other evidence makes it certain that it was only a short while before, not a thousand years.

Unit 16 (20:11-15)

In the ominous and mysterious comment under the opening of the seventh seal, "there was silence in heaven about the space of half an hour" (8:1), there is a sense of foreboding of an awful event. It should be obvious from the nature of the seals and the fact that Christ Himself opens them, in contrast to the fact that angels introduce the trumpets and vials, that the seals are all-comprehensive. They begin with the purpose of Christ to conquer and He does conquer (6:2). They end with this ominous and somber note in heaven (8:1) implying that His conquering purpose is at an end. The final event in winding up the affairs of the earth is the judgment of all, "small and great," and the execution of the penalty on the guilty. In the section under the general judgment (Chapter 2), I have discussed the principles to be served by a great general judgment where all the intelligent beings of the universe are present; where every knee shall finally bow, every voice will finally be silenced, and the whole plan and purpose of God will be vindicated.

This occasion called the great white throne judgment (20:11-15) is the general judgment and is parallel to Matthew 25:31f and other less detailed passages.

Unit 17 (21:1-22:20)

These two final chapters give us a picture of the eternal state. The new heaven and new earth, spoken of by Peter (2 Pet. 3:13), follow the destruction of this present universe comprised of the heavens and the earth at the revelation of Christ. I will not make a detailed explanation of these chapters, since they do not add much, if any, toward establishing a framework of eschatology relative to Christ's second advent. Almost everyone acknowledges these chapters describe the new heaven and new earth, and follow the second advent of Christ.

Now that we have completed this study of Revelation, it would be profitable to look at the major providential events as symbolized by the seals, trumpets, and vials in relation to each other. In Cluster Study 10 on page 237, this comparison is made.

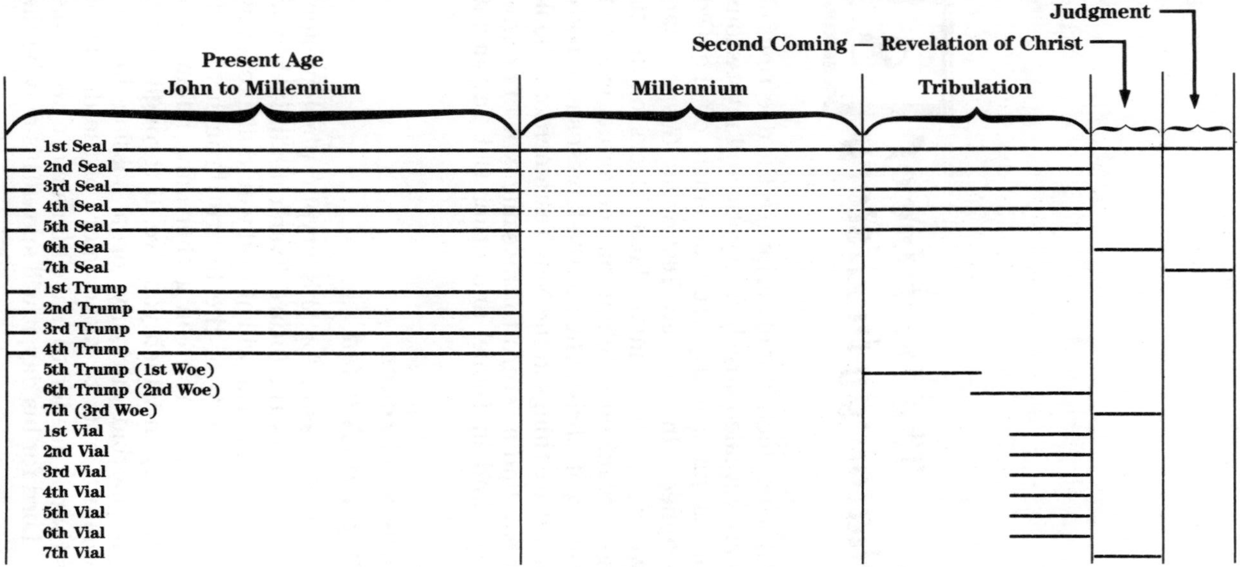

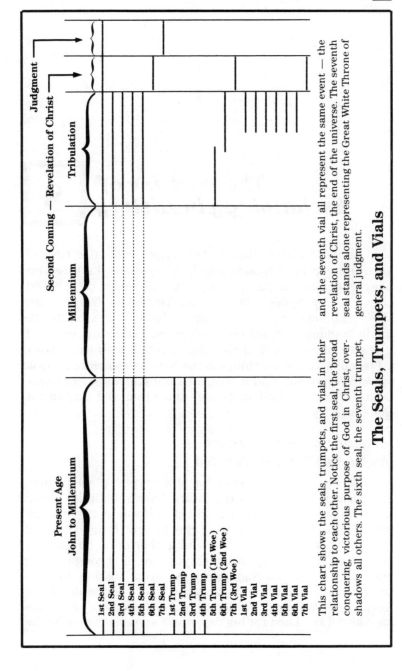

This chart shows the seals, trumpets, and vials in their relationship to each other. Notice the first seal, the broad conquering, victorious purpose of God in Christ, overshadows all others. The sixth seal, the seventh trumpet, and the seventh vial all represent the same event — the revelation of Christ, the end of the universe. The seventh seal stands alone representing the Great White Throne of general judgment.

The Seals, Trumpets, and Vials

The Doctrine of Eschatology in History 8

Unlike the other doctrines of Scripture, the doctrines of future things are revealed largely in cryptic and mysterious language. This is particularly true of much of the Old Testament prophecy. In the New Testament *Gospels* and *Epistles*, however, we have many large blocks of direct, plain-language, organized teaching on the actual event of the second coming of Christ. Then in the largest single body of teaching on future things in the New Testament, the book of *Revelation*, we find a return to the same type of cryptic writing that we find in Daniel and other Old Testament passages.

Cryptic Codes are Broken by God's People as Needed

Now there is a reason for this cryptic phenomenon. Everyone wants to know the future. Even rank infidels who have no interest at all in the will of God would like to know the future. But knowledge of the future through biblical prophecy is like manna. You can gather only the amount you need for the day in which you live. If through greed, carnal intrigue, morbid curiosity, or a passion for the sensational, one attempts to gather more of the details of future events than is needed to make him a more profitable servant of the Lord for his day, it will spoil. This may be the reason so many hold on to spoiled and corrupt systems of eschatology. We can have what we need, but what we do not need is skillfully hidden by the Holy Spirit in cryptic revelation. Now, however, two thousand years after the apostles said "it is the last time" (1 John 2:18), the need is upon us to settle at least the true framework of prophecy. Surely the millennium cannot be too far distant; and if we enter that period with the wrong understanding, it will be a great handicap to the work of the Lord and a serious problem for God's people.

As the events of history unfold, more and more we will be facing events that were once prophecy. As this continues, the codes can be broken to meet current needs; data are now available to help us see more clearly the meaning of the cryptic prophetic writings. Consider, for example, Daniel's situation. Although Daniel received and wrote some of the most significant prophecies of Scripture, we cannot miss his great consternation at being unable to understand the meaning of what he had written:

> And I heard, but I understood not: then said I, O my Lord, what shall be the end of these things? And he said, Go thy way, Daniel: for the words are closed up and sealed till the time of the end (Dan. 12:8, 9; see also 8:26, 27).[1]

Since the days of Daniel, history itself has helped us to see what is meant by much of what he wrote; e.g., Daniel 8:8f has seen partial fulfillment in the career of Antiochus Epiphanes, but the language of the passage looks, in type, beyond him to a future "man of sin" by Telescopic Prophetic Vision. Yet we are able to learn much in principle concerning the final "antichrist" by observing the nature of the prototype Antiochus.

But Daniel himself did not have this advantage. However, when the Jews, in the days of the Maccabees were under

---

[1] This passage and others clearly demonstrate the biblical principle that the development of a complete doctrine of eschatology is a long-range thing related to the needs of God's people and the development of God's purpose in time.

the cruel tyranny of Antiochus, they were emboldened to accomplish mighty deeds of valor by this much-needed "manna" for their own day.

So it goes. God in infinite love and wisdom has written prophecy which will come clear to those who stand in need of the knowledge, but not for the curiously idle or for the sensation seekers.

Sudden Early Development of a Full New Testament Eschatology was Not Feasible

It is clear from these things that the writers of Scripture did not always fully understand their own writings (1 Pet. 1:10-12). Peter remarks of Paul's prophetic writings that some things are "hard to be understood" (2 Pet. 3:16). Then too, they did not have the advantage of having the completed Scriptures. Significantly, God waited until last, after most of the apostles and early Christians had passed off the scene, to reveal the final chapter and perhaps the most significant body of prophecy in all the Scriptures — the book of Revelation.

This teaches us two significant things: 1) Even though each of the apostles perfectly understood what they taught, it is probable that none of them, with the possible exception of John, after receiving Revelation, had a full-blown, organized understanding of future things. Most of them died before Revelation was written. 2) It is certain that among the early church fathers of the first and second centuries, there was no mature, biblically organized doctrinal body of New Testament eschatology. So far from having arrived at an organized understanding of the prophetic truths found in the *Gospels*, the *Epistles*, and the *Revelation*, many of them were still trying to decide which of these books, especially Revelation, belonged in the canon of Scripture.

As we shall later see, those who set forth any early system of eschatology borrowed the salient features from the errors of the Jews. They just did not have the completed Scriptures to guide them. Moreover, it takes time — dialogue, thesis, antithesis, and generally synthesis — to arrive at a sound systematized body of major doctrinal truth. For the first two or three centuries after the death of Christ the questions concerning the incarnation of God in Christ and the question of the canon of the New Testament Scriptures preoccupied the churches primarily. Ecclesiology and eschatology became secondary issues in the latter half of the second and most of the third centuries.

Any elaborate system of eschatology set forth prior to the completion of and agreement upon the New Testament canon of Scripture should have been, and was, suspect. The earliest books of the New Testament — the synoptic Gospels and certain of the Pauline epistles — dealt primarily with the person and work of Christ and the nature of the churches as localized entities responsible for the spread of the Gospel. Eschatology is mentioned in these, but only in the basic, necessary truths that Christ would return, raise the dead, and judge the world. No millennium is mentioned in these early documents.

Any reliable systematic correlation of these New Testament truths with Old Testament prophecy had to await the final chapter of God's revelation to man, and then there would need to be time to digest it. When the New Testament was complete near the turn of the second century, it would yet be almost a century before any extensive biblical dialogue on the subject of eschatology would begin.

I do not mean by this that no one had proposed a system of eschatology — they had. But as might be expected, a system formulated before all the data was in would be in error and would be a disappointment to the more careful and objective saints. Such was the case. A few of the early Christians seized upon the Jewish notion that the messianic reign would be an earthly, corporeal reign from Jerusalem in a kingdom of this world. They would reign with Christ a thousand years in luxury and power over the nations of the world. When the book of Revelation furnished, for the Christian, a time frame for the millennium — a thousand years (Rev. 20) — those who had already borrowed the Jewish system seized upon the concept of a millennium and "christianized" the Jewish concept of an earthly messianic king. This became known as Chiliasm from the Greek *χιλιάσ* (from which is derived our prefix *kilo*, a thousand). Christ, in this view, would return to this present earth and establish an earthly monarchy over sinful, flesh-and-blood men for a thousand years. I will treat this development more fully later.

While some few held this notion prior to the rise and spread of the Montanist movement (latter second century), which was Chiliasts almost to a man, it was not much of an issue. But when this view grew widespread toward the end of the second century, many other churches began a dialogue against it. By the end of the third century Chiliasm, or premillennialism, once again had relatively few voices, and became a non-issue until the nineteenth century.

Presently I want to examine the eschatology of the early Christian writers and briefly discuss the development of this doctrine from the first century until now. But first I want to take note of the contemporary efforts on the part of premillennial writers to press down upon the Christian world the false notion that premillennialism was the official position of the early church — full-blown, direct from the apostles themselves.

Was Premillennialism the Universal Faith of the Early Church?

What then must we make of the extravagant claims popularly presented by premillennial writers that " . . . premillennial belief was the *universal* [Pentecost's italics] belief of the church for two hundred and fifty years after the death of Christ"?[2] Then Charles Ryrie wrote:

> Premillennialism is the historic faith of the Church. To prove that statement is the purpose of this chapter.[3]

---

[2] J. Dwight Pentecost, *Things to Come* (Findlay, Ohio: Dunham Publishing Co., 1958), p. 374.

[3] Charles C. Ryrie, *The Basis of the Premillennial Faith* (Neptune, New Jersey: Loizeaux Brothers), p. 17.

Both Ryrie and Pentecost then list a number of the early church fathers whom they present as proof of the claim.

Henry Thiessen also made this claim, prior to Ryrie or Pentecost, both in three articles in *Bibliotheca Sacra*[4] and in his *Lectures in Systematic Theology.*[5] All of these and others make reference to essentially the same list of works, which list I will examine in some detail below. But suffice it to say at this point that some premillennialist treatment of the historical evidence and of the beliefs of the early "fathers" on this issue is, I will say, highly misleading, that I might not say deceitful.

Eschatology until A.D. 150

The apostles themselves as we have already seen, held a simple, direct eschatology: 1) Christ reigns at God's right hand, until 2) the time when He returns to destroy the world and to put all enemies under His feet, including death, at 3) the resurrection of the dead, rapture of the saints, and 4) the general judgment of all men small and great; after which 5) the righteous will dwell with Him forever in a new heaven and new earth, and 6) the wicked will be consigned to the lake of fire forever. These are the salient features of New Testament eschatology prior to the writing of Revelation. It is true that Paul introduced the "man of sin" and Matthew the great tribulation. All this was wholly compatible with what John would later write. Then, as a very old man, John the Apostle received the book of Revelation, just about the turn of the second century. In this last prophetic work the concept of the millennium is first introduced to New Testament writings, but with very little elaboration.

Now, those who lived or wrote in the first or near the turn of the second century are going to reflect either this simple direct apostolic eschatology, or they will reflect an

---

[4] Henry C. Thiessen, "Will the Church Pass Through the Tribulation?", *Bibliotheca Sacra*, XCII, 1, 2, 3 (1937).

[5] Henry C. Thiessen, *Introductory Lectures in Systematic Theology* (Grand Rapids: Wm. B. Eerdmans Pub. Co., 1949), pp. 475-478.

eschatology, derived from "Jewish fables," not from the apostles.

I want to introduce now seven names or documents from this period. Five of these are mentioned by Ryrie[6] as proof of his claim that premillennialism is the historic faith of the early church. I will consider them in two groups: The first group reflects a simple, direct eschatology as do the apostolic writings. There are four of these, namely:

1. Clement, bishop of the church at Rome, A.D. 91-100. He wrote a letter to the Corinthians, A.D. 95-96.

2. Ignatius, bishop of the church at Antioch, who was martyred in Rome, A.D. 107-110. As he traveled from Antioch to Rome to be executed, he wrote letters to six churches along the way, and one to Polycarp, as follows:

"To the Ephesians"
"To the Magnesians"
"To the Trallians"
"To the Romans"
"To the Philadelphians"
"To the Smyrnaens"
"To Polycarp"

3. Polycarp, bishop of the church at Smyrna. He wrote a letter to the church at Philippi very shortly after the martyrdom of Ignatius, probably at the latest not much beyond A.D. 110.

4. *The Didache*, a primitive church manual of early Christianity. According to Lightfoot it was probably written in the first century or near the beginning of the second.

Now we will examine and see if these documents support the premillennial position that the eschatology of the early church was premillennial.

Clement. The letter commonly known as *The Epistle of Clement to the Corinthians* was sent in the name of the church of Rome to admonish the Corinthian church regarding a schism that had developed in the latter. There is not much material in the letter that deals with eschatology at all,

---

[6] Ryrie, pp. 19-21.

but what there is reflects no proof of premillennialism. To the contrary, it contains random comments that reflect the things that Christ and the apostles taught. But in all candor, we all must admit there is not a word uttered by Christ or any of the apostles that teaches that Christ will reign from an earthly throne over sinful men.

We find then that Clement makes one comment about the return of Christ in the context of the resurrection:

> Ye fools, compare yourselves unto a tree; take a vine. First it sheddeth its leaves, then a shoot cometh, then a leaf, then a flower, and after these a sour berry, then a full ripe grape. Ye see that in a little time the fruit of the tree attaineth unto mellowness. Of a truth quickly and suddenly shall His will be accomplished, the scripture also bearing witness to it, saying; He shall come quickly and shall not tarry; and the Lord shall come suddenly into His temple, even the Holy One, whom ye expect.
>
> Let us understand, dearly beloved, how the Master continuously showeth unto us the resurrection that shall be hereafter; whereof He made the Lord Jesus Christ the firstfruit, when He raised Him from the dead. Let us behold, dearly beloved, the resurrection which happeneth at its proper season.[7]

Although Clement mentions the Lord coming "into His temple," he does not appear in context to regard that as an earthly residency of Christ. He gives some illustrations of the resurrection from nature and holds forth the resurrection, not the pretribulation rapture or the earthly reign of Christ, as the essence of the Christian hope. For he continues:

> For He saith in a certain place; and Thou shalt raise me up, and I will praise Thee; and I went to rest and slept, I was

---

[7] Joseph Barber Lightfoot, *The Apostolic Fathers* (shorter), pp. 23, 24. Two different reprints of Lightfoot's translation of the Apostolic Fathers have been employed, hereafter referred to as Lightfoot (shorter) and Lightfoot (longer). Both were reprinted by Baker Book House in Grand Rapids, Michigan, the shorter in 1970 and the longer in 1981. Lightfoot in his translation uses italics to indicate when the writers are quoting or alluding to Scripture. I have changed these to regular type, using italics only for emphasis.

> awakened, for Thou art with me. And again Job saith; And Thou shalt raise this my flesh which hath endured all these things.
>
> With *this hope* therefore let our souls be bound unto Him that is faithful in His promises and that is righteous in His judgments.[8]

Now this has none of the special emphasis of a premillennial writer. Ryrie quotes only that portion which deals with the Lord coming quickly to His temple,[9] and gives none of the context. This is hardly sufficient to prove that his eschatology was premillennial. Clement's emphasis is upon resurrection, not rapture; he apparently did not expect to be living when the Lord returned. There is, however, another significant characteristic feature about the writing of Clement; more than once he quotes Old Testament passages which have clear reference to Israel and interprets them in a church context, for example:

> All the generations from Adam unto this day have passed away: but they that by God's grace were perfected in love dwell in the abode of the pious; and they shall *be made manifest in the visitation of the kingdom of God.* For it is written: Enter into the closet for a very little while, until Mine anger and My wrath shall pass away, and I will remember a good day, *and will raise you from your tombs.* Blessed were we, dearly beloved, if *we should be doing* the commandments of God in concord of love . . . .[10]

Clement's quote is a paraphrase of a combination of passages from Isaiah 26:20 and probably Ezekiel 37:12.[11] His application of these passages to the visitation of the "kingdom of God," to all generations, from Adam, to himself and those in the church relationship, and to the resurrection, shows clearly that he sees no revived Jewish theocracy apart from the church. Therefore, it seems rather presumptuous on

---

[8] Lightfoot (shorter), pp. 24, 25.

[9] Ryrie, p. 20.

[10] Lightfoot (longer), Pt. 1, Vol. 2, p. 297.

[11] Ibid., p. 151.

such scant evidence to put premillennialism in his mouth as Ryrie does. On the contrary, there is as much or more evidence that he is not speaking of an earthly reign. Again he writes:

> . . . through Him the Master willed that we should taste of the immortal knowledge; . . . For so it is written; Who maketh His angels spirits and His ministers a flame of fire; but of His Son the Master said thus; Thou art My Son, I this day have begotten Thee. Ask of Me, and I will *give Thee the Gentiles for Thine inheritance*, and the *ends of the earth for Thy possession.* And again He saith unto Him; *Sit Thou on My right hand, until I make Thine enemies a footstool for Thy feet.*[12]

Now *there* is pure apostolic eschatology. The Gentiles are given for an *inheritance* of Christ, and the whole earth for a *possession*; yet Clement sees this in true apostolic fashion as accomplished *during the Session of Christ at God's right hand*, making His enemies His footstool, not by an earthly reign.

As to the millennium, Clement's understanding would by necessity have been primitive and incomplete since he did not have, as yet, the book of Revelation. His eschatology was accurate but incomplete. Yet this letter by Clement is one of the purest and most inspiring pieces of Christian literature in existence apart from Scripture itself. It is a marvel of powerful admonition — an excellent model of speaking the truth in love. I heartily recommend it as reading for every Christian.

Ignatius. The date of the seven letters of Ignatius is between 107-110 A.D. Ryrie also lists him as a proof that premillennialism is the historic faith of the church, even though he admits that Ignatius says little about eschatology. But he thinks Ignatius is in "correspondence" with the premillennial doctrine because he "refers to the 'last times' and emphasizes the attitude of expectancy."[13]

Now even I, a postmillennialist, occasionally refer to the

---

[12]Ibid., p. 290.

[13] Ryrie, p. 21.

"last times." I believe "it is the last time" (1 John 2:18). It has been for two thousand years. I would not want to submit that kind of "proof" for a serious proposition of truth. The transparency of that logic surely weakens his case for premillennialism, and I call attention to this issue because the time is far past when Christian people should begin to demand substance to the process of indoctrination in premillennialism which has gone almost unchallenged for nearly a century. It has been treated as if it were the *Ark of the Covenant*, and could not be touched without sudden death.

But did Ignatius have an "attitude of expectancy"? He did indeed, but what did he expect? He expected to die for the testimony of his Lord, just as Peter did, and to be resurrected. He says characteristically:

> I write to all the churches, and I bid all men know, that of my own free will I die for God, unless ye should hinder me. I exhort you, be ye not an 'unseasonable kindness' to me. Let me be given to the wild beasts, for through them I can attain unto God.[14]

As to the "attitude of expectancy" Ryrie mentions, if expectancy of a "soon return" of Christ is meant as implied, there just is not a syllable of this in the whole of seven letters. Not once does he mention the second coming of Christ in any way. His comment on the "last times" is as follows:

> These are the last times. Henceforth let us have reverence; let us fear the long suffering of God, lest it turn into a judgment against us.[15]

This hardly represents an attitude of expectancy of the "soon coming" of Christ. Ignatius emphasizes the resurrection of Christ strongly. Citing Peter's witness to the resurrection of Christ, he said, "Wherefore also they despised death, nay they were found superior to death."[16] His faith and hope was in the resurrected Christ and his own resurrection to eternal life,

---

[14] Lightfoot (longer), Pt. 2, Vol. 2, p. 560.

[15] Ibid., p. 547.

[16] Ibid., . 568.

not in a rapture before death. There is no hint of it in his writings, and it is disturbing to have a learned man attempt to use the writings of Ignatius as proof of a premillennial faith in the early church.

Polycarp. This godly saint, who in his old age also paid for his faithfulness to Christ with his life, wrote a letter to the church at Philippi not long after the martyrdom of Ignatius, probably not much later than A.D. 110. Polycarp was a pastor of the church of Smyrna, and his letter to the Philippians is a gem of apostolic orthodoxy and Christian charity.

It is quite certain that Polycarp was a disciple of the aged Apostle John[17] who died about A.D. 100 when Polycarp was about thirty years old. It is almost certain, therefore, that Polycarp would have had access to the book of Revelation at the time of his writing. Hence if Revelation makes one a Chiliast, we should find it in Polycarp. This advantage Clement of Rome probably did not have when he wrote to the Corinthians, A.D. 95-96. Ignatius, writing A.D. 107-110, may possibly also have had access to Revelation by this time, but it is not likely that Ignatius personally knew John.

Henry C. Thiessen cites Polycarp as one who "... held the view that the Lord would come and set up an earthly Millennium."[18] As authorities for this statement he gives a modern writer, Silver, and an ancient writer, Eusebius (*Ecclesiastical History*, III, 39). I do not have Silver's work before me, but I have Eusebius, by far the better source. Now this reference gives not a syllable that says or implies that Polycarp believed in an earthly kingdom. Polycarp's name is mentioned by Eusebius only once in a quotation from Irenaeus as follows: "These things are attested by Papias, who was John's hearer and the associate of Polycarp . . . "[19] The only thing established about Polycarp is that he was acquainted with Papias. I find it very disconcerting when scholars of the reputation of Thiessen prove to be unreliable on such issues.

---

[17] Lightfoot (longer), Pt. 2, Vol. 1, pp. 440-441.

[18] Thiessen, "Will the Church . . . ", p. 192.

[19] *Eusebius*, III, 39.

Ryrie did not cite Polycarp as proof of the premillennial faith of the early church, although Polycarp says more on the subject of eschatology than does Ignatius. This omission will become easier to understand when we see what Polycarp has to say. While Polycarp's letter is short, we are able to gain some insight into his ideas on eschatology by one passage in particular. It reads:

> Wherefore gird up your loins and serve God in fear and truth, forsaking the vain and empty talking and the error of the many, for that ye have believed on Him that raised our Lord Jesus Christ from the dead and gave unto Him glory *and a throne on His right hand;* unto whom *all things were made subject* that are *in heaven and that are on the earth;* to whom every creature that hath breath doeth service; *who cometh as judge of quick and dead*; whose blood God will require of them that are disobedient unto Him. Now He that raised Him from the dead *will raise us also*; if we do His will and walk in His commandments and love the things which He loved . . . [20]

Polycarp sees no earthly throne, but he does see Christ ruling over all things in heaven and earth from the right hand of God — even as the apostles did. He also sees Christ coming, not to rule on earth, but to resurrect and judge both the living and the dead, the wicked and the righteous. This is pure apostolic eschatology; it cannot be premillennial.

Now these three men of the first century are considered to be soundly apostolic in their theology in all other regards with the single exception that Ignatius had drifted from the apostolic simplicity in the matter of episcopal authority. But there is nothing in any of them that suggests a premillennial eschatology. To the contrary, two of the three emphasize the *reign of Christ at God's right hand* — so reminiscent of the New Testament emphasis as we have seen. Clement and Polycarp both see Christ reigning in the heavens, and they expect to be resurrected from the grave at His return. That is the simple eschatology of the early church, and it is in perfect harmony with the New Testament Scriptures, but not a word of premillennialism.

---

[20] Lightfoot (longer), Pt. 2, Vol. 3, pp. 471-472.

Shedd remarks:

> There are no traces of Chiliasm in the writings of *Clement of Rome*, *Ignatius*, *Polycarp*, *Tatian*, *Athengoras*, and *Theophilus of Antioch*. The inference from these facts, then, is, that this tenet [Chiliasm] was not the received faith of the church certainly down to the year 150.[21]

The Didache. This work is of rather early origin. Lightfoot places it toward the end of the first century. It is written in two parts. The first is a moral treatise, not necessarily Christian in origin,[22] and the second part is comprised of teachings for the church. Its significance for eschatology is found in the following passage:

> *Be watchful* for your life; *let your lamps not be quenched and your loins not ungirded, but be ye ready; for ye know not the hour in which our Lord cometh.* And ye shall gather yourselves together frequently, seeking what is fitting for your souls; for the whole time of your faith shall not profit you, if ye be not perfected at the last season. For in the last days *the false prophets* and corrupters shall be multiplied, and the sheep shall be turned into wolves, and love shall be turned into hate. For as lawlessness increaseth, *they shall hate one another and shall persecute and betray. And then* the world-deceiver *shall appear* as a son of God; *and shall work signs and wonders*, and the earth shall be delivered into his hands; and he shall do unholy things, which have never been since the world began. Then *all created mankind shall come to the fire of testing*, and many shall be offended and perish; *but they that endure* in their faith *shall be saved* by the Curse Himself. *And then shall the signs* of the truth *appear;* first a sign of *a rift in the heaven*, then a sign of a *voice of a trumpet*, and thirdly a *resurrection of the dead; yet not of all*, but as it was said: *The Lord shall come and all His saints with Him. Then shall* the world *see the Lord coming upon the clouds of heaven.*[23]

---

[21] William G. T. Shedd, *A History of Christian Doctrine* (New York: Charles Scribner's Sons, 1897), Vol. II, p. 390, 391.

[22] Lightfoot (shorter), p. 121.

[23] Ibid., p. 129.

The salient points in this passage are as follows:

1. Exhortation to watchfulness and preparedness apparently based upon the parable of the wise and foolish virgins, etc.;

2. Warning of false prophets, the increase of lawlessness, and the appearance of the "world-deceiver";

3. A brief mention of the tribulation events or the "testing" of "all created mankind";

4. Finally a revealing description of the second coming of Christ.

This passage reveals an acquaintance with Matthew's Gospel and probably both Paul's books to the Thessalonians, and possibly Revelation. We gather from these things that the writer expects the church to see fulfillment of the prophecies relative to the tribulation and the revelation of Paul's "man of sin" (2 Thess. 2:3), who is to appear "as a son of God," prior to the return of Christ. He has no concept of a pretribulation rapture, and shows no signs of exposure to the idea of the millennium as introduced in Revelation.

He accurately places the second coming immediately after the tribulation. He sees the heavens dividing, "a rift," denoting a full destruction — the end. He notes the voice of a trumpet and the resurrection of the dead. He adds the ambiguous phrase "yet not of all" as if to acknowledge that the saints who are alive and remain would not be resurrected but raptured. He then notes that the "world" will "see the Lord coming upon the clouds of heaven," as implied in 1 Thessalonians 4:17; hence he, correctly, does not believe in a secret rapture.

All these things taken together show that the writer is not premillennial. He believes in the destruction of the heavens and earth, that the rapture and revelation are one event, apparently accompanied by a general resurrection. Ryrie quotes only three lines ending with the phrase "yet not of all." And although Ryrie admits this does not prove a premillennial belief, he claims it disproves a belief in a general resurrection. The statement taken as quoted by Ryrie apart from its full context could imply that, but the following sentence [the "world sees"] more likely suggests that he means all were not dead to be resurrected.

In a word the eschatology of this writer is consistent with that of Clement, Ignatius, and Polycarp, and so far we have not a word of proof of premillennialism in these.

Now, as I said earlier, I want to introduce seven names or works from the first century period. Of the seven, I have discussed four. Clement and Polycarp are perhaps the soundest of the early fathers. Ignatius is soundly apostolic in all matters except for his extraordinary exaltation of the "bishop" over the "elders" — which the New Testament presents as the same office. *The Didache* is not orthodox in every regard, but is in harmony with the other three in eschatology as far as it is discussed. The remaining three individuals of the first century do not at all reflect an apostolic view of eschatology. These three are Cerinthus, Papias, and the writer of a work called *The Epistle of Barnabas*. I will discuss all three of these under the following heading.

A Kingdom of This World — The Jewish Error

The three persons mentioned above each held a premillennial position in the first and early second century. Before we examine their respective views, it will be necessary to answer the question: what is the origin of the concept of an earthly messianic kingdom? The doctrine of a corporeal reign of the Messiah on earth is evident in the Jewish rabbinical and apocryphal writings and the Dead Sea Scrolls of the Qumran community of Jews. The historian Philip Schaff makes the following observation about Jewish Chiliasm (or millenarianism):

> The Jewish Chiliasm rested on a carnal misapprehension of the Messianic kingdom, a literal interpretation of prophetic figures, and an overestimate of the importance of the Jewish people and the holy city as the centre of that kingdom. It was developed shortly before and after Christ in the apocalyptic literature, as the Book of Enoch, the Apocalypse of Baruch,

> 4th Esdras, the Testaments of the Twelve Patriarchs, and the Sibylline Books. It was adopted by the heretical sect of the Ebionites, and the Gnostic Cerinthus.
>
> The *Christian chiliasm is the Jewish chiliasm spiritualized and fixed upon the second, instead of the first coming of Christ.*[24]

While not all Jews have held this view, the origin of the idea of chiliasm stems from a Jewish earthly mind-set that would not come to terms with the truth that God (or the Messiah) was in reality their king reigning from heaven. This mind-set goes back at least to the days of the Judges (cf. 1 Sam. 12:12, 17; 8:7-9, 19, 20; 10:19). God solemnly protested against this earthly mind-set through Samuel (1 Sam. 8:9), and again through the Messiah Himself (Luke 17:20, 21; John 6:15; 18:36). It is this earthly mind-set that played the major role in the Jewish rejection of their Messiah.[25] They wanted Him as an earthly king (John 6:15), but they would have none of Him as a spiritual king. They could not handle the truth that "The Lord hath prepared his throne in the heavens; and his kingdom ruleth over all" (Psalm 103:19; see also John 6:26, 27, 41, 42, 60-62, 66).

This same mind-set has continued to work to keep the Jews in unbelief to this day. I once had a lengthy discussion with the rabbi of a local Jewish synagogue. The bottom line of his argument against Jesus as Messiah was that the real Messiah must be a king on earth, and he correctly pointed out to me from the New Testament that Jesus rejected that idea and that nowhere did the apostles teach it. Whereupon I showed him from the Old Testament that he had wholly misunderstood the nature of the Messiah's reign — that it

---

[24] Philip Schaff, *History of the Christian Church* (Grand Rapids: Wm. B. Eerdmans Pub. Co., 1980), Vol. II, p. 614.

[25] Shedd in his *History of Christian Doctrine*, p. 389, says: "The Jews at the time of the Incarnation were expecting a personal prince, and a corporeal reign . . . and one of the principal grounds of their rejection of Christ was the fact that he represented the messiah's rule as a spiritual one in the hearts of men, and gave no countenance to their literal and materializing interpretation of the Messianic prophecies."

would be an eternal not an earthly reign (2 Sam. 7:16), and would be from the right hand of God (Psalm 110:1). He would have none of that. He made the same mistake as his earthly-minded fathers of the first century and remained in unbelief.

Aside from the pre-Christian apocalyptic literature we also see this mind-set in the Qumran community of Jews just prior to the time of Christ. From a liturgical fragment discovered in Qumran is this passage concerning the Messianic "Prince of the Congregation":

> May he make thy horns of iron and thy shoes of bronze! May thou toss like a young bull and trample the peoples like the mud of the streets! For God has established thee as a sceptre over the rulers . . . and all the peoples shall serve thee, and he shall exalt thee by His holy Name. And thou shalt be as a lion . . . .[26]

This passage shows the character of the messianic reign expected by the Jews of Qumran. Friebel summarizes in part the function of the Messiah as conceived by the Qumran community as follows:

> He is the eschatological military leader of the forces of the "people of God." As a military leader, he is spoken of as being warlike . . . .
>
> His position is that of ruler, not only of the community of the righteous remnant, but of the whole earth . . . .[27]

Friebel further concludes:

> Thus, it would seem from the terminology used and the functions performed, that the Messiah and the beliefs held about him were very similar to those of the mainline Judaism contemporary with the Qumran community, that the Messiah was to be the ideal king who would deliver God's people from their enemies.[28]

---

[26] Quoted by Kelvin G. Friebel in "The Qumranian Doctrine of the Messiah: (paper read at the Hebrew Graduate Seminar, University of Wisconsin-Madison, 1980-81), p. 14.

[27] Ibid., p. 20.

[28] Ibid., p. 22.

I would not want to leave the impression that none of the early Jews held any notion of the "kingdom of heaven" in the abstract or spiritual sense. Some of them did, as evidenced from the Talmudic and Hebraic writings. Several examples are given to this effect by John Lightfoot.[29] Still they believed in a resurrection prior to the first advent of the Messiah:

> The righteous, whom the Lord shall raise from the dead in the days of the Messiah, when they are restored to life, shall not again return to their dust, neither in the days of the Messiah, nor in the following age: but their flesh shall remain upon them till they return and live . . . to eternity (Gloss. in Bab. Berac. fol. 9.2)[30]

Lightfoot summarizes from Talmudic writings the Jewish understanding of the coming[31] of the Messiah as follows:

> See here the doctrine of the Jews concerning the coming of the Messiah:
>
> 1. That at that time there shall be a resurrection of the just:... *The Messias shall raise up those that sleep in the dust* (Midr. Tillin, fol. 42.1).
>
> 2. Then shall follow the desolation of this world:... *This world shall be wasted a thousand years* (Gloss. in Bab. Berac. fol. 9.2). Not that they imagined that a chaos, or confusion of all things, should last the thousand years; but that this world should end and a new one be introduced in that thousand years.

---

[29] John Lightfoot, *A Commentary on the New Testament from the Talmud and Hebraica* (Grand Rapids: Baker Book House, 1979, reprinted from 1859 edition by Oxford Univ. Press), Vol. 2, pp. 50-52.

[30] Ibid., p. 310.

[31] This refers to the first advent of the Messiah, since the Jews had no concept of a second coming. Also, it should be remembered that these Talmudic concepts were committed to writing in their present form some time between the second and fifth centuries. However, the concepts themselves are more ancient. Some arose before the time of Christ, but it is uncertain when the idea of the "thousand years" arose among the rabbis. It existed before the book of Revelation was written. It probably arose as an extrapolation from the analogy of the first seven millennia with the seven-day week — the seventh being the Sabbath.

3. After which . . . *eternity should succeed.*[32]

These Talmudic doctrines then show the culmination of the growth of an earthly mind-set of Messianic kingship starting at least in the time of judges, through the Qumran community, the New Testament period, finalized and written in the rabbinic writings up to the fourth century. The Jews came to hold the notion of a resurrection prior to the coming of the Messiah, and this notion had pervaded the minds of almost all the early Jews (many of whom later became Christians) from their youth. Such a notion ingrained from childhood was difficult to purge from the minds of many of the early Jewish Christians, especially before the full revelation of the New Testament Scripture was complete and widely distributed. This mind-set prompted the sincere but naive question of Acts 1:6. In this light it would seem almost inevitable that during the century-long period of time prior to the broad availability of the New Testament, that such an error as chiliasm would rise from this vestigial Jewish mind-set.

This should not be thought strange. The same attitude lingered among the early churches concerning circumcision. Many could not believe one could be saved apart from it (see Acts 15). Likewise also the inclusion of the Gentiles within the church (see Acts 10:45-47; 11:4-17) was a problem even to the apostles until God convinced Peter by a vision.

The New Testament Scriptures corrected all three of these errors, but that did not prevent some considerable number among the early Christians from embracing them. Therefore, we would expect a Chiliastic aberration to break out sooner or later among the early Christians. Shedd notes:

> There being this affinity between Millennarianism and the Later-Jewish idea of the Messiah and his kingdom, it is not surprising to find that Millennarianism was a peculiarity of the Jewish-Christian, as distinguished from the Gentile-Christian branch of the church, at the close of the first

---

[32] Lightfoot, *Commentary*, p. 311.

century. It appears first in the system of the Judaistic-Gnostic *Cerinthus.*[33]

This brings us to the discussion of the first three Chiliasts of the first and early second centuries: Cerinthus, the writer of the *Epistle of Barnabas*, and Papias.

Cerinthus. Aside from mainline Judaism, the quasi-Christian Gnostic Cerinthus is the earliest known to have held a Chiliastic view of the *second* coming of Christ. Cerinthus is called the "Heresiarch" (archheretic) by Eusebius.[34] His public ministry was contemporaneous with the latter days of the Apostle John well before Revelation was written. They were antagonists theologically, and the heresies of Cerinthus and other Gnostics, some think, occasioned the writing of John's Gospel. To say the least there is no writing more suited to answer the Gnostics than John's Gospel.

Cerinthus was a Jew born in Egypt. Though he left Judaism, he was not properly a Christian at all. He held Jesus to be the Christ, but he considered Him to have been born naturally of Joseph and Mary, and to have received a heavenly messianic nature at baptism. This heavenly nature left Jesus at His passion and was to return to Him in an earthly messianic millennial kingdom centered at Jerusalem.[35]

Schaff adds a significant footnote to his discussion of Cerinthus:

> The chiliastic eschatology of Cerinthus is omitted by Irenaeus, who was himself a chiliast, though of a higher spiritual order, but it is described by Caius, Dionysius (in Eusebius), Theodoret, and Augustin.[36]

During the earthly reign of Christ, in the view of Cerinthus, there would be opportunity to indulge in sensual pleasures:

> . . . he conjectured that it would consist in those things that he

[33] Shedd. Vol. II, p. 390.

[34] Eusebius, Book 3, Chapter XXVIII

[35] Schaff, Vol. II, pp. 465, 466.

[36] Ibid., p. 466.

> craved in the gratification of appetite and lust, i.e., in eating, drinking, and marrying, or in such things whereby he supposed these sensual pleasures might be presented in more decent expressions; viz. in festivals, sacrifices, and the slaying of victims.[37]

Such was the eschatology of the first known premillennialist. Cerinthus did not derive these views from Scripture, nor from any contemporaneous Christian. At that time only the Jews taught a view of the earthly reign of Christ. It is not difficult, therefore, to discern that the Judaistic background of Cerinthus came over into his quasi-Christian eschatology, not only in the concept of an earthly reign, but even to the reinstitution of animal sacrifice. Some premillennialists even today expect the reinstitution of the Old Testament theocracy right down to the slaying of animal sacrifices — in spite of all the book of Hebrews teaches to the contrary.

Barnabas. Among the early Christian documents is a writing called *The Epistle of Barnabas.* The exact date of the writing is not known; it has been dated by various writers from A.D. 70 to A.D. 132.[38] If this work, as some have claimed, was by the Barnabas of *Acts*, he never made such a claim for himself. The Barnabas of *Acts*, who broke with Paul over his nephew John Mark, went to Cyprus and never appears in the New Testament narratives again. Lightfoot believes the author to be a Barnabas of Alexandria who writes against Judaism, and he suggests the date of the work is between 70-79 A.D.[39]

As to the eschatology of this Barnabas, he holds a very rare position. It does not lend itself well to classification by any of the three broad contemporary positions — premillennial, postmillennial, or amillennial. It is not properly premillennial because Barnabas does not see an earthly kingdom on this *present* earth with the Lord ruling

---

[37] Dionysius of Alexandria as quoted by *Eusebius*, XXVIII.

[38] Lightfoot (shorter), p. 134.

[39] Ibid., p. 135.

over flesh-and-blood men. He says:

> *He ended* [creation] *in six days.* He meaneth this, that in six thousand years the Lord shall *bring all things to an end;* for the day with him signifieth a thousand years; . . . *Behold, the day of the Lord shall be as a thousand years.* Therefore, children, in six days, that is in six thousand years, *everything shall come to an end. And He rested on the seventh day.* This He meaneth; *when His Son shall come,* and shall abolish the time of the Lawless One, and shall judge the ungodly, and shall *change the sun and the moon and the stars,* then shall He truly rest on the seventh day.[40]

This is not amillennial in that Barnabas recognizes a distinctive thousand-year millennial period. It is not properly postmillennial in that the Lord comes before the millennium, but is compatible with it only in that the Lord's return terminates this present universe. Actually, Barnabas appears also to be compatible with the eschatology of *Clement, Ignatius, Polycarp,* and *The Didache* in that they look to share in a resurrection when Jesus leaves the right hand of God as this present earth comes to an end.

Barnabas probably had not seen the book of Revelation, hence his millennial idea, as that of the Jews, is derived from the idea that a day with the Lord is as a thousand years and analogous to the 7-day creation week with the millennium corresponding to the 7th day or sabbath. He reflects characteristics of the Jewish eschatology, but none of the Christian writers (excluding Cerinthus) prior to Papias gives any hint of an earthly reign of Christ over flesh-and-blood men on this present earth.

Papias. Papias was born probably not later than A.D. 70. He lived to a ripe old age and was martyred about the same time as Polycarp. The lives of these two men were nearly coterminous. Papias was a bishop at Hierapolis and, like

---

[40] Lightfoot (shorter), pp. 151-152. Barnabas openly explains that his concept of the thousand years is extrapolated from the seven-day week and seven millennia analogy. The probability that this Alexandrian Jew derived the salient features of his eschatology from contemporary Judaism is very strong indeed.

Cerinthus, was a strong Chiliast. But unlike Cerinthus he was considered orthodox in most other matters of the faith.

Irenaeus says of Papias that he was "John's hearer and the associate of Polycarp . . . ." Eusebius, however, shows that it is more likely that the John of Papias' acquaintance was one John a Presbyter of Ephesus and not the Apostle. He quotes Papias to this effect:

> But if I met with anyone who had been a follower of the elders anywhere, I made it a point to inquire what were the declarations of the elders. What was said by Andrew, Peter or Philip. What by Thomas, James, John, Matthew, or any other of the disciples of our Lord. What was said by Aristion, and the presbyter John, disciples of the Lord . . . [41]

Papias seems to imply here that he got his information from people who had known the apostles, but, as Eusebius points out, he does not claim to have heard them for himself. Yet the question has never been settled, and it matters little for our purposes. Many who heard and knew the apostles were in error about various doctrines; Cerinthus definitely knew the Apostle John, but he was an "archheretic."

Papias wrote, late in life (c. 130-140 A.D.),[42] a work in five books called *Exposition of Oracles of the Lord.* He was an avid compiler of the stories and sayings that came to him by word of mouth. He seemed not to have been impressed by the written word saying:

> . . . for I do not think that I derived so much benefit from books as from the living voice of those that are still surviving.[43]

Papias seemed to have had an appetite for the sensational. Eusebius again comments:

> The same historian [Papias] also gives other accounts, which he says he adds as received by him from unwritten tradition, likewise certain strange parables of our Lord, and of his doctrine and some other matters rather too fabulous. In these

---

[41] *Eusebius*, Book 3, Chapter XXXIX

[42] Lightfoot (shorter), p. 262.

[43] *Eusebius*, Book 3, Chapter XXXIX

> he says there would be a certain millennium after the resurrection, and that there would be a corporeal reign of Christ on this very earth; which things he appears to have imagined, as if they were authorized by the apostolic narrations, not understanding correctly those matters which they propounded mystically in their representations. For he was very limited in his comprehension, as is evident from his discourses; yet he was the cause why most of the ecclesiastical writers, urging the antiquity of the man, were carried away by similar opinions; as, for instance, Irenaeus . . . [44]

This statement tells much about the reputation of Papias as well as the development of premillennial doctrine among the early fathers. It was considered an aberration popularized by Papias,[45] but by no means apostolic — as anyone can tell by reading the New Testament. Just where Papias derived his premillennialism is impossible to tell exactly, yet it would be naive to rule out all influence from Cerinthus. However, the famous account by Papias of the millennial conditions as given in *Irenaeus*, suggests the Jewish apocalyptic writings as at least one source. Irenaeus quotes Papias as follows and claims the apostles heard these things from the Lord. But it is actually from the Jewish Apocalypse of Baruch:[46]

> The days will come, in which vines shall grow, each having ten thousand shoots, and on each shoot ten thousand branches, and on each branch again ten thousand twigs, and on each twig ten thousand clusters, and on each cluster ten thousand grapes, and each grape when pressed shall yield five and twenty measures of wine.[47]

---

[44] Ibid.

[45] It is difficult not to notice the parallel in the roles played by Papias in the second century and by J. N. Darby in the nineteenth century in the spreading and popularizing of the premillennial position in their respective times.

[46] W. F. Farrar, *The Early Days of Christianity* (New York: Casell, Petter, Galpin, & Co., 1883), p. 397. Also see J. E. H. Thomas, "Apocalyptic Literature" *International Standard Bible Encyclopedia* (1937), Vol. I, p. 166.

[47] Lightfoot (shorter), p. 269.

The account goes on to ascribe like marvelous production to wheat and other plants and animals. It appears then that Papias was a student of the Jewish apocalyptic literature, or some of his oral sources were; and since his millennial views are so similar to the Jewish ideas, and also to Cerinthus' views, the evidence that they had a common source is very strong. There is no mistake that these are the beginnings of the premillennial doctrines among Christians. This doctrine spread widely in the second century and some of its extravagant views were modified, but no responsible historian has ever claimed to trace this doctrine to the apostles or the main-stream first century church. The evidence is positively clear that it was not in fact so derived.

In view of these things do we then have any intellectual or moral right to put these foreign doctrines into the mouths and teachings of our Lord, the apostles, Clement, Ignatius, Polycarp or the early apostolic church?

Neander comments:

> When we find Chiliasm in Papias, Irenaeus, J. Martyr, all this indicates that it arose from one source, and was propagated from one spot.[48]

Early Christian Chiliasm is clearly an aberration arising from Jewish eschatology.

We have seen then that Irenaeus got his Chiliasm from Papias, and that Eusebius claims most of the later Chiliasts sprang from Papianism. Chiliasm in the later second century and early third became rather widespread.

The Shepherd of Hermas. This is one other work which might be regarded as an early second century writing. Some have supposed that this Hermas is the same as the one mentioned in Romans 16:14. However, the most definite information as to the author of this work comes from the *Muratorian Canon* (c. A.D. 180)[49] which states that the work

---

[48] Augustus Neander, *General History of the Christian Religion and Church*, tr. Joseph Torrey (11th ed., New York: Hurd & Houghton, 1871), p. 404.

[49] Lightfoot (shorter), pp. 161-162.

was written between A.D. 140 and 155 by one Hermas, the brother of Pius bishop of Rome.

A passage from Hermas is quoted by Henry C. Thiessen both in an article in *Bibliotheca Sacra*[50] and in his *Lectures in Systematic Theology*[51] and part of the same passage is quoted by Ryrie.[52] Hermas is set forth, particularly by Thiessen, as not only an example of one holding a premillennial position, but also as one holding a pretribulation rapture position.

A vision is set forth by Hermas in which he is said to have seen a great and furious beast. The beast is identified as representing the great tribulation. At first Hermas was fearful of it, but upon reflecting on the faith and works of the Lord, he says, "I took courage and gave myself up to the beast." Then when Hermas came near the beast, "it stretched itself on the ground, and merely put forth its tongue, and stirred not at all until I had passed by it." Then Hermas met a virgin which he identifies as representing the church. At this point Thiessen picks up the account and continues as follows:

> . . . a virgin met him and saluted him thus: "Hail, O man!" He returned her salutation, and said, "Lady, hail!" Then she asked him, "Has nothing crossed your path?" To this Hermas replied: "I was met by a beast of such a size that it could destroy peoples, but through the power of the Lord and His great mercy I escaped from it." Then the virgin said, "Well did you escape from it, because you cast your care on God, and opened your heart to the Lord, believing that you can be saved by no other than by His great and glorious name. . . . You have escaped from great tribulation on account of your faith, and because you did not doubt in the presence of such a beast. Go, therefore, and tell the elect of the Lord His mighty deeds, and say to them that this beast is a type of the great tribulation that is coming."[53]

---

[50] Thiessen, "Will the Church . . . ?, pp. 195-196.

[51] Thiessen, *Lectures*, p. 476.

[52] Ryrie, p. 20.

[53] Thiessen, "Will the Church . . . ?", pp. 195-196.

Following this Thiessen draws a conclusion on the strength of this passage from Hermas. He says:

> . . . we seem to have in the Shepherd of Hermas a fairly clear indication of the fact that there were those who believed that the Church would be taken away before that period of judgment begins.[54]

As weak as that conclusion is as it stands, I am compelled to point out another fact which not only destroys the conclusion but casts a shadow on the intent of the writer. In the long quotation above, there is an ellipsis between "glorious name" and "you have escaped" indicating an omission from the text quoted. Now this is a very common and proper thing to do — unless the words omitted are such that, when withheld, would rob the reader of information relevant to the issue or, worse yet, would mislead the reader and allow a false conclusion to be drawn.

Ryrie also quotes from Hermas and also omits the same relevant information that Thiessen does. Ryrie begins his quotation with the words "You have escaped . . . ",[55] and like Thiessen withholds relevant information concerning Hermas' position.

Now we look to the work, *The Shepherd of Hermas*, itself to see what the omission says. There is one sentence in the place of the ellipsis that changes Thiessen's conclusion completely. I will quote the part of that portion as it would be without the omission:

> . . . His great and glorious Name. *Therefore the Lord sent His angel, which is over the beasts, whose name is Segri, and shut its mouth, that it might not hurt thee.* Thou has escaped . . . (Italics indicate the omitted sentence.)[56]

What then does this tell us? It makes clear that Hermas expected to go through the tribulation but that God in His

---

[54] *Ibid.*

[55] *Ryrie, p. 20.*

[56] *Lightfoot (shorter), p. 180.*

providential care would keep him safely through it. It shows he did not expect to be "taken away before that period of judgment begins" as Thiessen tries to prove. Not only this sentence, but the statement I quoted above that Hermas "took courage and gave myself up to the beast" and that he "passed by it" unharmed shows no thought of a rapture, but he expected courageously to go through it. Thiessen, on the strength of this quotation from Hermas, had hoped to disprove the truth that there remains no evidence of a belief in the pretribulation rapture "from Polycarp down, until the strange utterances given out in the Church of Edward Irving."[57] Actually, he has confirmed it!

This same "misquotation" appears in Thiessen's *Lectures* as a continuous quotation. The reader is not even warned by an ellipsis.[58]

Christians have almost universally expected to go through the tribulation, but they have also expected to be providentially protected during this time (Rev. 3:10).

Now we have seen that premillennialism was not the faith of the early church for the first and early second centuries. Shedd summarizes this period as follows:

> It [Chiliasm] appears first in the system of the Judaistic-Gnostic *Cerinthus*, the contemporary and opponent of the apostle John. Of the Apostolic Fathers, only *Barnabas*, *Hermas*, and *Papias* exhibit in their writings distinct traces of this doctrine, — the latter teaching it in its grossest form, and the first two holding it in a less sensuous manner. There are no traces of Chiliasm in the writings of *Clement of Rome*, *Ignatius*, *Polycarp*, *Tatian*, *Athengoras*, and *Theophilus of Antioch*. The inference from these facts, then, is, that this tenet was not the received faith of the church certainly down to the year 150. It was held only by individuals . . . . And in the

---

[57] Thiessen, "Will the Church . . . ?, p. 196, quoting Robert Cameron, *Scriptural Truth about the Lord's Return*, p. 72.

[58] Thiessen, *Lectures*, p. 476. It should be noted that the last two-thirds of this work was edited from Henry C. Thiessen's notes posthumously by John Caldwell Thiessen, and this may have been an innocent oversight on his part.

instance of those whose general catholicity was acknowledged — as Barnabas, Hermas, and Papias, — there was by no means such a weight of character and influence, as would entitle them to be regarded as the principle or sole representatives of orthodoxy. On the contrary, these minds were comparatively uninfluential, and their writings are of little importance. The ecclesiastical authority of Clement of Rome, Ignatius, and Polycarp is certainly much greater than that of Barnabas, Hermas, and Papias.[59]

The Doctrines of Eschatology from A.D. 150 to the Present — A Summary

The last half of the second century saw the influence of Papias' views of eschatology spread. Irenaeus was a student of Papias, and he wrote widely and influenced many others. But the rise of Montanism in the late second century gave the Chiliastic doctrine wings, and it spread widely and rapidly. Many of the churches began to oppose it openly as it grew.

The influential Alexandrian school of theology opposed Chiliasm; but as a pendulum swings to extremes, they polarized to a spiritualizing, allegorical, and platonic theology which, in eschatology, finally sowed the seeds of historic Catholic and Protestant amillennialism.

It was Dionysius of Alexandria who finally sounded the death knell for Chiliasm in the early church and brought peace. Dionysius was a superintendent of the Alexandrian school. Since the supposed literalism[60] of premillennialism stood in an antagonistic position to the allegorical and spiritualizing tendencies of the Alexandrian school, Dionysius

---

59 Shedd, Vol. II, pp. 390-391.

60 I say "supposed literalism" because the premillennial position cannot stand on a truly *literal* interpretation of the meaning of the words of Scripture. Almost all historians uniformly, and erroneously, put forth the notion that apart from a spiritualizing or allegorical mode of interpretation, premillennialism must stand! Such, as I have shown, is not the case. Premillennialism arises not from a literal interpretation of the words of Scripture, but from an earthly philosophical mind-set which arose among the Jews before the first advent of Christ and continues today in premillennialism.

opposed it. Because of a special gift of reasoning ability, his tact, and a charitable spirit, he was successful in winning over some of the leading proponents of Chiliasm, and thereafter the view declined.

A full account of this conflict is given by Neander. One Nepos, a zealous partisan of premillennialism, wrote a book called *A Refutation of the Allegorists* setting forth his Chiliast doctrine. It became a very popular book among the Chiliasts. Neander writes:

> . . . Many occupied themselves more with the book and theory of Nepos than with the Bible and its doctrine . . . . After the death of Nepos, Korakion, the pastor of a country place stood at the head of this party . . . . Dionysius did not, like others, forget the Christian in the bishop; his love for souls induced him to repair in person to those churches, and to call the clergy, who defended the opinions of Nepos, together to a conference . . . . The book of Nepos was laid before them, and the bishop discussed its contents with those clergy for three days, from morning to evening; he listened quietly to all their objections, endeavoring to answer them out of the Scripture, and conducting the discussion by quoting fully from Scripture on every point; and the consequence was a result which seldom, indeed, proceeds from theological disputes; namely, that the clergy were thankful for the instruction they had received, and Korakion himself, in the presence of them all, honestly retracted his former opinions and declared himself persuaded of the truth of the contrary to them, A.D. 255.[61]

While this conference did much toward quieting the debate on Chiliasm, there were at least three other reasons for its decline. One was the strong opposition to Montanism. Then later when Pagan persecution subsided there was not such a strong sentiment that longed for Christ to intervene by an earthly reign, and as the Catholic party gained power and influence in alliance with the state, the spiritualizing tendency seemed to be confirmed by this great "success." Amillennialism therefore came to be firmly established, in the Catholic wing, holding that the millennium was nothing more

---

[61] Neander, pp. 405-406.

than the normal Gospel era. Because of the Catholic alliance with the Roman state, it seemed to them as if they were entering the millennium. Amillennialism then became the historic eschatology of the Catholics and the Reformers because it is a natural human conclusion for a sacral church.

Now as time passed the non-Catholic churches of the fourth century and following — primarily the Donatists of North Africa and later the Paulicians of Armenia, Cappadocia and the Caucasus Mountains — were driven from their homes under the new Catholic persecution. They migrated for safety to the valleys of the Alps Mountains and other locations in southern Europe. The eschatology they took with them is difficult to ascertain. These non-Catholic churches lay sequestered in the peaceful Alpine valleys for centuries. They came to be known generally as Waldenses.[62] Not enough information concerning their eschatology exists to put together a clear picture. However, in A.D. 1100 a poem was written by a Waldensian author called *The Noble Lesson.* From this and a few other documents we are able to get some idea of their eschatology.

Once again Ryrie attempts to convey the impression, without actually stating it, that they were premillennial.[63] He says:

> *The Noble Lesson*, one of their writings, *certainly* shows their expectation of *the coming kingdom* (emphasis mine).

Yet he quotes not a syllable from *The Noble Lesson.* We turn to this ancient document to see what this Waldensian actually said:

> We ought always to watch and pray,
> For we see the World nigh to a conclusion.
> We ought to strive to do good works,
> Seeing that the *end of this World* approacheth.[64]

---

[62] For a more complete account of these churches, see William Jones, *The History of the Christian Church* (Wetumpka, Ala.: Charles Yancey, 1845), and W. R. Downing, *The New Testament Church* (Sunnyvale, Calif.: Lakewood Baptist Church, 1982).

[63] Ryrie, p. 27.

[64] Quoted in Samuel Morland, *History of the Evangelical Churches of*

From this we can see that they were expecting the end of the world, not an earthly kingdom of this world. Furthermore the writer says:

> As also, that no man living can know the end.
> And therefore we ought the more to fear,
> as not being certain,
> Whether we shall die to day or to morrow.
> But when *the day of Judgment* shall come,
> *Every one shall receive their full Reward.*
> Those that shall have done *either well or ill.*
> Now the Scripture saith, and we ought to believe it,
> That all men shall pass two ways.
> *The good to glory, and the wicked to torment.*[65]

From this passage it is clear that they held the scriptural idea of "the day of Judgment" in which there would be a general judgment of both the righteous and the wicked and the respective rewards and destinies settled. This is far from premillennial doctrine. Furthermore, the Waldensians believed in a general resurrection in connection with "the day of Judgment." In a brief statement of some of the tenets of their faith, dating A.D. 1120, article 8 says:

> And as for the Virgin Mary, that she was holy, humble, and full of grace: and in like manner do *we believe concerning all the other Saints*, viz. that being in Heaven, *they wait for the Resurrection of their Bodies at the Day of Judgment.*[66]

It is clear from these things that they believed in both a general resurrection in connection with a general judgment of both classes together at the end of the world. How then can the implication be made by Ryrie that they expected "the coming kingdom" in the way Ryrie expects it? Their beliefs, so far, are compatible with amillennialism. However, it seems

---

the Valleys of Piedmont (London: Henry Hills, 1658), p. 99. (In quoting this work, as in others, I have used italics to highlight issues for discussion; thus the italics are mine unless otherwise noted.)

[65] Ibid., pp. 99-100.

[66] Ibid., p. 33.

impossible that they could have consciously held a true amillennial view in the traditional Catholic sense. Surely, under the continual persecution they bore, they could hardly have believed that Satan was bound or viewed those times as the millennium.

The writer of *The Noble Lesson* apparently believed the second coming was imminent, but that it would end all things by a general resurrection or judgment. Actually, he does not seem to have taken account of a millennium, or only vaguely so. He exhibits the same impressions that almost all people get from a sincere but surface, devotional, non-analytical reading of the New Testament Scriptures. His understanding, however, is very compatible with that of Clement of Rome, Ignatius, Polycarp, and the non-Chiliast fathers who had not had opportunity to have worked out a complete eschatology relating to the millennium (since its time span is only mentioned in Revelation).

As to the Waldensians, they certainly had the book of Revelation, but it is likely their time was used up surviving persecution and preserving the faith once delivered to the saints. They apparently had not had opportunity to formulate a detailed eschatology around the millennium. I think it is regrettable that they were not able to give more time to it, because they seemed to be readily able to see the true teachings of Scripture in all matters that urgently claimed their attention. Actually, they may have had a sound eschatology. Almost all their works were destroyed by their persecutors; very little survived.

Their concept of the "king of heaven" was biblical also in that they expected the full inheritance of heaven at the end — not an earthly kingdom:

> Having hope in the King of Heaven,
> *That at the end he may receive us into his glorious habitation.*
> Now he that shall not do what is contained in this Lesson,
> Shall never enter into this house.[67]

Again their idea of the kingdom as expressed in *The Noble*

[67] Ibid., p. 101.

Lesson shows through in this statement as well:

> But to be content with Food and Raiment.
> To love one another, and to be at peace.
> Then he promised them *the heavenly kingdom*,
> And to those which were spiritually poor:[68]

But one final passage, I think, should settle the question forever that these saints (whom all Catholic and Protestant historians call heretics) which comprised the true churches of the Lord in those dark ages, were not premillennialists:

> Now according to the Scripture, there are already many Antichrists.
> For, all those which are contrary to Christ, are Antichrists.
> Many Signs and great Wonders
> Shall be from *this time forward* until the Day of Judgment,
> The Heaven and *the Earth shall burn*, and all the Living die.
> After which *all shall arise to everlasting Life*,
> *And all Buildings shall be laid flat.*
> *Then shall be the last Judgment*,
> When *God shall separate his People, according as its* [sic] *written*,
> To the wicked he shall say, *Depart ye from me into Hell Fire, which never shall be quenched* . . .
> And give us to hear that which he shall say to his Elect without delay;
> *Come hither ye blessed of my Father*,
> Inherit the Kingdom prepared for you from the beginning of the World.[69]

Now I leave these words to the conscience of those who attempt to lead God's people to believe that the writer of *The Noble Lesson*, or the Waldensians, were premillennial. This last passage is unmistakably an illustration that the Waldensians had thoroughly understood the principles expressed in the "first rigorous propositional truth" (see Chapter 2) that dominates biblical eschatology: that when

---

[68] Ibid., p. 110.

[69] Ibid., p. 120. (Due to a misprint in Morland's book, this page is numbered 120, but is actually page 118).

Christ returns this earth shall be destroyed and will be inhabited no more by flesh and blood. All the righteous will go into everlasting life as glorified saints, and all the wicked will go into hell.

Before closing this section, I want to say a word about reformation eschatology. When the times are satisfactory to a given church movement, there is a tendency to ascribe a millennial character to them. Thus it was that amillennialism was born among the Catholics. When Constantine decreed the Catholic brand of Christianity to be the official religion of the state, the "world" was instantly "won," though not to Christ, but to Catholicism. The Catholics saw this as the ultimate measure of success. This sacral order, they thought, was the very epitome of millennial blessing. Wherever the state of Rome had power, the world was "Christian" — the society was the church.

Since the Protestant denominations adopted the same sacral, state-church order, protestantism was also an instant "success" in the areas where it had power. Thus the "millennial" character of Protestant society came suddenly to Germany at the decree of Luther and the German princes. Calvin brought the "millennium" to Geneva, Henry VIII to England, and John Knox to Scotland. It was a natural heritage, like sacralism, that Catholic amillennialism would also accrue to the Reformers, and it has been the traditional eschatology of protestantism until this day.

Whence Postmillennialism?

If I should make an attempt to demonstrate that a postmillennial eschatology was a fully thought-out and organized doctrine of either the apostles or the early apostolic fathers, it would be as transparent (but no more so) as the attempts of the premillennial writers to press premillennialism upon Paul, Peter, Clement of Rome, Ignatius, or Polycarp.

Since none of these but Polycarp had access to the book of Revelation, they could not have been made conscious of a distinct millennium by means of the New Testament Scriptures. The apostles may have known about it from the Lord's private teachings, but if so there is no direct expression of it in their New Testament teachings until Revelation, traditionally the last book of the canon to be written, near the end of the first century. The only other way such a doctrine could likely have arisen was by borrowing from the Jews as did Cerinthus, the writer of *The Epistle of Barnabas*, and Papias who actually quoted material from the Jewish apocalyptic writings, even though he by that time doubtless had access to Revelation.

Just how far from a biblical eschatology men like Clement, Ignatius, and Polycarp were, is impossible to tell. Assuming they had never heard of the concept of a distinctive millennium period, they were, as near as we can tell, perfectly true to the light they had. However, what we do know about their eschatology reveals that they looked forward to being resurrected from the dead — hence did not hold to imminency. It is implicit also in their writings that they expected the resurrection and second coming at the very end of the world. Now, a person holding these two principles: 1) that the second coming of Christ, resurrection, and judgment are at the end (destruction) of the world, and 2) that the second coming is not imminent (because some prophecies are yet to be fulfilled), needs only to have the concept that there is a distinctive millennial period and he is, *per se*, a postmillennialist. It is entirely probable that this was the actual understanding of these early orthodox fathers as well as the apostles.

Many individuals who never wrote a line on the subject and many individual church congregations scattered in obscure places may well have had this simple, direct understanding of biblical eschatology. The Paulicians who inhabited the regions of Armenia, Cappadocia, and the Caucasus Mountains until the ninth century had no Chiliasm among them, but surely they had some notion of a millennium.

However, it would take giants of faith to be able to build a strong doctrine of a millennium while struggling under terrible persecution as those faithful churches did who did not follow the Catholics into Roman sacralism. The Paulicians from the east and the Donatists from the west, and other groups who made their way to the protective valleys of southern Europe, in all likelihood had some vague hope of millennial condition at some future time. We have seen from one of their writers that they expected Christ's return at the end of the world at the resurrection and general judgment. Therefore any notion of a distinctive earthly millennium they might have had would have been a postmillennial view. And I cannot believe that such a studious people had no notion of a millennium among them. But this cannot, to my knowledge, be documented.

The sad fact is that before the death of the last apostle the seeds of eschatological error had already been sown in the early church. During that critical time between the writing of the final book of the New Testament Scripture (c. A.D. 98) and the time when all these inspired writings were collected and accepted by the early church (well into the fourth century), there was a period of vulnerability when false doctrines were difficult to treat; and they arose in profusion. There was the Judaism of Paul's day; there was Gnosticism, Chiliasm, later the Paracletism of the Montanists. But in eschatology there arose two influences, both of which were unscriptural, that polarized the churches into two extreme positions and obscured the true biblical eschatology. These influences were 1) the widespread doctrine of Chiliasm primarily by and among the Montanists, and 2) the spiritualizing and allegorical philosophy of the Alexandrian school which opposed, and finally overcame Chiliasm.

The zeal of these two opposing factions had such a polarizing effect that most of the leaders aligned with one or the other, and the surviving writings on eschatology are concerned with one or the other of them. This does not mean, however, that among the early churches some did not quietly hold a scriptural view, just as some have in this past half-century. A number of years ago, I knew of a wise old preacher, acknowledged everywhere to be an excellent Bible expositor. But he was a loner; he had no place to feel at home. He was invited to speak occasionally and tolerated as a curiosity. He was a postmillennialist. He will never make the pages of history, but he lived, believed and taught the Scriptures.

Two thousand years from now, if the world should stand, it might be difficult to produce a postmillennial document written between 1925 and 1985. It is difficult now. But the fact that none, to my knowledge, can be certainly produced from the first until about the seventeenth century does not mean no one believed it or taught it. It is enough that the Scriptures set it forth very clearly.

Now, just as with premillennial views, there are many variations among postmillennial views. To reduce this term *postmillennial* to its broadest possible definition only two items must be noted: 1) belief in a distinctive millennial period in human history on this present earth; 2) belief that at the second coming of Christ this present earth will be destroyed. I believe that many saints have held this simple understanding, and never realized it could have a label. With this definition in mind then, I want to look at the period of history when this view began to be consciously set forth in an organized body of doctrine.

Among the earlier writers to set forth an eschatology departing from the Augustinian or Reformed concept of the millennium was an Englishman, Thomas Brightman (1562-1607). His scheme was very complicated, the details of which I could never accept. He expected actually two special millennial periods, but that Christ would return at the very end of the world.

The significant thing about the period from about 1600 and for the next two centuries was that the Christian world, particularly the Baptists, Puritans, and other non-conformist movements (as opposed to the establishment churches), were longing for revival. Their changing eschatology was a message of hope out of great confusion and centuries of oppression. Brightman wrote:

> ...thou mayest more fully rejoice, receive with all tidings of the final destruction of the Turks presently, after the destruction of Rome (Papacy). For she must first be defeated.... After that the Christian world shall be purged from the wicked abominations of Rome by the last and universal slaughter thereof as this Revelation declareth. And lest anything should yet be

> wanting to the full heap of joy, there thou mayest know that the calling of the Jews to be a Christian nation is hereunto joined and with all a most happy tranquility from thence to the end of the world. . . .[70]

Toon remarks that, "Brightman's eschatological scheme may be described as a form of postmillennialism . . . ."[71]

Simultaneous with the rise of this eschatology, which later came to be known as "the latter day glory," was a strong hope of revival that also began to arise in the seventeenth century. Among the strong expectations was the conversion of the Jews and a general revival of the power of the Gospel. Others, after Brightman, promoting this theme were Henry Finch, William Gouge, John Cotton, and John Owens. The doctrine of the latter-day glory became a part of the Congregationalists' confession of faith entitled the *Savoy Declaration of Faith and Order*. In chapter 20 of that confession there appears a paragraph, probably written by John Owens, which reads in part as follows:

> . . . so according to his promise we expect that in the latter days Antichrist being destroyed, the Jews called, and the adversaries of his dear Son broken, the churches of Christ being enlarged and edified through a free and plentiful communication of light and grace, shall enjoy in this world a more quiet, peaceable and glorious condition than they have enjoyed.[72]

Toon further says:

> The development of the doctrine of the latter day glory of the church on earth also took place in Scotland . . . . Perhaps the most persuasive advocate of this pristine postmillennialism

---

[70] Thomas Brightman, *A Revelation of the Revelation* (1615), as cited by Peter Toon, *Puritan Eschatology 1600 to 1650* (Cambridge: James Clark & Co., Ltd., 1970), p. 27.

[71] Ibid., p. 31.

[72] Toon, p. 37. A full treatment of Congregationalist eschatology as it later developed may be seen in Samuel Hopkins, *A Treatise on the Millennium* (New York: Arno Press, 1972). This is a reprint of the original work of Hopkins, a Congregationalist pastor, first published in 1793.

was James Durham (1622-1658) . . . .[73]

The postmillennial position continued to develop and spread:

> In both Old and New England as well as in Scotland the eschatological doctrine now usually called postmillennialism has continued to the present day [1970] to have many supporters. Some of its more famous advocates include Jonathan Edwards in his *History of Redemption*, Daniel Whitby in his *Paraphrase and Commentary on the New Testament*, Charles Hodge and Augustus Strong in their works on *Systematic Theology* and Patrick Fairbairn in his *The Interpretation of Prophecy*. Of course the attitudes to the contents of Daniel and Revelation have greatly changed as the years have passed by, but the belief in the conversion of the Jewish people to Christ accompanied by world-wide rich spiritual blessing for the church of Christ before the Second Coming of Christ has remained constant.[74]

I would add a few more prominent names who held a postmillennial position: Dr. J. L. Dagg, an early Southern Baptist professor; Dr. B. H. Carroll, author of *An Interpretation of The English Bible;* J. M. Pendleton who wrote the tract, *An Old Landmark Reset* which triggered the "Landmark" controversy; Calvin Goodspeed, author of *The Second Advent of Christ;* and Dr. J. L. Vipperman, Pastor of Southside Baptist Church, Spartanburg, South Carolina.

Interestingly, Vipperman was a classmate with J. Frank Norris who was an avid premillennialist. Both Vipperman and Norris were classmates under B. H. Carroll.

As young men Norris and Vipperman opposed each other on the millennial question. In some sense the sensationalism and rise to popularity of Norris paralleled that of the premillennial doctrine since the turn of the twentieth century.

The idea of the latter day glory, which came to be known generally as postmillennialism, played a powerful role in the

---

[73] Ibid., p. 40.

[74] Ibid., p. 41.

great awakenings of the 18th and 19th centuries. Until early in the 18th century a pall of deadness had generally pervaded the Christian world. The evangelistic spirit of Gospel preaching and revival power since the first century had been largely limited to the so-called "heretical" movements in the middle ages, the Waldensians, etc., when God was pleased to lift the yoke of their persecutors from time to time. The Reformation was not the result of a "grass-roots" revival movement. It worked itself out politically and established the same state-church sacralism of the Catholics which is the enemy of Holy Spirit revival and a hot-house for corruption, self-satisfaction, and deadness.

This was the state of affairs as the doctrine of the latter day glory began to take root among the Puritans, Baptists, and other non-conformists as well as some in the establishment churches. The longing and prayerful attitude for revival in those days is well expressed in the words of Thomas Boston (1716):

> Are you longing for a revival to the churches, now lying like dry bones, would you fain have the Spirit of life enter into them? Then pray for the Jews. "For if the casting away of them be the reconciling of the world; what shall the receiving of them be, but life from the dead."[75]

In America also the earnest expectation for the outpouring of God's blessing continued. A Mr. Adams of New London urged:

> Oh! that the Lord would arise and have mercy upon Zion, that the time to favour it, the set time may come, that the whole earth may be filled with the knowledge of the glory of the Lord, as the waters cover the sea![76]

Under the influence of the hope of the latter day glory, in the mid-eighteenth century Daniel Marshall, a Baptist preacher, is typical of many among the Baptists in the great

---

[75] Iain Murray, *The Puritan Hope* (Carlisle, Pa.: The Banner of Truth Trust, 1975), p. 114

[76] Ibid.

awakening period. We can easily see in his life the zeal and godly impulse a biblical eschatology gives to the preaching of the Gospel. His son, Abraham Marshall, writes of his father and of others:

> Firmly believing in the near approach of the "latter-day glory," when the Jews, with the fulness of the Gentiles, shall hail their Redeemer, and bow to his gentle scepter; *a number of worthy characters* ran to and fro, through the eastern states, warmly exhorting to the prompt adoption of every measure tending to hasten that blissful period... One, and not the least sanguine, of these pious missionaries, was my venerable father ....
>
> It may possibly be thought that Mr. Marshall was the subject of delusive hope; and culpably enthusiastic when he left New England, with a family, to roam under the rising beams of the latter-day glory, as he supposed, for the conversion of souls. But let this matter be fairly considered, and it will appear, that his most sanguine expectations must have, so far, been fully realized. Since the period at which Mr. Marshall commenced his career, those burning and shining lights, Rev. Messrs. Whitefield and Wesley, with their zealous associates and numerous followers, have aroused a slumbering world, and liberally shed the luster of truth in its darkest recesses; thousands of able and evangelical writers and preachers have been raised up, and as many gospel churches formed; a revolution in America has bestowed religious liberty on one quarter of the globe; the system of the Man of sin has been almost demolished; liberty of conscience has made rapid advances in Europe ... missionaries have gone out, literally, into all the world; and sinners, of all descriptions, have fallen, by thousands, beneath the sword of the Spirit, which is the word of God.[77]

Murray wrote:

> Though a number, like the Simeons and Annas of another day, thus waited for a divine visitation, when the great revival of the eighteenth century at last began in the late 1730's, it was unexpected by the mass of nominal Christians. And even those who had long prayed for a new out-pouring of the Spirit

---

[77] James B. Taylor, *Lives of Virginia Baptist Ministers* (Richmond: Yale & Wyatt, 1838), pp. 15, 20, 21.

> were to be astonished at both the extent and power of the work.[78]

There was a second wave to the revivals that accompanied this biblical hope. The God-ordained means of faithful preaching of the Gospel by the power of God is the means for revival in any age, and when God's people have held this eschatology of hope there have been powerful results. On into the nineteenth century this hope inspired churches in local communities to powerful revival. In Virginia in the early nineteenth century a Baptist minister, John Jenkins, exhorted his people:

> While we are often hearing of the triumphs of the cross in foreign countries; while our ears are cheered with the animating news, that the gracious work is spreading in every direction in our highly favored country; while thousands of heaven-born souls are daily emerging from darkness into the marvelous light of the gospel, mingling their prayers with the elders saints, and uniting their voices in lofty songs to God and the Lamb, — we remain still and inactive; our harps are hung upon the willows; and we pass it off, by faintly saying, "we wish we could see a revival amongst ourselves," [sic] But why is it thus with us? Is the Lord's ear heavy, that he cannot hear? or, is his arm shortened, that he cannot save? Not so, we must look for the cause at home. Let every preacher, every deacon, and every private member of the church, examine himself strictly, as in the presence of the living God, and if he finds that he has been remiss, or negligent in any Christian duty, let him repent, return, and do his first works; let every church be stirred up to use all diligence in all the duties of her charge. In short, a reformation must first begin amongst professors, before we can expect to see it among the unconverted.[79]

Early in this book I said a biblical eschatology would focus the attention of churches on the harvest, on correcting wrongs, purging corruption, cleansing the churches, and sharpening the implements of harvest. John Jenkins' work is an example. One must first have a biblical hope before he can

---

[78] Murray, p. 114.

[79] Taylor, pp. 352-353.

seriously make this response. The latter day glory principle says more than that there is coming a day when the Gospel will have power. It says that because the Gospel *is* the power of God unto salvation to be preached in hope by normal, clean, human agencies, these same principles and agencies will work for, not only a millennium, but a revival *at any time* they are truly exercised *in faith* with a *zealous confidence.* John Jenkins, sometime after the above sermon, baptized over 250 converts in one country church in 1801-1802.[80]

Now without multiplying examples, it is more than clear that the principles inherent in a postmillennial eschatology have demonstrated their power. The only periods of time when God's people have predominantly held this simple biblical eschatology, there has been powerful revival, i.e., the 1st century and the 18th and 19th centuries. God has demonstrated His pleasure toward this eschatology of hope that accords with the truth of God's plan and purpose. I submit the proposition that in the days when the first century church held to the biblical outlook of future things according to the revelation given them, they had vast success. When premillennialism and amillennialism arose as widespread doctrines, the power and effectiveness of the early church witness waned. When in the eighteenth and nineteenth centuries these false doctrines gave way to a biblical eschatology of hope for the power of the Gospel, the churches again had a powerful revival. These are the stubborn facts.

The Pall of Gloom Returns

Then accordingly, as it was in the second century, when the gloom of premillennialism and amillennialism again spread itself abroad in the late nineteenth and twentieth centuries, the impulse of true Holy Spirit revival also nearly disappeared from the scene. The "revivals" since those days have not been primarily spontaneous grass-roots movings of the Holy Spirit, but shallow substitutions — planned campaigns — produced by promotional efforts and built around

---

[80] Taylor, p. 353.

popular personalities to circumvent the distressing absence of the powerful visitation of the Spirit at the grass-roots of communities and churches.

Those who have ascribed failure to the church — the very institution that God Almighty designed, empowered, and ordained for a world-wide harvest — have been forced by their errors to the sorry business of bribery with hot-dogs, bubblegum, ten-ton banana splits, games, and contests to maintain the external appearance of success. They have built "churches" that are giant, undisciplined hot-beds of immorality and sassy pride. No man having a biblical understanding and faith in the truth that God's work of salvation is accomplished *only* through the power of the Holy Spirit in conjunction with the Gospel of Christ, will ever cheapen the Gospel with these carnal expedients.

Iain Murray in his excellent book, *The Puritan Hope*, after showing the development of the doctrine of the latter day glory, illustrating the power of it in the great revival periods and the ensuing missionary activities, then came to the part of history that saw the revival of premillennialism. This chapter he appropriately entitles, "The Eclipse of Hope."

This eclipse of hope is becoming more apparent every day that passes. The following statement illustrates quite well what it has come to be:

> Why is there such a pessimistic vein in many sectors of evangelical Christianity? Is it because most of us are a-millenarians or pre-millenarians? Is it because we expect the world to grow worse and believe we can do very little about it, apart from praying for the return of our Lord?[81]

How did we come to this state of affairs? How did the churches move from the impulse of the latter day glory to the pessimism of today?

In the early nineteenth century premillennialism was at a very low ebb. But beginning about 1825-30 a movement began that would eventually spread a pall of pessimism over

---

[81] Klaas Runia, "Evangelical Responsibility in a Secularized World," *Christianity Today*, Vol. XIV, No. 19 (June 19, 1970), p. 13.

thousands of the very churches born under the power and hope of the latter day glory.

"The leader of this change of direction was Edward Irving."[82] Irving became the founder of the Catholic Apostolic Church, now nearly extinct. In the early days of this church we find the seeds of the modern resurgence of premillennialism. More remarkable than that, Irving's church and some of his acquaintances, particularly J. N. Darby, became the incubator of a new doctrine — pretribulation rapturism — which not one of the ancient Chiliasts held.

For over a century it has been generally known that the germ of the idea of the pretribulation rapture was expressed in a special "revelation" or vision seen by a woman in Irving's church.[83] But the details of this have only as of c. 1970-1975 been thoroughly researched and documented by Dave MacPherson, a Christian journalist. I will only cite one statement from this work wherein MacPherson quotes a Rev. Robert Norton[84] who was very much involved with the development of these new doctrines in Irving's church. Norton wrote:

> Marvellous light was shed upon Scripture, and especially on the doctrine of the second Advent, by the revived spirit of

---

[82] Murray, p. 188.

[83] For example, Dr. Oswald J. Smith, early in the twentieth century, in a tract *Tribulation or Rapture — Which?* p. 7, tells of his experience in turning from pretribulation rapturism. In this tract he discussed the Irvingite "revelation" and quoted H. A. Baker, *Tribulation to Glory*, as follows: "Beginning with the Irvingite woman, then propagated by John N. Darby about 1830, this new 'spirit-inspired' doctrine during the last century has come down to us until it has become popular. George Mueller opposed it; so did Benjamin Willis Newton; so did Dr. S. P. Tragelles and other brethren, but all in vain."

[84] Dave MacPherson, *The Incredible Cover-Up* (Plainfield, N.J.: Logos International, 1975), p. 37. For those who desire to understand the true origin and development of this pretribulation rapture aberration, two modern works are indispensable. First was MacPherson's work (1975) and the second, adding new important information, is a little booklet by John L. Bray, *The Origin of the Pre-Tribulation Rapture Teaching* (Lakeland, Fla., John L. Bray Ministries, Inc., 1982).

> prophecy. In the following account by Miss M. M. [Margaret Macdonald], of an evening during which the power of the Holy Ghost rested upon her for several successive hours, in mingled prophecy and vision, we have an instance; for here we first see the distinction between that final stage of the Lord's coming, when every eye shall see Him, and His prior appearing in glory to them that look for Him.[85]

Then MacPherson comments:

> There are two astonishing admissions in this paragraph. Norton says Margaret Macdonald saw a two-stage coming, and that this was the *first* time such a distinction was made![86]

Now, turning to the work of John L. Bray which came some few years after McPherson's, it appears that Miss Margaret Macdonald was not the very first to conceive such an idea. In fact, the seeds of the idea may have been planted in her mind and in Edward Irving's mind by a book written in 1812 by a Jesuit priest. Bray gives the following account:

> The book to which I refer is entitled, "The Coming of Messiah in Glory and Majesty," written by Emmanuel Lacunza, a Jesuit priest from Chile, writing under the assumed name of Rabbi Juan Josafat Ben-Ezra as a converted Jew, and first published in Spain in 1812. This book was later translated into English by Rev. Edward Irving and published in London, England, in 1827.
>
> When this book was first published, the seeds were sown for the development and growth of a pre-tribulation rapture. . . .
>
> In this book Lacunza taught that Christ will appear in the sky, raise certain of the Christian dead and catch up the living ones; then bring judgments and wrath upon the earth; and then at least 45 days after his appearance and when all these judgments are over and antichrist and his followers are destroyed, He will descend to the earth itself with his saints to set up his millennial kingdom.[87]

---

[85] Ibid.

[86] Ibid.

[87] Bray, p. 2.

The facts are these: Edward Irving thought so much of Lacunza's book that he translated it into English (900 pages in two volumes with a long introductory discourse by Irving) and published it in 1827. It would be difficult to believe that Irving never preached on these things, or that Margaret Macdonald had never been exposed to them before her "vision." Thus, an embryonic form of the present-day pre-tribulation rapture theory grew up in Irving's church from 1827-1830.

J. N. Darby, who was a leader in another movement —the Plymouth Brethren — arising about the same time (c. 1830), knew about Irving's teaching, about Margaret Macdonald's revelation, and Lacunza's book. Darby claimed to have conceived the doctrine of the two-phase pretribulation rapture in 1827, the same year in which Lacunza's book was published in English.[88] It was Darby who first gave form, organization, and publicity to the present-day theory of the pretribulation rapture and taught it publicly. There are thousands who claim that Darby simply "saw" these things from personal study of the Scripture. But Darby formulated his theory after having been a sympathetic observer in the Macdonald home at about the time Margaret Macdonald received her "revelation," and Macdonald was in Irving's church at a time when Irving was republishing Lacunza's work which had the first known germ of the pre-tribulation rapture. You may draw your own conclusions, but there are several "smoking guns" in this story.

Darby modified the Lacunza/Irving/Macdonald theory, provided a quasi-scriptural basis for it, and spread it abroad. Then C. I. Scofield picked it up and implanted this theory into the notes of the *Scofield Reference Bible* putting it into the hands and minds of thousands of fundamentalists right down to the grass roots. Many fundamentalist preachers to this day stand and announce their sermon texts by page number from the *Scofield Reference Bible* — promoting this and other grievous errors.

---

[88] Ibid., p. 28.

Whither Now?

I submit these things now to be searched, I trust with charity and sincerity, by the people of God. This doctrine of a postmillennial eschatology has not been an issue in nearly a century. In the beginning of this book, I said I wanted to be candid — to open the issue directly as it relates to Scripture truth. I said I would be hard on the things I considered to be in error but would want to be charitable toward every sincere brother.

I know that many have vested interests, long-standing relationships, some with position, prestige, income, or millions of dollars in brick and mortar and real estate, which they feel would be in jeopardy should they change their eschatology. To those I would say God can bless any man who would dare to honestly search His Word with a view to changing to whatever the Scriptures teach. The greatest religious empire in the world is not worth compromising one syllable of God's truth. Only with a bold courage can God's people ever hope to obey and come to a unity of the faith on all the things that divide us. In this we can trust, that if truth destroys an empire, it *should* be destroyed. If a good work *should* survive, God is able to sustain it even though its leader may change his eschatology.

The need of the hour for those who believe the Bible is for each to be willing to submit himself and his doctrines to be candidly and charitably searched by others through sincere dialogue. According to the prayer of Christ — ". . . that they also may be one in us: *that the world may believe that thou hast sent me*" (John 17:21) — nothing but truth could be more important than unity. Upon this unity *visible to the world* turns the real success of the Gospel.

But is it not true that most Christians are so busy building empires that God has not commanded to be built, that there is no time to accomplish the one important thing He has commanded — the building of churches unified according to truth? The greatest need of evangelical and fundamental Christianity is courage and vision:

How is the gold become dim! how is the most fine gold

> changed! the stones of the sanctuary are poured out in the top of every street. The precious sons of Zion, comparable to fine gold, how are they esteemed as earthen pitchers, the work of the hands of the potter!... For this our heart is faint; for these things our eyes are dim (Lam. 4:1, 2; 5:17).

The latter day glory, the millennium, will come in God's own time as He has outlined in prophecy. However, the principles of righteousness, unity, and peace which will then prevail are available to us now, though Satan hinders. The deliberate search for them and the apprehension of them in the greatest measure possible by the millions of Christians now living could but fill the earth with a revival of gladness, hope, joy, and peace which will suffice until the day when "the knowledge of the Lord will cover the earth as the waters cover the sea."

Bibliography

Biederwolf, William E. *The Second Coming Bible.* Grand Rapids: Baker Book House, 1972.

Bray, John L. *The Origin of the Pre-Tribulation Rapture Teaching.* Lakeland, Fla.: John L. Bray Ministries, Inc., 1982.

Carroll, B. H. *Daniel and the Inter-Biblical Period.* Nashville: Broadman Press, 1947.

——— . *Revelation*, Vol. XVII of *An Interpretation of the English Bible.* Grand Rapids: Baker Book House, 1973.

Downing, W. R. *The New Testament Church.* Sunnyvale, Ca.: Lakewood Baptist Church, 1982.

Eusebius. *Ecclesiastical History*, trans. Christian Frederick Cruse. Grand Rapids: Baker Book House, 1955.

Farrar, W. F. *The Early Days of Christianity.* New York: Cassell, Petter, Galpin & Co., 1883.

Friebel, Kelvin G. "The Qumranian Doctrine of the Messiah." Paper read at the University of Wisconsin-Madison Hebrew Graduate Seminar, 1980, Madison, Wisconsin.

Gibbon, Edward. *The Decline and Fall of the Roman Empire.* The Great Books, Vol. XLI. Chicago: Encyclopaedia Britannica, Inc., 1952.

Goodspeed, Calvin. *Christ's Second Advent.* Toronto: William Briggs, 1900.

Hawkins, William C. and Willard A. Ramsey. *The House of God.* Simpsonville, S.C.: Hallmark Baptist Church, 1980.

Hopkins, Samuel. *A Treatise on the Millennium.* New York: Arno Press, 1972.

Jones, William. *The History of the Christian Church.* Wetumpka, Ala.: Charles Yancey, 1845.

Josephus, Flavius. *Antiquities of the Jews*, trans. William Whiston. New York: Leavitt & Co.

Larkin, Clarence. *Dispensational Truth.* Philadelphia: Author, 1920.

Lightfoot, John. *A Commentary on the New Testament from the Talmud and Hebraica.* Grand Rapids: Baker Book House, 1979.

Lightfoot, Joseph Barber. *The Apostolic Fathers.* Grand Rapids: Baker Book House, 1970 (shorter) and 1981 (longer).

MacPherson, David. *The Incredible Cover-Up.* Plainfield, N.J.: Logos International, 1975.

Mauro, Philip. *The Gospel of the Kingdom.* Swengel, Pa.: Reiner Publications, 1974.

McDaniels, David K. *The Sun.* New York: John Wiley & Sons, 1979.

Morland, Samuel. *The History of the Evangelical Churches of the Valleys of the Piemont.* London: Henry Hills, 1658.

Morris, Henry M. *The Revelation Record.* Wheaton, Il.: Tyndale House Publishers, Inc. and San Diego: Creation-Life Publishers, 1983.

Murray, Iain. *The Puritan Hope.* Carlisle, Pa.: The Banner of Truth Trust, 1975.

Neander, Augustus. *General History of the Christian Religion and Church.* New York: Hurd & Houghton, 1871.

Pentecost, J. Dwight. *Things to Come.* Findlay, Ohio: Dunham Publishing Co., 1958.

Porter, H. "Scythians," *International Standard Bible Encyclopedia,* 1937, Vol. IV.

Runia, Klaas. "Evangelical Responsibility in a Secularized World," *Christianity Today,* XIV (June 19, 1970), 13.

Rusk, Roger. "The Day He Died," *Christianity Today,* XVIII (March 29, 1974), 4-6.

Ryrie, Charles C. *The Basis of the Premillennial Faith.* Neptune, N.J.: Loizeaux Brothers, 1953.

Schaff, Philip. *History of the Christian Church,* Vol. II. Grand Rapids: Wm. B. Eerdmans Publishing Co., 1980.

Shedd, William G. T. *A History of Christian Doctrine,* Vol. II. New York: Charles Scribner's Sons, 1897.

Smith, Oswald J. *Tribulation or Rapture — Which?* The Sovereign Grace Advent Testimony.

Taylor, James B. *Lives of Virginia Baptist Ministers.* Richmond: Yale & Wyatt, 1838.

Thiessen, Henry C. *Introductory Lectures in Systematic Theology.* Grand Rapids: Wm. B. Eerdmans Publishing Co., 1949.

———. "Will the Church Pass Through the Tribulation?", *Bibliotheca Sacra,* XCII (January, April, July, 1937), 39-54, 187-205, 292-314.

Thomas, J. E. H. "Apocalyptic Literature," *International Standard Bible Encyclopedia,* 1937, Vol. I.

Toon, Peter. *Puritan Eschatology 1600 to 1650.* Cambridge: James Clark & Co., Ltd., 1970.

Verduin, Leonard. *The Reformers and their Stepchildren.* Grand Rapids: Baker Book House, 1980.

Walvoord, John F. *The Revelation of Jesus Christ.* Chicago: Moody Press, 1966.

Index

Scripture Index

Revelation (Cont.)